Data-Driven Decision Making in Fragile Contexts

DIRECTIONS IN DEVELOPMENT
Public Sector Governance

Data-Driven Decision Making in Fragile Contexts

Evidence from Sudan

Alexander Hamilton and Craig Hammer, Editors

© 2017 International Bank for Reconstruction and Development / The World Bank
1818 H Street NW, Washington, DC 20433
Telephone: 202-473-1000; Internet: www.worldbank.org

Some rights reserved

1 2 3 4 20 19 18 17

This work is a product of the staff of The World Bank with external contributions. The findings, interpretations, and conclusions expressed in this work do not necessarily reflect the views of The World Bank, its Board of Executive Directors, or the governments they represent. The World Bank does not guarantee the accuracy of the data included in this work. The boundaries, colors, denominations, and other information shown on any map in this work do not imply any judgment on the part of The World Bank concerning the legal status of any territory or the endorsement or acceptance of such boundaries.

Nothing herein shall constitute or be considered to be a limitation upon or waiver of the privileges and immunities of The World Bank, all of which are specifically reserved.

Rights and Permissions

This work is available under the Creative Commons Attribution 3.0 IGO license (CC BY 3.0 IGO) http://creativecommons.org/licenses/by/3.0/igo. Under the Creative Commons Attribution license, you are free to copy, distribute, transmit, and adapt this work, including for commercial purposes, under the following conditions:

Attribution—Please cite the work as follows: Hamilton, Alexander, and Craig Hammer, eds. 2017. *Data-Driven Decision Making in Fragile Contexts: Evidence from Sudan.* Directions in Development. Washington, DC: World Bank. doi:10.1596/978-1-4648-1064-0. License: Creative Commons Attribution CC BY 3.0 IGO

Translations—If you create a translation of this work, please add the following disclaimer along with the attribution: *This translation was not created by The World Bank and should not be considered an official World Bank translation. The World Bank shall not be liable for any content or error in this translation.*

Adaptations—If you create an adaptation of this work, please add the following disclaimer along with the attribution: *This is an adaptation of an original work by The World Bank. Views and opinions expressed in the adaptation are the sole responsibility of the author or authors of the adaptation and are not endorsed by The World Bank.*

Third-party content—The World Bank does not necessarily own each component of the content contained within the work. The World Bank therefore does not warrant that the use of any third-party-owned individual component or part contained in the work will not infringe on the rights of those third parties. The risk of claims resulting from such infringement rests solely with you. If you wish to re-use a component of the work, it is your responsibility to determine whether permission is needed for that re-use and to obtain permission from the copyright owner. Examples of components can include, but are not limited to, tables, figures, or images.

All queries on rights and licenses should be addressed to World Bank Publications, The World Bank Group, 1818 H Street NW, Washington, DC 20433, USA; e-mail: pubrights@worldbank.org.

ISBN (paper): 978-1-4648-1064-0
ISBN (electronic): 978-1-4648-1065-7
DOI: 10.1596/978-1-4648-1064-0

Cover illustration: © Jomo Tariku. Used with permission. Further permission required for reuse.
Cover design: Naylor Design, Inc., Washington, DC

Library of Congress Cataloging-in-Publication Data has been requested.

Contents

Foreword		*xi*
Preface		*xiii*
Acknowledgments		*xv*
About the Editors and Authors		*xvii*
Abbreviations		*xxi*

	Introduction: What Contribution Can Survey Data Make toward Evidence-Based Policy Making in Fragile and Conflict-Affected Contexts?	1
PART 1	**General Theory and Principles of Survey Design and Political Economy Dynamics**	**5**
Chapter 1	The Political Economy of Data Collection and Evidence-Based Policy Making in Fragile Contexts *Alexander Hamilton*	7
	Introduction	7
	Literature	8
	A Simple Model of the Political Economy of Data Collection and Availability	10
	Robustness Tests	11
	Limitations	13
	Conclusion and Policy Implications	13
	Notes	14
	Bibliography	14
Chapter 2	Understanding and Preparing Survey Data for Quantitative Analysis *Chandni Raja, Naomi Crowther, and Ella Spencer*	17
	Introduction	17
	Literature Review	18

	Data Collection	18
	Sampling Design	19
	Sample Weighting	21
	Data Cleaning	23
	Missing Responses	23
	Ordering of Responses	25
	Recoding of Responses	26
	Merging or Appending of Data	27
	Conclusion	29
	References	29
Chapter 3	**Working with Incomplete Data Sets**	**31**
	Chandni Raja, Naomi Crowther, and Ella Spencer	
	Case Study: Conflict	32
	Case Study: Access to Finance	41
	Suggestions for Future Data Collection	49
	Conclusion	50
	Bibliography	50
Chapter 4	**Quantitative Analysis Using Household Survey Data**	**53**
	Chandni Raja, Naomi Crowther, and Ella Spencer	
	Case Study: Public Services	53
	Advanced Quantitative Analysis–Factor Analysis and Structural Equation Modeling	62
	Conclusion	72
	Notes	73
	Bibliography	73
PART 2	**Detailed Analysis of the Survey's Modules**	**75**
Chapter 5	**Using Survey Data from Sudan for Policy Making: The Determinants of Trust and the Perceived Effect on Gender of Decisions by the Tribal Leader**	**77**
	Alexander Hamilton and John Hudson	
	The Data Set	78
	Background to the Analysis: Sudan	80
	Literature	82
	Theory: Perceived Fairness and Trust	86
	Regression Results	94
	Conclusions and Implications	99
	Annex 5A: Generating Locational Variables in Stata	102
	Notes	103
	Bibliography	104

Chapter 6	The Vicious Circle of Poverty, Poor Public Service Provision, and State Legitimacy in Sudan	107
	Alexander Hamilton and Jakob Svensson	
	Introduction	107
	Background: Sudan	108
	The 2013 DFID Sudan Household Survey Data	109
	Discussion	116
	Notes	116
	References	117
Chapter 7	Geography and Correlates of Attitudes toward Female Genital Mutilation in Sudan: What Can We Learn from Successive Sudan Opinion Poll Data?	119
	Alexander Hamilton and Ngianga-Bakwin Kandala	
	Background	119
	Methods	121
	Results	127
	Discussion	150
	Notes	157
	References	157
Chapter 8	The Effect of Decentralization Policies on Inequalities of Public Service Delivery in Sudan	159
	Zintis Hermansons and Bashir Ahmad	
	Existing Research on Governance and Service Delivery in Sudan and Proposed Methodology	160
	Governance in Sudan: A Macro Perspective on Service Delivery	162
	Theoretical Framework: Decentralization and Service Delivery	164
	Fiscal Decentralization and Service Delivery in Sudan: Exploring Institutional Design and Available Data	165
	Decentralization and the Center–Periphery Hypothesis	169
	Conclusions	173
	Annex 8A Distribution of Responsibilities among Different Levels of Government in Sudan	173
	Notes	174
	References	174
Chapter 9	Still Far from Development: Humanitarian Assistance Policy and Practice in Darfur between 2004 and 2014	179
	Dragana Marinkovic	
	Introduction	179

	Methodology	181
	Darfur in Context	181
	Effects of the Conflict on Livelihoods in Darfur	182
	Shrinking Humanitarian Space and Security and the Effect on Assistance	184
	Politicization of Humanitarian Aid, Push for Long-Term Solutions, and Effect on Assistance	187
	Effect of Political Pressure on Returns and Reintegration	191
	Conclusion	194
	Notes	194
	References	194
	Conclusion: Can We Use Survey Data?	**199**

Box

5.1	Questionnaire Structure	79

Figures

2.1	Distribution of Responses to Two Questions in the Data Set	24
3.1	Experiences of Conflict in the Past Year, by Gender	39
3.2	Biggest Issues Facing Sudan Today at the State Level	42
3.3	Access to Financial Services, by Income Group	45
3.4	Access to Financial Services, by Center–Periphery Dynamic	46
3.5	Access to Financial Services, by Center–Periphery Dynamic and Income	47
3.6	Access to Financial Services, by Gender	48
4.1	Perceptions of Service Quality, by Rural–Urban Location	56
4.2	Perceptions of Service Quality, by Income Group	57
4.3	Monthly Household Income, by Gender and Center–Periphery Location	58
4.4	Ratings of Public Services for Three States	59
4.5	Average Overall Perception of Quality versus Average Overall Level of Trust, at the Individual Level	61
4.6	Theoretical Framework for the Determinants of Service Quality	62
4.7	Regression of Service Quality Rating on Demographics and Trust Factors, with Trust Factors as "Mediators"	66
4.8	Regression of Service Quality Rating on Socioeconomic and Demographic Variables	66
4.9	Regression of Service Quality Rating on Socioeconomic and Demographic Variables and Trust Factors	66
4.10	Structure of Governance and Public Resource Flows in the Education Sector	71
5.1	Trust in Tribal Leader	90

5.2	Location-Based Tribal Trust and Location-Based Education	93
5.3	Location-Based Tribal Trust and Location-Based Fairness	93
5.4	Regression Coefficients on State Variables	98
6.1	Political Participation and State Legitimacy	115
7.1	Share of Study Participants, by Educational Attainments	131
7.2	Share of Study Participants, by Reasons That FGM Should Continue	131
7.3	Proportion of Study Participants, by Self-Perceived Identity	132
7.4	Likelihood of Pro-FGM Attitude, by Educational Attainments, 2012/13	143
7.5	Likelihood of Pro-FGM Attitude, by Educational Attainments, 2014	143
7.6	Likelihood of Pro-FGM Attitude, by Trust in Local Government, 2012/13	144
7.7	Likelihood of Pro-FGM Attitude, by Trust in Local Government, 2014	144
7.8	Likelihood of Pro-FGM Attitude, by Self-Perceived Identity, 2012/13	145
7.9	Likelihood of Pro-FGM Attitude, by Self-Perceived Identity, 2014	145
7.10	Estimated Nonparametric Effect of Respondent's Age	149
8.1	Worldwide Governance Indicators for Sudan, Percentile Ranks	162
8.2	Public Education Spending, 2005–08	163
8.3	Per Capita Central Government Transfers, by State, 2000–10 Average	168
8.4	Perceived Quality of Services	168
9.1	Reasons for Leaving Home, Darfur	185
9.2	Total Humanitarian Aid to Sudan, by Year, 2002–14	189
9.3	Funding for Reintegration and Recovery, 2010–15	190
9.4	Funding for Food and Livelihoods Sector, 2002–14	190

Maps

3.1	Distribution of Monthly Household Income, State Level	33
3.2	Populations of Internally Displaced Persons	34
3.3	Experience of War at the State Level	37
3.4	Displacement at the State Level	38
3.5	Food Insecurity in Sudan	40
3.6	Starting a Business at the State Level	43
7.1	The Observed Proportion of People with Positive Attitudes Surrounding FGM Continuation (Pro-FGM), by State	138
7.2	Adjusted Total Residual Spatial Effects of Positive Attitudes Surrounding FGM Continuation (Pro-FGM), State Level, 2012/13	140
7.3	Spatial Residual Effects of Positive Attitudes Surrounding FGM Continuation (Pro-FGM), State Level, 2012/13	140

7.4	Adjusted Total Residual Spatial Effects of Positive Attitudes Surrounding FGM Continuation (Pro-FGM), State Level, 2014	141
7.5	Spatial Residual Effects of Positive Attitudes Surrounding FGM Continuation (Pro-FGM), State Level, 2014	141

Tables

2.1	DFID Sudan Household Surveys Design, 2013	21
2.2	Sampling Weights Based on Gender and Geographical Strata	22
2.3	Example of a Data Set in Wide Form	28
2.4	Example of the Same Data Set in Long Form	28
4.1	Nonresponse for Questions on Public Service Ratings	54
4.2	Correlation Matrix of Trust in Public Institutions	64
4.3	Factor Analysis of Trust in Public Institutions	65
4.4	Regression Results for Rating Public Schools	67
4.5	State-Level Regression Results for Rating Public Schools	69
5.1	Data Definitions	89
5.2	Summary Data on Identification in 2013 and 2014 DFID Sudan Household Surveys	91
5.3	Regression Results	94
5.4	Regressions Based on Location Variables Only	98
6.1	Summary Statistics	111
6.2	Summary Statistics: Urban vs. Rural and Poor vs. Nonpoor	112
6.3	State Legitimacy: Summary Statistics	113
6.4	Political Participation: Summary Statistics	114
7.1	Baseline Characteristics of the Study Population	124
7.2	Baseline Characteristics of the Study Population, by Intent to Continue FGM	128
7.3	Unadjusted and Fully Adjusted Odds Ratios of Intent to Continue FGM across Selected Covariates	133
7.4	Fully Adjusted and Bayesian Odds Ratios of Intent to Continue FGM across Selected Covariates	146
8.1	Three Layers of Problem-Driven Governance and Political Economy Analysis	161
8.2	Three Layers for Analyzing Service Delivery in Sudan by Applying Problem-Driven Governance and Political Economy Analysis	161
8.3	Strategies of Subversion Regarding Decentralization	161
8.4	Sudan's Central Government Revenues	163
8.5	Contingency Table on Party Affiliation in Sudan	172
9.1	Returned and Existing IDPs by Year, 2006–13	192

Foreword

It is a tragedy that the countries that need data the most are the least likely to have it. Good data lead to good decisions. But in fragile and conflict-affected states, collecting reliable data and applying them to improve people's lives can be incredibly difficult.

The Sustainable Development Goals challenge us to "leave no one behind" and ensure data represent all segments of society. This not only means having statistics on fragile states and their citizens, but ensuring that women, girls, minorities, and other marginalized groups within them are well represented in the data that are used in the governance processes that affect their lives.

The World Bank and the U.K. Department for International Development (DFID) recognize this and are at the forefront of supporting individuals and institutions in these difficult environments. This volume makes a significant contribution to the nascent field of governance statistics by demonstrating new methods for conducting surveys in fragile contexts and using the results to make evidence-based decisions.

Using a DFID household survey focused on governance issues in Sudan, academics and practitioners, from both the statistics and the governance fields, have mapped insights into the perceptions and beliefs of the Sudanese population. These data have helped an interdisciplinary group of researchers to glean insights into what ordinary Sudanese think about everything from female genital mutilation to the link between poor service provision and trust in government.

This work shows that while producing and using data in fragile contexts is difficult, it is eminently possible. New methods for creating and analyzing data in Sudan can yield an inclusive picture of society. I look forward to seeing these approaches studied, refined, and scaled into new settings.

Haishan Fu
Director, Development Data Group
The World Bank

Preface

The idea for this edited volume emerged from collaborative operational work by the World Bank and the U.K. Department for International Development (DFID) in Sudan on data collection, analysis, statistical capacity development, and data literacy capacity development for government and nongovernment actors. Sudan has long been characterized by weak public institutions, skills shortages, slow rates of gross domestic product growth, and macroeconomic instability, all of which are exacerbated by a lack of timely and reliable statistics on the basis of which policies can be formulated. Conflict and other major shocks not only have brought about great hardship but also have set back years of investment in public institutions and public infrastructure, perpetuating a cycle of underdevelopment. The aim of the collaborative work by the World Bank and DFID has been to enable more access to and use of good-quality evidence for improved decision making.

The premise that motivated this work might seem intuitive: although fragile states could benefit from the availability of evidence to help improve policy-making decisions, the paucity of data is likely to be most acute in these contexts. Although data alone cannot have a transformative effect without the proper contextual incentives, such information is an essential and necessary prerequisite for greater accountability and more efficient decision making.

In Sudan, the first step was a DFID-launched and -led multiyear household survey program. The analyses in this volume focus on that opinion poll data. By painstakingly running a variety of robustness tests, triangulating the data, and working with independent researchers to review and develop insights from the first and subsequent polls, the sponsors saw clearly that, despite some significant political economy dynamics, the evidence from these opinion polls could, in the first instance, be used to improve DFID Sudan programs. Over time, through capacity building and dissemination, the data could have a wider effect on policy makers and social accountability actors across the country, and potentially in other fragile contexts.

Specifically, this volume begins with big questions around the political economy of data, which provide readers with a framework of critical questions they always need to consider when trying to assess the validity, reliability, and potential effect of a data set on decision making. It then explores the efforts to assess how and if the DFID Sudan household surveys, given the political and conflict challenges present, can be considered to provide valid and reliable data for decision making. Following these more general chapters, the volume then explores specific areas covered by the household survey, including female genital mutilation; public service delivery; and the interplay of governance, service quality, and state legitimacy.[1]

Alexander Hamilton
DFID

Craig Hammer
World Bank

Note

1. Because of the evolution of political dynamics over the period covered, the number of states in Sudan has changed, something that affects the analysis of this volume.

Acknowledgments

This book is a product of the joint collaboration of the World Bank's Development Data Group and the U.K. Department for International Development (DFID) in Sudan. The publication of this volume was made possible through funding provided by the DFID Sudan Evidence Base Programme,[1] which was implemented jointly by DFID and the World Bank. The editors of the manuscript are Alexander Hamilton (DFID) and Craig Hammer (World Bank).

This volume would not have been possible without the insights of Kate Fearon (DFID), who commissioned the first polling in Sudan that formed the basis of this work, and Jackie French, who as the first program manager of the Evidence Base Programme, ensured that subsequent polling was possible. Likewise, support from the subsequent DFID programme manager Kate Viner, as well as from Martin Dyble (DFID), Omayma Ibrahim (DFID), and Alice Motion (DFID), together with Xavier Furtado (World Bank), Fareed Hassan (World Bank), Nada Amin (World Bank), and Kawther Berima (World Bank), greatly facilitated the publication of this book.

The manuscript benefited greatly from the immensely helpful input provided by its formal reviewers, Wei Huang and Varvara Lalioti. Skillful editorial support was provided by Olivia Robinson. In addition, the volume benefited from the insights and support provided by Alyson King (U.K. Foreign and Commonwealth Office), Laura James (University of Cambridge), and Pasqualino Okello (Youth and Women Empowerment Programme, Uganda), as well as the personal support provided by Renata Bernardo, Sara Jensen, and Sonya Ramian. The editors also wish to thank Mary Fisk and Jewel McFadden for their tireless support throughout the publication process; Jomo Tariku for creating the cover art; and Bruno Bonansea for creating the maps. Finally, we would like to thank the Central European University, the U.K. Department for International Development, the University of California–Los Angeles, the Internal Displacement Monitoring Centre, the London School of Economics and Political Science, The MIT Press, the *Spatial and Spatio-Temporal Epidemiology* journal, the United Nations, and the World Bank for their kind permission to reproduce their work and diagrams.

Note

1. See the Evidence Base Programme website, http://devtracker.dfid.gov.uk/projects/GB-1-204021/.

About the Editors and Authors

Editors

Alexander Hamilton is an economic and statistics adviser for the U.K. Department for International Development (DFID), where he leads research and policy regarding governance statistics. Before this posting, he was based in DFID Sudan and Ethiopia, where he worked on developing an evidence base for decision making and on providing technical assistance to the Ministries of Finance and National Statistics offices. Before joining DFID, Hamilton was a quantitative political economy consultant for the World Bank. He is the author of numerous working papers, peer-reviewed journal articles, and two books, *African Parliamentary Reform* (Routledge, 2012) and *Understanding Policy Change: How to Apply Political Economy Concepts in Practice* (World Bank, 2012). He holds an MPA in public and economic policy from the London School of Economics and Political Science and a DPhil (PhD) in politics (positive political economy) from the University of Oxford.

Craig Hammer is program manager and senior operations officer at the World Bank. He specializes in governance reforms and, in particular, open government and open information initiatives. His work at the World Bank has included strengthening laws, policies, and regulations focused on access to information, open government data, and data-driven decision making for improved public service delivery to traditionally marginalized and underserved communities in more than 30 countries in Africa, the Middle East, Latin America, South Asia, and Central Europe. He is a member of the Council on Foreign Relations, a member of the Society for the Policy Sciences, a fellow of the World Academy of Art and Science, and a member of the Council of Editors for the *Journal of Law and Politics*. He has published books, chapters, and refereed journal articles on topics including governance, law, and development.

Authors

Bashir Ahmad is a freelance consultant promoting human rights and fighting against terrorism and extremism in the Federally Administered Tribal Areas (FATA), Pakistan. He has more than seven years of working experience in culturally diverse, politically sensitive, and challenging environments. He uses cinema as a tool to highlight social and religious issues and to promote peace. He worked for more than three years with the British Council and United Nations Population Fund Pakistan to promote cultural diversity, women's and children's rights, and equality. He is the producer and director of a short documentary film on gender discrimination and women's empowerment in FATA. His interests are identifying policy gaps and developing relevant policies to address the issues of terrorism, political violence, and religious extremism in Asia, the Middle East, and Africa. He holds an MPA from the School of Public Policy at the Central European University.

Naomi Crowther is a consultant with the World Bank Group Development Impact Evaluation Unit, working on the randomized controlled trial of a labor market intervention targeting high-risk youth in high-violence municipalities of Honduras. Before this project, she worked for the Grameen Foundation in Colombia, where she conducted a project to identify the factors that affect poverty outreach of microfinance institutions across Latin America. She has authored papers for the *Journal of Public and International Affairs*, the U.K. Department for Work and Pensions, and the International Finance Corporation. She holds an MPA in public and economic policy from the London School of Economics and Political Science.

Zintis Hermansons is a project expert at ESPON EGTC (European Grouping on Territorial Cooperation) based in Luxembourg, dealing with research on European regional and urban development. Previously, he was a national expert at the Ministry of Environmental Protection and Regional Development of Latvia, where he was involved in several international projects financed by the European Commission, Organisation for Economic Co-operation and Development, and Norway Grants that explored how regional development can be measured using statistics and spatial data. He is the author of several academic publications, and his research interest is evidence-based policy and its role in decision making in public administration. He holds an MPA from the School of Public Policy at the Central European University.

John Hudson is a professor of economics at the University of Bath. He has published almost 100 academic papers in the leading academic journals of the world, including *The Economic Journal, Journal of Economic Perspectives, World Development*, and *Social Science and Medicine*, as well as several books. Much of his work relates to development economics, with a particular focus on the effectiveness of development aid. He also has done research for public sector bodies such as DFID and the Planning Bureau in Nicosia, Cyprus; he advises the Commonwealth Scholarship Commission; and he is a past vice president of the European Academy for Standardization. He holds an MA and PhD in economics from the University of Warwick.

Ngianga-Bakwin Kandala is professor of biostatistics at Northumbria University, U.K., and head of the Health Economics and Evidence Synthesis Research Unit at the Luxembourg Institute of Health. He is also a distinguished professor at the University of Witwatersrand, South Africa. He has published more than 100 academic papers in leading academic journals, including *British Medical Journal, American Journal of Tropical Medicine and Hygiene, International Journal of Public Health, Social Science and Medicine,* and *Applied Health Economics and Health Policy,* as well as two books. His most recent book is titled *Advanced Techniques for Modelling Maternal and Child Health in Africa* (Springer Science, 2014). Previously, he was an associate professor in health technology assessment, a joint appointment with the University of Oxford and University of Warwick; he also has worked at the University of Lagos, Nigeria, and the University of Botswana. His research addresses maternal and child health and a variety of health-related inequalities in both developing countries and command economies, using large-scale household data. He also has conducted research for public sector bodies such as DFID and the United Nations Children's Fund on torture and female genital mutilation. He holds an MSc from the University of Lagos and PhD from the Ludwig-Maximilians University (LMU), Munich.

Dragana Marinkovic is a project manager at Komaza Kenya, a social enterprise focused on poverty alleviation of farmers in rural Kenya. Previously, she was a quantitative research assistant at the School of Public Policy, Central European University, where she worked on a research project focused on political economy of program evaluation (randomized controlled trials). Before that, she worked at the Center for Conflict Negotiation and Recovery, where she conducted research on best practices in conflict prevention and peace building in fragile states and was an Open Society Foundations' Rights and Governance intern in Ghana, conducting research on sustainability of Ghanaian civil society organizations. She holds an MPA from the School of Public Policy at the Central European University.

Chandni Raja is an economist in the antitrust and competition economics practice of Compass Lexecon. Before joining Compass Lexecon, she was a research assistant in development economics at the Suntory and Toyota International Centres for Economics and Related Disciplines at the London School of Economics and Political Science, where she conducted research on perceived returns to education in the labor market in South Sudan and was a consultant for DFID Sudan. She is one of the authors of the winning entry to the Financial Inclusion Insights Open Data Analysis Challenge, in which she analyzed financial inclusion in India using livelihood groups and patterns of income generation. She has also produced research on the consumption patterns of unemployed households. She holds an MPA in public and economic policy from the London School of Economics and Political Science.

Ella Spencer is the evaluation manager and an economist at the International Growth Centre (IGC). Before joining IGC, she worked as an independent development consultant, specializing in research on sustainable livelihoods in the fragile-state context. She has completed a number of evaluations in South Sudan, including those on behalf of the International Rescue Committee regarding its gender-based violence programming, and for the World Bank looking at skills development and training opportunities. Alongside this work, she founded and now runs GCSE Success, a charitable organization focused on reducing educational inequalities in the United Kingdom. She has more than four years of private sector experience, working as an actuary in the insurance sector for a number of multinational companies. She holds an MPA in public and economic policy from the London School of Economics and Political Science.

Jakob Svensson is professor of economics at the Institute for International Economic Studies, Stockholm University. He has published numerous academic papers in the leading academic journals of the world, including the *Quarterly Journal of Economics* and the *American Political Science Review*. Before his academic career, he was a senior researcher at the World Bank. In 2009, he was awarded the Assar Lindbeck Medal, which is awarded biannually to a young researcher who has made significant contributions to economic thinking and knowledge. He holds an MA and PhD in economics from the University of Stockholm.

Abbreviations

CI	confidence interval
CPA	Comprehensive Peace Agreement
CR	credible region
DDPD	Doha Document for Peace in Darfur
DFID	U.K. Department for International Development
DHS	Demographic Health Surveys
EFA	exploratory factor analysis
EU	European Union
FCAS	fragile and conflict-affected states
FGM	female genital mutilation
GDP	gross domestic product
GPE	governance and political economy
IDP	internally displaced person
INC	interim national constitution
JEM	Justice and Equality Movement
MICS	Multiple Indicator Cluster Survey
MSc	master of science
NGO	nongovernmental organization
OR	odds ratio
PhD	doctor of philosophy
POR	posterior odds ratio
SDG	Sudanese pound
SEM	structural equation modeling
SMEs	small and medium enterprises
SOE	state-owned enterprise
SPLM	Sudan People's Liberation Movement
SPSC	Sudan Polling Statistics Center
UN	United Nations

UNAMID	African Union–United Nations Hybrid Mission in Darfur
UNICEF	United Nations Children's Fund
UN OCHA	United Nations Office for the Coordination of Humanitarian Affairs
WAS	water and sanitation
WHO	World Health Organization

Introduction: What Contribution Can Survey Data Make toward Evidence-Based Policy Making in Fragile and Conflict-Affected Contexts?

Can the use of perceptions-based survey data facilitate evidence-based decision making in fragile and conflict-affected states? Survey data can, potentially, provide insights into the perceptions and experiences of not only a representative member of a population but also, depending on design, specific subgroups, enabling an analysis of the role of gender, educational, socioeconomic, geographic, and age-related variables. If such survey information is reliably and validly collected, it could provide useful information regarding the design of development programs by helping map out the context and some of the consequences of specific policy or program interventions. For example, survey data can help identify the demographic groups that are most in need in a particular area or the possibility of opposition to or support for certain interventions; the intended and unintended effect of interventions; and the potential distributional effects of a policy on different groups. Critics of survey data argue that self-reported experiences or perceptions are not likely to be a reliable or valid source on which to base decision making. Respondents may intentionally or unintentionally misreport their perceptions or experiences, and, especially in fragile and conflict-affected states, the reliability of surveys may be questionable because certain areas of the country or certain groups cannot be reliably reached at any given point in time.

The aim of this volume is to demonstrate, through the analysis of a series of surveys conducted in Sudan, how such survey tools can, under certain conditions, be used as effective instruments for understanding and designing programs and policies to produce better decision making. Sudan is a good example of a country with which to assess this proposition, because if it can be demonstrated that valid and reliable data can be collected in one of the most challenging places on earth, then arguing that such an approach would not be feasible in more benign contexts becomes more difficult. Of course, given the paucity of surveys in Sudan, this case study is somewhat likely to overstate the value added of a single survey instrument in other contexts in which data collection is more frequent. Nevertheless, the insights of the Sudan case are still likely to be, at least partially, illustrative of the power of using survey data in other contexts, whether many or a few valid and reliable survey instruments exist for use.

This volume essentially explores the stated objective—unpacking the potential role of survey data in decision making. Specifically, part 1 begins with a very simple political economy model of how and under what conditions more data, such as that collected through surveys, might serve to make decision making more effective and equitable (chapter 1). Through development of this formal model of the political economy of data collection and dissemination, deriving a set of hypotheses about whether and under what conditions data collection and generation might be able to facilitate a better understanding and more effective and inclusive policy making becomes possible. After this theoretical framework, chapter 2 concerns itself with the overall question of how to ensure that survey data collected in politically challenging and conflict-afflicted states can be used for quantitative (mostly regression-based) analysis. Through the example of the Sudan survey data sets, the chapter introduces how such surveys, in combination with the tools of econometric analysis, can provide useful insights into the context and challenges of policy making in fragile states like Sudan. Chapter 3 then delves into some of the very practical considerations that must be addressed when trying to collect reliable and valid perceptions data in contexts such as that of Sudan. This chapter therefore provides the reader with a practical roadmap for database generation and survey design. The final chapter in part 1, chapter 4, then applies the general principles of survey design and econometric analysis outlined in the previous two chapters to the case of the 2013 and 2014 U.K. Department for International Development (DFID) Sudan household surveys to demonstrate how, in practice, one can make an assessment of the utility of a given survey data set to inform decision making—in this case, focusing on the general issue of trust in public services.

Part 2 moves from the general to the specific, focusing on different thematic topics found in the DFID Sudan household surveys to illustrate how careful econometric analysis of the data can yield interesting insights into Sudan's policy-making context and political economy dynamics. Chapter 5 looks at two factors (gender and socioeconomic background) that help explain trust in tribal leaders, who play a vital institutional role in many parts of rural Sudan. Chapter 6 explores the link between government performance and state legitimacy further by examining how perceptions of service delivery and quality affect levels of trust in different types of government institutions. Chapter 7 examines what demographic factors (for example, education, gender, geographical location, and income) determine self-reported support for female genital mutilation. Chapter 8 focuses on the issue of decentralization, and chapter 9 focuses on the humanitarian and conflict contexts, which remain major concerns given the protracted humanitarian crisis. The volume concludes with an overall assessment of how and under what conditions surveys can be useful in informing our decision making, the specific strengths and limitations of the case of the DFID Sudan household surveys, and, by extension, avenues for further research.

PART 1

General Theory and Principles of Survey Design and Political Economy Dynamics

CHAPTER 1

The Political Economy of Data Collection and Evidence-Based Policy Making in Fragile Contexts

Alexander Hamilton

Introduction

In a world of scarce resources, effective decision making requires knowledge of the trade-offs between different choices. Only by knowing the pertinent facts affecting a given decision—both the costs and the benefits, intentional and unintentional—is it possible to select a policy that achieves the most feasible desired outcome. In practice, most policy is made with imperfect knowledge, especially regarding the full consequences of a decision maker's actions. This problem of imperfect knowledge is particularly pertinent with respect to public policy because the decisions of policy makers affect the incentives and behaviors of a large and diverse number of actors over a potentially long timescale. Specifically, imperfect information can enable policy makers, or the organized interest groups that are able to lobby politicians, to use public resources to generate rents rather than to provide pro-development goods and services demanded by large (and hence more disorganized) groups of citizens.

In fragile states, this problem of complexity and rent seeking in decision making is compounded by two main factors: (a) the higher costs of data collection attributable to technical factors and (b) the more pronounced political economy dynamics usually in play, such as poor accountability mechanisms, institutionalized incentives for corruption and rent extraction, and exclusionary social or political settlements. Despite those challenges, effective data collection and the evidence-based decision making that it might engender can have a transformational effect on the feasibility of pro-poor development. The transformation can occur because, on the margin, those larger and less organized groups (for example, taxpayers and the general public) that are most likely to have a preference for public goods generation and pro-development policies can be empowered by the public availability of data, thereby becoming more effective in translating their latent preferences into effective demands (Besley 2007; Olson 1971).

Consequently, availability of public data can partly offset the relative advantage of those more organized and narrow interest groups, such as lobby groups or vested interests, that are likely to favor the use of scarce public resources to produce excludable goods that are less conducive to pro-poor development.

By developing a very simple exploratory model for understanding the potential effect of public data availability on decision making, this chapter will provide a conceptual framework for understanding the conditions under which widespread availability of data can result in more pro-development decision making. Of course, as already noted, the availability of such information asymmetry–mitigating data sets is no panacea for bad decision making by itself. However, a clearer understanding of how and under what conditions the availability of better quality data can foster more pro-development decision making on the margin may make it possible to understand when and how, in practice, the political economy of data collection and decision making can play a role in fostering pro-poor development.

The rest of this chapter is organized as follows: First, a brief review of the literature on the role of data in decision making is carried out—a process that highlights both the benefits and the perils of data-driven decision making. Following that discussion, a simple formal model is developed that seeks to capture how the availability of data for decision making can affect outcomes. That process generates some basic predictions about when and how the availability of data can result in more pro-development decision making. The chapter then considers how the insights of the simple framework can be operationalized and tested in practice and also highlights the framework's limitations. The process reveals the critical and practical role for testing the importance of data-driven decision making in various contexts. The chapter concludes with a critical appraisal of the framework and suggests future avenues of theoretical and empirical research.

It is important to note that although the aim of this theoretical exercise is to illuminate the "big picture" questions that may be answered by survey data, most empirical survey data will only provide concrete but derivative evidence in support of the model. Thus, although survey data may directly be able (a) to show whether or how different groups, especially politically marginalized groups, might be affected or (b) to support a policy intervention—thereby addressing the collective action dynamics previously noted—the survey data do not explore how the policy process and lobbying process are subsequently affected. However, providing a clear theoretical framework that is consistent with survey result findings sets the stage for subsequent research to test the more refined hypotheses generated by the model offered in this chapter.

Literature

The centrality of statistics (the "science of the state") as the cornerstone of developing viable public policies has long been documented (Ball 2004; Tooze 2001). Without data, the ability to allocate resources effectively becomes increasingly difficult, especially in complex decision-making environments. Once made publicly available, statistics for decision making become a public good, exhibiting the properties of both *nonrivalry* (the consumption of statistical data by one actor not impinging on the ability of another actor to also consume the data) and *nonexcludability* (because once data sets are made public, it is not easy to restrict access to them). The more information available to help voters and other groups ascertain the actions of decision makers, the easier it is for voters to hold decision makers accountable or to challenge their decisions (Alt and Lassen 2005).

A number of skeptics dispute this narrative. They argue that the potential benefits of using data in decision making should not be overstated. According to this argument, policy making is inherently political, and transparency alone may not significantly diminish the incentives of policy makers to pursue narrow rent-seeking agendas. In fact, the argument follows, by encouraging risk aversion or even fatalism, increasing access to data may in practice reduce the quality of good governance under some conditions (see, for example, Smart and Sturm 2013). Certainly, the relative transparency of data availability across Organisation for Economic Co-operation and Development (OECD) countries has not resulted in the elimination of incentives for corruption (Hamilton 2012, 2013).

Which of these two accounts is closer to the truth? A growing corpus of work in political economics suggests that the effect depends on the context (Besley 2007). Contexts (such as liberal democratic regimes) where other factors provide at least some incentives for decision makers to be responsive to the needs of large latent groups will be far more affected by the availability of better and more accessible data than contexts (such as some highly repressive authoritarian states) in which the incentives to take into account these preferences are limited (Persson and Tabellini 2000). Therefore, the magnitude of the effect of better-quality data and better access to data may be highly contingent on other factors. Even if it is less effective in some contexts, though, it is difficult to argue, given the findings of a large body of empirical evidence, that such access to data is not usually accompanied by a relative increase in empowerment of larger latent groups (Alt and Lassen 2005).

However, even in contexts in which decision makers have an incentive to cater to the preferences of pro-development coalitions, the development of better data does not guarantee better-quality decision making. For example, because of unintended consequences, a decision aimed at achieving a positive outcome may result in negative net consequences (Hayek 1945). A good example of this unintended consequences effect is the way in which donor priorities in many African countries skewed the production of official statistics to meet donor priorities. Policy makers prioritized the development of data that complement donor evaluation and assessment needs over other data sets that were not linked to such externally funded programs. Thus, the system created perverse incentives and led to poor decision making, even as more data were actually generated and made available (Jerven 2013).

If the use of data and statistics is potentially impeded in many ways, then under what specific conditions might investing in data generation and availability be more likely to foster better decision making? At least in the case of large data sets (especially surveys and censuses, for example), the answer may lie in the free publication, dissemination, and accessibility of such data. The availability of such information may, on the margin, empower relatively large groups, such as taxpayers or civic organizations, with useful information that can help further their agendas. Conversely, smaller groups, such as lobbies or vested interest groups, tend to be better able to overcome collective action problems than their larger counterparts, meaning that they are more likely to collect private information that they can use to influence policy makers (Olson 1971; Persson and Tabellini 2000). It is important to note that whereas the magnitude of this effect may vary significantly by context (regime type, for example), the availability of more data should, on the margin, still have a positive effect and thus reduce the information inequality between small and large groups. The magnitude of this effect may vary significantly because of a host of other factors.

In short, the availability of public data at the point of demand mitigates the information asymmetries between different stakeholders in policy making. Although that factor in itself may not eliminate all the differences in the ability to incentivize decision makers, it does provide a logically consistent narrative for why the availability of large data sets can result in decision making that is more focused on large latent groups such as taxpayers, civil society, or the poor, and hence is less skewed toward the preferences of smaller, organized groups.

A Simple Model of the Political Economy of Data Collection and Availability

Let us assume a polity in which the decision maker (i) allocates tax revenue (τ), which is a proportion of national income (Y, and $\tau < Y$), to generate goods and services.[1] The decision maker (that is, politician) makes her allocation on the basis of the effective demands (lobbying efforts) of two groups. The first is a relatively large and politically disorganized group of citizens (j) who wish that tax revenue would be used to generate pro-development public goods (g). The second is a relatively small and more politically organized special interest group (γ) with a preference for private goods that furthers the interests of its own group but no one else's (r). By definition, given that N is the total population, it is assumed that N_j is greater than N_γ. The two groups noncooperatively and simultaneously lobby the decision maker for the use of tax revenues in the first period, and the decision maker makes an allocation on that basis in the second period. The decision maker therefore allocates tax revenue to maximize her utility function:

$$U_{i[max]} = (1-N_\gamma)r + (1-N_j)g.$$

$$\text{s.t } 0 < \tau < Y \quad (1.01)$$

Expression (1.01) has a very intuitive interpretation. Because, by definition, N_j is greater than N_y, the decision maker has an incentive to provide relatively more private (r) than pro-development (g) goods given the collective action dynamics at play. This situation captures the intuition expressed by Olson (1971) that small groups, because they are better able to organize, face fewer collective action problems and are actually in a better position to lobby decision makers than are large groups that suffer from more pronounced free-rider constraints.

How can the provision of large-scale, publicly available data affect the incentives of decision makers? When citizens face greater collective action issues and data collection is costly, the absence of such data indicates a significant information asymmetry: the smaller lobby group is more likely to be able to collect and selectively communicate data to serve its purpose. The availability of publicly available data is, therefore, likely to strengthen the relative bargaining position of citizens (N_j) because (a) the citizen group has access to data on the effects on and needs of the broad population and (b) the ability of special interest groups to selectively communicate specific elements of information is diminished. Thus, expression (1.01) can be rewritten as follows:

$$U_{i[max]} = [(1-\alpha)(1-N_\gamma)r] + [\alpha(1-N_j)g],$$

$$\text{s.t} < \tau < Y \qquad (1.02)$$

where α is an index, $0 \leq a \leq 1$, of the public availability of valid data for evidence-based decision making. Intuitively, as the level of such data increases, so does the relative bargaining power of citizens in relation to the organized lobby. Consequently, the relative informational asymmetries between the two groups diminish. Thus, expression (1.02) shows that the greater availability of data can result in a more effective allocation of public resources because policy makers have, on the margin, a greater incentive to take into account the preferences of large latent groups over those of organized lobbies.

Expressions (1.01) and (1.02) very simply illustrate that in the presence of collective action problems, where policy makers have an incentive to allocate tax revenues to optimize joint effective demand, the availability of public data can, by diminishing the information asymmetries between large latent groups and smaller organized lobbies, result in more pro-development outcomes. Thus, we can derive a simple testable implication for the model that the growth in the availability of public data sets should, on the margin, result in more pro-development spending.

Robustness Tests

The simple formalization in the previous section makes several assumptions that can be relaxed to derive more sophisticated hypotheses about the effect of public data availability on decision making. First, the assumption that decision makers have no agenda of their own, but simply respond to the effective demand of different groups, may be unrealistic. Second, even if the generation of public data may be desired, technical constraints in data collection may mean that the data sets generated are misleading and cannot be used for effective decision making. The growing literature on ways in which statistical data are compiled demonstrates that second possibility (see, for example, Jerven 2013).

Nonbenevolent Decision Makers

Like interest groups, decision makers may prefer to use public finances to serve their own agenda: the generation of their own private goods (r_i). This scenario can be modeled by modifying expression (1.02) as follows:

$$U_{i[max]} = (1-\beta)\{[(1-\alpha)(1-N_\gamma)r] + [\alpha(1-N_j)g]\} + \beta(r),$$

$$\text{s.t } \tau < Y \quad (1.03)$$

where β ($0 \leq \beta \leq 1$) represents the taste of the decision maker to allocate resources to satisfy either (a) her individual needs or (b) the private needs of interest groups and the pro-development needs of the public. Expression (1.03) is intuitively interesting because unless the decision maker is entirely nonbenevolent, $\beta = 0$, the existence of publicly available data (α) should still result in an improvement in the provision of pro-poor development. However, the magnitude of this result will clearly be affected by the level of nonbenevolence of decision makers, which in itself may be a function of other institutions (regime type, for example).

Biased Information

As documented extensively by Jerven (2013, 2014), if the data developed and used are biased, then using the data can have a detrimental effect because biased data can skew decisions. Interestingly, the welfare implications of such a skew may not be detrimental to large latent groups. If the biased data (incorrectly) make the evidence appear to be more conducive to the priorities of large latent groups than would otherwise be the case, then such biases can benefit those groups. Of course, as also documented by Jerven (2013, 2014), smaller groups are more likely to have the resources and ability to assess data quality and ensure that the facts are not inconsistent with their private agenda. Therefore, such an outcome is unlikely. The effect of biased data can be modeled by incorporating the term ε into expression (1.02), where $-\infty \leq \varepsilon \leq \infty$. The extent to which policy will favor any group will depend on the relative bias of data in favor of a group's agenda. Because there is a resource constraint ($\tau < Y$), the group that has the highest realization of ε will have the greatest ability to benefit from biased data sources.

$$U_{i[max]} = \varepsilon_\gamma (1-\beta)\{[(1-\alpha)(1-N_\gamma)r] + \varepsilon_j [\alpha(1-N_j)g]\} + \varepsilon_i \beta(r).$$

$$\text{s.t } \tau < Y \quad (1.04)$$

Limitations

This simple model provides a basic conceptual framework for linking political economy dynamics with the effect of better data collection and dissemination. Although it can capture the effect of known technical and nontechnical factors on the effect of data, it assumes knowledge of the full effects of increased (valid) data on public policy making. However, in complex (multidimensional) decision-making environments, the distribution of unintended (positive and negative) consequences may be unknown (Riker 1982), and as a result, it may be difficult to anticipate the full welfare effects of greater data availability. For example, data transparency may incentivize extreme risk aversion if such data make the short-term costs of initiatives, but not their long-term benefits, more visible. Moreover, a misinterpretation of key data could result in an unexpectedly strong public reaction. The effect of low-probability extreme events could be disproportionately negative. For example, perverse political economy incentives could arise if manipulated results from clinical trials were used to persuade policy makers to approve products that were not safe or did not yield the benefits suggested. Such a result would completely negate the overall expected utility of data dissemination. Although under certain conditions and assumptions, then, we may be able to anticipate the effect of greater data openness and availability, we must remember that such expectations do not always prove accurate.

Conclusion and Policy Implications

How does the availability of data affect the incentives for pro-poor decision making? Differential collective action capabilities that tend to favor small privileged groups suggest that the public availability of data should, on the margin, help empower larger groups to provide incentives for policy makers. Such incentives should shift resources toward the provision of more pro-developmental public goods favored by diffuse interests. How and to what extent this dynamic occurs depend on the totality of incentives faced by decision makers. Therefore, although more data availability is likely to be conducive to pro-poor development, its effect will also be determined by how other institutional factors (personal preferences of decision makers, for example) and technical factors (that generate biases in data sets, such as outright manipulation, poor design, and so on) affect outcomes. The practical implications are that the generation and public availability of data are likely to be critical in fostering pro-poor development but that the effect is likely to be determined by other contextual and technical factors.

One important way in which we can begin to explore whether the implications of this simple model are consistent with realities on the ground is by examining general population survey data across a range of development issues: from governance to service delivery to economic development in fragile states. Large-scale population surveys could provide useful insights into the perceptions of the population on a range of critical issues, especially in those states with little history of polling such as Sudan and, to a much lesser extent, Ethiopia. Furthermore, disaggregation based on gender, regional, socioeconomic, ethnic, and cultural variables can allow us to identify how perceptions vary across groups. Thus, we can gain a more nuanced understanding of the needs and perceptions of elements of the population, as well as the potential role of institutional and contextual factors (marginalization or discrimination, for example) in explaining variations in perceptions. Such surveys, therefore, have a potentially critical role to play in enhancing the possibility of evidence-based decision making.

Of course, such surveys also pose significant challenges. For example, respondents may intentionally or unintentionally choose not to respond truthfully to survey responses. Some population groups may be poorly represented regardless of sample sizes (nomadic people, for example). Moreover, standard error of surveys over time could make comparisons difficult or unfeasible, and multiple factors that determine responses might make it difficult to attribute changes in perceptions over time to specific interventions.[2] Despite these potential limitations, as the ensuing chapters demonstrate, as long as survey data are rigorously and critically reviewed and assessed alongside other data sources, they can provide a critical contribution to the development of a robust evidence-based ecosystem.

Notes

1. The model in this section is based on Persson and Tabellini's (2000, 172–77) model on lobby groups. We thank MIT University Press for permission to reproduce elements of this model.
2. For a review of the benefits and limits of survey-based data, see Hamilton (2012).

Bibliography

Alt, J., and D. Lassen. 2005. "The Political Budget Cycle Is Where You Can't See It: Transparency and Fiscal Manipulation." EPRU Working Paper 05–03, Economic Policy Research Unit, Department of Economics, University of Copenhagen.

Ball, P. 2004. *Critical Mass: How One Thing Leads to Another*. New York: Farrar, Straus and Giroux.

Besley, T. 2007. *Principled Agents? The Political Economy of Good Government*. Oxford, U.K.: Oxford University Press.

Bowden, R. 1989. *Statistical Games and Human Affairs: The View from Within*. Cambridge, U.K.: Cambridge University Press.

DFID (U.K. Department for International Development). 2005. "Reducing Poverty by Tackling Social Exclusion: A DFID Policy Paper." DFID, London.

Hamilton, A. 2012. "Elections, Context and Institutions: The Determinants of Rent Extraction in High-Income Democracies." PhD thesis, Oxford University, Oxford, U.K. http://ethos.bl.uk/OrderDetails.do?uin=uk.bl.ethos.570703.

———. 2013. "Small Is Beautiful, at Least in High-Income Democracies: The Distribution of Policy-Making Responsibility, Electoral Accountability, and Incentives for Rent Extraction." Policy Research Working Paper 6305, World Bank, Washington DC.

Hayek, F. A. 1945. "The Use of Knowledge in Society." *American Economic Review* 35 (4): 519–30.

Jerven, M. 2013. *Poor Numbers: How We Are Misled by African Development Statistics and What to Do About It*. Ithaca, NY: Cornell University Press.

———. 2014. "The Political Economy of Agricultural Statistics and Input Subsidies: Evidence from India, Nigeria, and Malawi." *Journal of Agrarian Change* 14 (1): 129–45.

Muller, D. 2003. *Public Choice III*. Oxford, U.K.: Oxford University Press.

Niskanen, W. 2007. *Bureaucracy and Representative Government*. Chicago: Aldine Transactions.

Olson, M. 1971. *The Logic of Collective Action: Public Goods and the Theory of Groups*. Cambridge, MA: Harvard University Press.

Persson, T., and G. Tabellini. 2000. *Political Economics: Explaining Economic Policy*. Cambridge, MA: MIT University Press.

Riker, W. H. 1982. *Liberalism Against Populism: A Confrontation Between the Theory of Democracy and the Theory of Social Choice*. San Francisco: Freeman and Company.

Smart, M., and D. Sturm. 2013. "Term Limits and Electoral Accountability." *Journal of Public Economics* 107: 93–102.

Tooze, A. 2001. *Statistics and the German State, 1900–1945: The Making of Modern Economic Knowledge*. Cambridge, U.K.: Cambridge University Press.

CHAPTER 2

Understanding and Preparing Survey Data for Quantitative Analysis

Chandni Raja, Naomi Crowther, and Ella Spencer

Introduction

This chapter provides an overview of the data collection process and the initial steps for data cleaning and organization for data collected in fragile and conflict-affected states (FCAS), using household survey data collected by the Department for International Development (DFID) Sudan in 2013 as a case study. The decision to focus our discussion of data analysis in fragile states on the Sudan was guided by the internal and external conflict the country has suffered over the past several decades. Thus, the main issues that will be discussed regarding the validity of data collected in this context of violence and conflict have crystallized across institutions and actors. The long-standing disruption to Sudan's economy and population entails that each aspect of the data collected—from the way the questions were worded, to the ethnicity and gender of the enumerator, and the location of conflict hot spots at the time each interview took place—must be taken into account in the methods of data analysis and interpretation of the results. The case of Sudan enables us to demonstrate a significant number of the most common obstacles in a given data set. The 2013 DFID Sudan household survey was designed to obtain a representative view of the Sudanese citizens' perceptions of public institutions, public service provision, the economy, conflict, and more to inform evidence-based policy making.

We discuss, first, the collection of representative survey data using sampling methods, and describe how these methods can be used to produce a

---

Authors' Note: This chapter is based on the joint U.K. Department for International Development (DFID)–London School of Economics Capstone Project (2013), "Inequalities in Public Services in the Sudan: Using a Perceptions-Informed View to Drive Policy in Education, Health and Water Provision," https://www.gov.uk/dfid-research-outputs. Permission to reproduce large parts of this work was granted by DFID.

survey design. We then turn to the initial steps for data cleaning and data organization, highlighting the key stages, the intuition behind each, and the methods used to undertake them. We pay particular attention to handling missing responses, ordering responses, recoding responses, and merging and appending data sets. Each of these sections addresses the particular challenges that arise in data collected from FCAS and, more specifically, that arose in the collection of the 2013 DFID Sudan household survey data. The intuition behind the adjustments that were made is explained such that the readers may understand the reasoning and adapt the recommendations to their own specific data sets.

Literature Review

Several authors have written on the quantitative analysis of household survey data, particularly data from developing countries and FCAS. Deaton's work (1997) on the microeconometric analysis of household survey data discusses, in a comprehensive fashion, methodologies for using household survey data from developing countries and the potential issues that researchers may run into while doing so, including survey design and regressions, simultaneity, measurement error, and use of instrumental variables. He also provides an in-depth look at data from several countries including Côte d'Ivoire, India, and Thailand. This chapter will draw from Deaton's discussions of survey design and sample weighting.

The United Nations Department of Economic and Social Affairs (2005) published "Household Sample Surveys in Developing and Transition Countries," which covers basic to advanced techniques in working with survey data and pays special attention to the needs of developing countries. Such needs for the implementation of surveys in those countries include the training of staff, financing, pilot tests, data management, and preparation of the final data set. We do not discuss those issues in this chapter but recommend this publication as a good resource to address the administrative and logistical issues of collecting and organizing data in developing states.

Data Collection

In July 2013, DFID Sudan commissioned the collection of public opinion survey data to inform evidence-based policy making. The surveys (hereafter "the DFID Sudan household surveys") aimed to garner perceptions held by Sudanese citizens on a range of topics from their levels of trust in public institutions to ratings of public service provision, police, legislators, and other public servants; and from their perceptions of the economy and the conflict setting to indications of their personal financial and economic behaviors. DFID Sudan hired a polling company, the Sudan Polling Statistics Center (SPSC), to collect the data by carrying out personal interviews at the household level.

Sampling Design

Household survey data are traditionally collected through a sample of responses from a frame or national list of households. The sample size depends on the size of the frame and the accuracy of the sample statistics for different sample sizes. Deaton (1997) argues that the accuracy of sample statistics does not increase proportionally with the sample size; rather, data validity normally increases proportionally with the square root of the sample size. This implies that larger populations will tend to have smaller sampling fractions than do smaller populations. The frame is often constructed using census data, but this is not possible in states where no recent census exists or where census data may not be accurate for any of several reasons. In cases in which the census data used for the sample frame are not representative of the population at large, issues of noncoverage of certain populations can arise. For example, displaced persons are a major group that may not be represented in a national census, especially in fragile states. If the sampling design of a household survey uses the census as the frame, groups such as these may not be represented accurately. This was the case in Sudan, where the most recent nationwide census of 2008 was widely contested, particularly with respect to displaced population estimates for the Darfur region (*Sudan Tribune* 2009).

The context of data collection must be considered when analyzing any data sourced from conflict states. First, if possible, the inaccuracy of the data sets should be mitigated by cross-checking significant differences in response rates and total observations to the same questions across years and regions. If any significant differences are found, the researcher should search for contextual reasons, and if none can satisfactorily explain the variation, measurement error may have occurred. This possibility should be considered when using the results from the data analysis for policy and decision making. Errors could render the results biased toward a subsection of the population and could make the findings both internally and externally invalid.

The most common statistical sampling method is two-stage cluster sampling, wherein clusters of households are randomly selected from the frame during the first stage, with households then randomly selected from those clusters at the second stage. The DFID Sudan household surveys used a multistage cluster sampling, with stratification of the sample on state and gender. Stratification is a step taken to collect data from fewer people while retaining a representativeness based on a set of predefined variables. Stratification ensures that the strata in question are represented in the data with enough observations to obtain reliable estimates from them, a result that is not guaranteed by simple random sampling. Stratification is particularly important in fragile states where certain areas of a country will likely be more affected by conflict than others, and therefore, without additional effort to collect data from these conflict areas, the results would be biased by *easier access* data from the less conflicted areas of the country.

Stratification not only ensures that certain groups are represented in the sample but also often improves the efficiency of statistical estimates. The variance of statistical estimates, calculated using simple random sampling, consists of both within-strata and between-strata variance. Between-strata variance arises because there may be unequal representation of different strata in the sample. However, the variance of statistical estimates with stratification is dependent on within-strata variation only. Hence, in cases in which there is large variation across strata and in which within-strata variation is limited, stratification will have the greatest effect on reducing the variance of statistical estimates (Deaton 1997). In the case of the DFID Sudan household surveys, following stratification on state, a multistage sampling process was used to randomly select respondents. First, four localities were randomly selected from each stratum, the probability of selection proportional to size. A cluster was then randomly selected from each of the four localities in each state. Households were randomly selected from each cluster using systematic random sampling. Finally, one individual over age 18 was selected from within each household using the Kish table method. At this stage, to ensure fair gender representation and to follow the stratification based on gender, a female respondent was chosen from alternate households. Table 2.1 illustrates the survey design for the DFID Sudan household surveys.

Although the procedure described was the sampling strategy intended for the DFID Sudan household survey data collection process, we are uncertain how closely it was followed. The two main causes for concern are (1) in certain regions, there were high rates of refusal to participate in the survey, possibly because the survey included several sensitive questions relating to political affiliation, personal opinion on female genital mutilation, and the taking of bribes; and (2) there were reportedly challenges in collecting data in conflict regions.

On the first point, the polling company (SPSC) field report suggests that interviewers encountered challenges during the data collection process. In Khartoum and across the Darfur states, more than 40 percent of people approached refused to participate in the survey. This is distinct from nonresponse to particular questions, which will be discussed in the following section.

On the second point, data collection in conflict areas is logistically challenging. Polling staff encountered problems reaching people living in certain regions, including both a lack of infrastructure and greater social fragmentation caused by the large diversity of cultures and religions in Sudan. In addition, we expected high numbers of people to have been displaced as a result of the conflict so were cautious when analyzing data coming from regions in conflict, including Darfur states. A number of quick statistics can be used to check when looking for *rogue* data. These include running density plots of responses across different regions to check they are normally distributed. If variations are uncovered, simple tests of statistically significant differences in means can be informative. If the researcher's contextual knowledge of the country does not yield an explanation of the variation, the data may be biased. In that case, the researcher should set up a meeting with the data collectors and carry out additional statistical tests.

Understanding and Preparing Survey Data for Quantitative Analysis

Table 2.1 DFID Sudan Household Surveys Design, 2013

Region (population in thousands)	State	DFID Sudan 2013 Survey			2008 Census	
		Number of localities sampled	Number of clusters sampled	Number of households sampled	Population in thousands	Geographical weights
Total		70	238[k]	2,365	30,894	n.a.
North (1,820)	Northern	2	15	150	699	0.357
	River Nile	3	15	150	1,120	0.572
East (4,534)	Red Sea	6	15	150	1,396	0.713
	Kassala	2	14[a]	140[e]	1,790	0.979
	Al Qadarif	4	15	150	1,348	0.688
Khartoum	Khartoum	6	26	258[f]	5,274	1.565
Al-awsut (7,423)	Al Jazirah	6	18[b]	172[g]	3,575	1.591
	White Nile	4	16[c]	150	1,731	0.883
	Sennar	4	16[d]	150	1,285	0.656
	Blue Nile	2	15	150	832	0.425
Kurdufan (4,327)	North Kurdufan	3	15	150	2,921	1.491
	South Kurdufan	6	15	143	1,406	0.753
Darfur (7,515)	North Darfur	9	10	102	2,114	1.586
	West Darfur	2	15	151[h]	1,308	0.663
	South Darfur	11	20	199[j]	4,094	1.575

Source: Based on data from the 2013 U.K. Department for International Development Sudan household surveys and the 2008 Sudan National Census.
Note: Numbers with superscript letters are different from the original survey design by the Sudan Polling Statistics Center, where the design stipulated that a = 15, b = 17, c = 15, d = 15, e = 150, f = 257, g = 174, h = 150, I = 200, and j = 2,375. Furthermore, in the collected data, some clusters belonged to different states, possibly because of coding errors. Thus, the sum of the numbers for the clustered samples does not match the total number of clusters (k). DFID = U.K. Department for International Development; n.a. = not applicable.

Sample Weighting

Although the construction of a survey design attempts to accurately represent a population as a whole, the probability of selection differs across individuals in that population. Each household surveyed in the data represents a different number of households in the population (Deaton 1997). These sample weights ensure that when a sample is used to calculate statistical estimates, these estimates reflect the population by addressing and correcting for the sampling design used to collect the data. Deaton (1997, 15) explains:

> The rule here is to weight according to the reciprocals of sampling probabilities because households with low (high) probabilities of selection stand proxy for large (small) numbers of households in the population.

The sampling weights that were used in the analysis of the DFID Sudan household survey data are presented in table 2.2. They reflect the stratification of the population based on gender and state. They do not, however, reflect the multistage cluster sampling strategy that was used to collect the data. To accurately account for the sampling strategy, we need details that include the number of

Table 2.2 Sampling Weights Based on Gender and Geographical Strata

Region (population in thousands)	State	2008 Census						DFID Sudan 2013 survey						Sampling weight (gender x state)	
		Total population in thousands	Male		Female			Total sample	Male		Female			Male	Female
Total		30,894	15,767	51%	15,127	49%		2,365	1,181	50%	1,184	50%		n.a.	n.a.
North (1,820)	Northern	699	354	1.1%	345	1.1%		150	76	3.2%	74	3.1%		0.3563	0.3572
	River Nile	1,120	572	1.9%	549	1.8%		150	72	3.0%	78	3.3%		0.6080	0.5385
East (4,534)	Red Sea	1,396	801	2.6%	595	1.9%		150	74	3.1%	76	3.2%		0.8283	0.5997
	Kassala	1,790	991	3.2%	799	2.6%		140	75	3.2%	65	2.7%		1.0113	0.9410
	Al Qadarif	1,348	670	2.2%	679	2.2%		150	73	3.1%	77	3.3%		0.7024	0.6746
Khartoum	Khartoum	5,274	2,800	9.1%	2,474	8.0%		258	131	5.5%	127	5.4%		1.6362	1.4914
Al-awsut (7,423)	Al Jazirah	3,575	1,724	5.6%	1,851	6.0%		172	85	3.6%	87	3.7%		1.5530	1.6287
	White Nile	1,731	849	2.7%	881	2.9%		150	74	3.1%	76	3.2%		0.8784	0.8878
	Sennar	1,285	626	2.0%	659	2.1%		150	74	3.1%	76	3.2%		0.6473	0.6641
	Blue Nile	832	422	1.4%	410	1.3%		150	73	3.1%	77	3.3%		0.4423	0.4080
Kurdufan (4,327)	North Kurdufan	2,921	1,407	4.6%	1,514	4.9%		150	75	3.2%	75	3.2%		1.4357	1.5458
	South Kurdufan	1,406	695	2.2%	712	2.3%		143	74	3.1%	69	2.9%		0.7188	0.7894
Darfur (7,515)	North Darfur	2,114	1,080	3.5%	1,034	3.3%		102	51	2.2%	51	2.2%		1.6210	1.5516
	West Darfur	1,308	640	2.1%	668	2.2%		151	77	3.3%	74	3.1%		0.6362	0.6914
	South Darfur	4,094	2,138	6.9%	1,956	6.3%		199	97	4.1%	102	4.3%		1.6872	1.4678

Source: Based on data from the 2013 U.K. Department for International Development Sudan household surveys and the 2008 Sudan National Census.
Note: DFID = U.K. Department for International Development; n.a. = not applicable.

localities in each state, villages in each locality, and households in each village in Sudan. Because the polling company only provided this information for a limited number of states, we could only incorporate the probability of selection on the basis of the stratification by state and gender. Researchers are always advised to investigate which polling companies have ensured stratified sampling in their surveys when deciding which data sets to use (when there is a choice). That data quality check step is particularly important in fragile states where the potential bias of having certain parts of the population missing from data collection could be largest and greatly mislead policy recommendations. Moreover, stratified sampling enables the researcher to undertake robust analysis of particular subsets of interest because that particular subset has been sampled in sufficient numbers.

Data Cleaning

Once the data have been collected using a sampling design that took into account sampling weights, initial data organization and cleaning must be performed. In the case of the DFID Sudan household survey data, data cleaning was needed to address the presence of missing responses, the ordering of responses and miscoded responses, and the merging or appending of data sets across different time periods.

Missing Responses

Analyzing the presence of missing responses was critical given the sensitive nature of the questions within the Sudanese data set and the complexity of the content addressed in the survey. Respondents were offered the option of responding "Don't know" for all questions. Any responses that were not one of the options provided or "Don't know" were coded as "Refuse." We then were able to identify how those missing responses were distributed with respect to a respondent's location, educational background, and political affiliation. For example, were respondents of a particular political persuasion more nonresponsive on average than their counterparts? Were there more nonresponses in certain areas compared with others?

We also analyzed whether certain questions attracted more nonresponses. We found that questions on respondents' political affiliation and on their level of trust in public institutions were particularly sensitive to missing responses. An avenue explored was whether questions that we thought more politically sensitive had more missing responses than others. A high number of missing responses to political questions could belie an atmosphere of censure. A following step would be to determine whether those nonresponses were uniform across sociodemographic groups of the population and then seek to contextualize this information given knowledge of the country's political landscape. Variation within subgroups of the population could imply that certain groups may feel particularly intimidated. Figure 2.1a shows the

Figure 2.1 Distribution of Responses to Two Questions in the Data Set

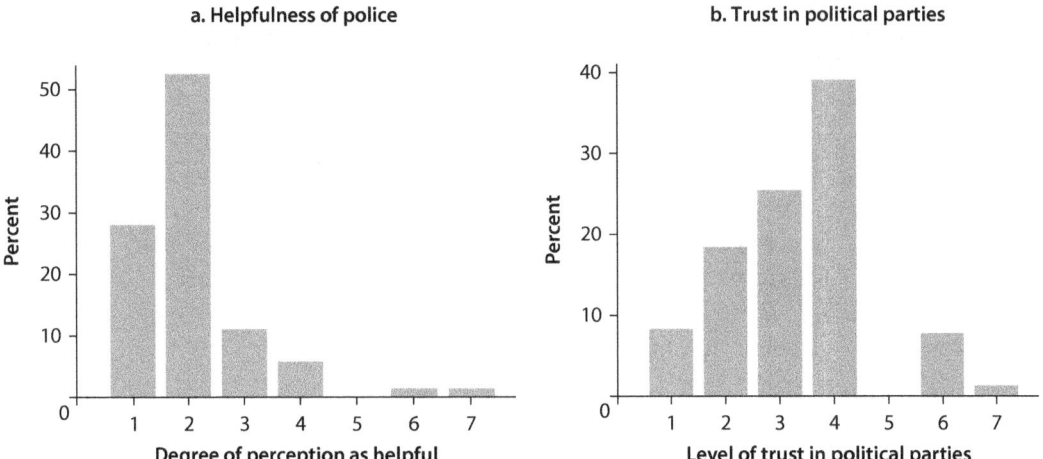

Source: Based on data from the 2013 U.K. Department for International Development Sudan household surveys.
Note: In panel (a), 1 = "Strongly agree," 2 = "Agree," 3 = "Disagree," 4 = "Strongly disagree," 6 = "Don't know," and 7 = "Refused to answer."
In panel (b), 1 = "A lot," 2 = "Some," 3 = "A little," 4 = "Not at all," 6 = "Don't know," and 7 = "Refused to answer."

rating of police helpfulness according to participant responses; figure 2.1b shows the rating of levels of trust in political parties by participants. Specifically, figure 2.1a shows the responses to the question "The police in my area are helpful," ranging from "Strongly agree" (1) to "Strongly disagree" (4), "Don't know" (6), and "Refused to answer" (7). Responses to how much trust respondents had in political parties are shown in figure 2.1b, ranging from "A lot" (1) to "Not at all" (4), "Don't know" (6), and "Refused to answer" (7).

The statistical software, Stata, automatically drops observations that have missing values for any of the variables included in a regression analysis. The decision to continue using variables that have significant numbers of missing values in a quantitative analysis is at the discretion of the researcher. At times, the sample is reduced to such a small size that conducting a quantitative analysis on a given variable risks misleading a researcher if he or she treats responses as representative. In the analysis of the DFID Sudan household survey data, we used some questions that had significant numbers of missing responses, but we acknowledged them and provided an analysis for how ignoring those responses could bias results. Indeed, using a question that has attracted many missing responses is a delicate matter. If missing responses are nonrandom, the researcher is working with information from a biased subsample of the population. If the results are assumed to be representative of the entire population, the research could produce misleading results. Uncovering whether a certain area or a certain demographic of the population has not answered the question is essential as the reason for the missing response may be a key to a more complete and accurate understanding of the context.

Missing responses pose an obvious challenge to data analysis, but the existence of social or cultural norms that result in social expectancy bias is a challenge that is more difficult to detect. We expected questions on topics related to social norms, such as female genital mutilation, to be subject to social expectancy bias. As a result, we were especially cautious in how the responses to those questions were used to inform and develop policy recommendations.

Tests can be used to determine the substantive validity of survey data, in terms of the variance of response and nonresponse, by comparing responses to *critical questions*, in which the respondent can express criticism of the regime, and *noncritical questions*, in which the respondent does not have an opportunity to do so (Horne 2011; Horne and Bakker 2009). Further information on how survey data can be used in conjunction with other data sources to assess the validity of the data, a method known as *triangulation*, is discussed in the next two chapters.

Ordering of Responses

In statistical analysis, considering whether the responses to survey questions are coded as continuous, ordinal, nominal, or binary is pivotal. Responses that are coded differently also should be interpreted accordingly and, in the case of nominal variables, should be modified for use in quantitative analysis. Continuous variables are always numeric and can take on any values in a range. That is distinct from categorical variables, which can also be numeric but must take on values that are categorized. We will provide examples of the different types of coding from the variables in our data set.

A clear example of a categorical variable in the DFID Sudan household surveys is that of the household income variable, described as "IncHH." It refers to the question, "What is your household income?," and is expressed in Sudanese pounds (abbreviated as SDG in the surveys). The possible responses to the question are "1—100–500 SDG," "2—500–1,000 SDG," "3—More than 1,000 SDG," "6—Don't know," and "7—Refuse." IncHH is not a continuous variable given that when the variable takes on a value between SDG 100 and SDG 500, for example, it is not coded as its exact value. Rather, it is coded as the category in which that value falls. Categorical variables that take on only one of two potential values are called binary variables. In this case, IncHH is an ordinal rather than a nominal categorical variable, because the income categories have an intrinsic ordering, defined numerically.

An ordinal categorical variable is not necessarily numeric. For example, the variable "IncSituation," referring to the question, "Which of the following statements most closely reflects [sic] your situation about your household income?," has the following possible responses: "1—Enough to cover my household bills"; "2—Not enough to cover my household bills"; "3—Enough to cover my household bills and to save"; "4—Cover my necessary expenses, there is nothing left over"; "6—Don't know"; and "7—Refuse." Though the categories are not defined numerically, "Not enough to cover my household bills,"

"Enough to cover my household bills," and "Enough to cover my household bills and to save" clearly correspond to increasingly higher levels of relative income (measured by this variable). However, this variable does need to be recoded so that the intrinsic ordering of the responses matches the coding. This will be discussed in the next section on miscoded variables.

Finally, some variables are both categorical and nominal, meaning that the categories do not have an intrinsic ordering. An example from Sudan's household survey data set is "notWork163b," referring to the question, "If you're not working, why not?," for which the possible responses are "1—House wife," "2—Student," "3—Retired," "4—Incapable," "5—Other," "6—Don't know," and "7—Refuse." These categories cannot be ordered in the same way as income or education categories, for example. They are therefore classified as nominal variables. To use nominal variables in regression analyses, they must be converted into binary variables. For example, to estimate the correlation between one member of the household's being "incapable" of working and the household's income, a binary variable would be generated—let it be called "incapability"—which takes on a value of 1 if notWork163b is equal to 4 and has a value of 0 otherwise. IncHH could then be regressed on incapability, which would allow an estimate of the correlation between these two variables.

Recoding of Responses

Response options may not always be coded in accordance with their intrinsic ordering, as is the case for the variable "HouseholdIncome140." Indeed, the original coding of response options was as follows:

- "1—Enough to cover my household bills"
- "2—Not enough to cover my household bills"
- "3—Enough to cover my household income and to save"
- "4—Cover my necessary expenses, there is nothing left over"

The HouseholdIncome140 variable needed to be recoded to match the order of the rest of the dataset responses, such that "2—Not enough to cover my household bills" took the lowest value (1); "4—Cover my necessary expenses, there is nothing left over" came next in the series (2); "1—Enough to cover my household bills" moved to the third-highest position (3); and "3—Enough to cover my household income and to save" became (4) under the new coding. Notice, however, whether "Cover my necessary expenses, there is nothing left over" represents greater or lesser income than "Enough to cover my household bills" is still ambiguous. The responses could be worded more clearly in future research to deter this ambiguity and preferably could be coded consistently into the questionnaire layout.

The codebook is normally a spreadsheet of some sort that links the question numbering of the data output of the survey to the exact wording in the questionnaire. It is a crucial piece of information that must be checked before any in-depth analysis is undertaken. Sometimes responses are coded as values that are not specified in the codebook. Those are most likely errors in the coding process, unless possible responses given in the survey were left out of the codebook. Working with the DFID Sudan household survey data, we referred to the codebook supplied by the polling company. For data in which response codes were not listed in the codebook, we presumed that the data had been miscoded. Because the proper coding of those responses was unclear, we chose to drop miscoded observations from the data set rather than recode them as missing values. Although miscoded observations can be recoded as "missing," that action could bias the results. If several responses were miscoded nonrandomly and recoded as missing values, then a researcher could possibly infer an inaccurate pattern regarding nonresponses. For example, in the case of the DFID Sudan household survey data collected from the Darfur states, we could have inaccurately inferred that both miscoded responses (if recoded as "missing") from the state of West Darfur and truly missing responses from North Darfur reflected systematic nonresponse to a particular question. In reality, it only reflected nonresponse from North Darfur.

Merging or Appending of Data

Often, survey data collected will be provided as multiple data sets that need to be brought together. There are a few potential scenarios: (1) the data sets in question consist of repeated observations spanning several time periods and asking the same or similar questions, that is, they form a panel data set; (2) the data sets consist of repeated observations spanning one or several time periods but ask different questions in each of the sets; (3) the data sets do not consist of repeated observations; or (4) some combination of the scenarios occurred. In any of these cases, there are two main options for data organization—*merging* or *appending*. Merging data sets creates a *wide* data set, whereas appending creates a *long* data set. For example, in scenario (1), in which two data sets with the same observations are repeated in different time periods, the two data sets can be either merged or appended. Merging the two data sets would create a single line entry for each observation but separate variables that are specific to each year. For example, an observation #1,321 and a variable "Income166" were found in both Data Set 2012 and Data Set 2013, and then merging Data Set 2013 with Data Set 2012 would result in one line entry under observation #1,321 with two income variables, hypothetically, Income166.2012 and Income166.2013. This would be an example of a wide data set.

Alternatively, appending data sets is possible as long as they have identical column headers, that is, they share the same variable list. When appending a data set—for example, in the case of a time series survey in which the same individual has been surveyed at different time periods—a researcher would create two line entries for a given observation. However, before merging the two data sets, the researcher must create a new variable in each data set with variable names—year, for example—in which all observations of the first data set are given a value, say 2012, and all observations in the second data set another value, say 2013. This will allow the researcher to differentiate the two values of a given observation. In this example, observation #1,321 would be repeated in the data set with a new variable "Year" that would take on the values of 2012 and 2013 for the two lines of observation #1,321. Each of the entries for this observation would take on potentially different values of a single variable Income166. Variables found in 2012 data but not in 2013 data would register missing values for all of the 2013 data points and vice versa. This would be an example of a long data set. Tables 2.3 and 2.4 provide a visual example of the same data set in wide form and long form, respectively.

In the case of the DFID Sudan household surveys, we were supplied with two data sets: one from 2012 and the other from 2013. However, neither data set was a panel data set. Thus there were no repeated observations between the two years, and if they were repeated, it was not intentional. Furthermore, identifying repeated observations was not possible. We therefore appended the data such that the variables found in both data sets became one variable entry in the new data set and the number of observations doubled, assuming an equal number of observations was found in each of the two data sets. Depending on the formats of the existing and desired data sets, a researcher can determine whether merging or appending is the more appropriate data organization tool to aggregate the data into a format that will allow full econometric analysis.

Table 2.3 Example of a Data Set in Wide Form

	famid	faminc96	faminc97	famince98
1.	1	40000	40500	41000
2.	2	45000	45400	45800
3.	3	75000	76000	77000

Source: UCLA Statistical Consulting Group 2006.

Table 2.4 Example of the Same Data Set in Long Form

	famid	year	faminc
1.	1	96	40000
2.	1	97	40500
3.	1	98	41000
4.	2	96	45000
5.	2	97	45400
6.	2	98	45800
7.	3	96	75000
8.	3	97	76000
9.	3	98	77000

Source: UCLA Statistical Consulting Group 2006.

Conclusion

This chapter provides a step-by-step breakdown of the key stages to be undertaken when dealing with a data set from a fragile state: from data collection to merging of data sets to creation of time series or panel data. To illustrate each step, we provide evidence from our preparation of the DFID Sudan household surveys. These data collection, cleaning, and organization steps are invaluable to the preliminary stages of data analysis. Though they do not form an exhaustive list, the steps provide guidelines for preparing the data for the analysis that will be discussed in later chapters. One of the crucial takeaways for a reader should be to fully understand the sampling strategy of the data collection agency, because doing so will shed light on any biases early in the process. It will also inform whether subgroup analysis can occur and whether the results are externally or internally valid, or both, and it will provide context to the next steps of checking for missing variables and the density plots of responses. Another takeaway should be the importance of planning for the analysis during the setup stage of the survey. Tasks include inputting the responses of questions in the correct order (if ordinal) and creating a clear and comprehensive codebook. An understanding of these steps also will enable the researcher to identify the limitations of working with data collected in FCAS and to determine how those challenges can be overcome.

References

Deaton, A. 1997. *The Analysis of Household Surveys: A Microeconometric Approach to Development Policy*. Baltimore, MD: Johns Hopkins University Press.

Horne, C. 2011. "Measuring Public Opinion under Political Repression." *American Diplomacy: Foreign Service Despatches and Periodic Reports on U.S. Foreign Policy*. April. http://www.unc.edu/depts/diplomat/item/2011/0104/comm/horne_measuring.html.

Horne, C., and R. Bakker. 2009. "Public Opinion in an Autocratic Regime: An Analysis of Iranian Public Opinion Data 2006–2008." Paper presented at the annual meeting of the Midwest Political Science Association, Chicago, IL, April 2–5.

Sudan Tribune. 2009. "Census Head Confirms Count of Southerners in North Sudan Is Incorrect." May 24. http://www.sudantribune.com/spip.php?article31275.

UCLA (University of California, Los Angeles) Statistical Consulting Group. 2006. "Stata Learning Modules: Combining Data." http://www.ats.ucla.edu/stat/stata/modules/combine.htm.

United Nations Department of Economic and Social Affairs. 2005. "Household Sample Surveys in Developing and Transition Countries." Studies in Methods, Series F No. 96.

CHAPTER 3

Working with Incomplete Data Sets

Chandni Raja, Naomi Crowther, and Ella Spencer

In this chapter, we discuss how to address and use data that have one or more of the problems outlined in chapter 2. We focus on obtaining a representative sample, obtaining complete responses from the sample, and being able to use the responses from questions in the survey to inform evidence-based decision making. To investigate these issues, we use two case studies drawn from the Department for International Development (DFID) Sudan household survey data: (a) respondents' experiences of conflict and (b) their access to financial services, experience with business creation, and perceptions of the economy. They are based on the section of the DFID Sudan household survey on humanitarian issues and the subsection of development issues on the economy and corruption, respectively.

From among the other sections covered in the survey—sections on political and social issues, public service access and quality, and development issues (with subsections on governance and rule of law and on social development and infrastructure) and on Darfur—we selected our two sections for the following reasons. With respect to the initial case study, we first recognize that collecting and analyzing data on respondents' experiences of conflict are a challenge specific and inherent to fragile and conflict-affected states, and we believe that reviewing and addressing this challenge is a valuable endeavor. Second, we find value in addressing evidence-based decision making in policy areas where respondents in fragile and conflict-affected states have limited experience, and therefore where data are limited. In considering the second case, the limited access to financial services and limited experience of business creation in Sudan present challenges in using data from these policy areas in decision making. We will look

---

Authors' Note: This chapter is based on the joint Department for International Development (DFID)–London School of Economics Capstone Project (2013), "Inequalities in Public Services in the Sudan—Using a Perceptions-Informed View to Drive Policy in Education, Health and Water Provision," https://www.gov.uk/dfid-research-outputs/inequalities-in-public-services-in-the-sudan-using-a-perceptions-informed-view-to-drive-policy-in-education-health-and-water-provision-lse-master-of-public-administration-mpa-capstone-report. Permission to reproduce large parts of this work was granted by DFID.

at each case study in turn and explain how we identified problems with the data, how we attempted to address those problems, and how they might be resolved in future surveys of this kind.

Case Study: Conflict

Concerns surrounding the collection, cleaning, and organization of data outlined in the previous chapter become more pronounced in conflict situations. As a result, working with data that aim to understand conflict or data that have been collected from respondents who have experienced conflict requires sensitivity to the social, economic, and political environment in conflict-affected regions. In this case study, we discuss the suitability of these data for informing policy and program design and for making inferences about conflict-affected populations. We show how the data can be used descriptively and otherwise and provide suggestions for the design of future data collection, and we emphasize that data collected in conflict areas should be subject to serious caution and sensitivity.

Background

Being cognizant of the issues with data collected in conflict settings is particularly important in the case of Sudan. During the past half century, Sudan has experienced two civil wars: war in Darfur and, more recently, war in the states of South Kurdufan and Blue Nile. Each conflict has had its own detrimental effects on the country's unity, economy, and social structures. The effects of conflict have been most prominent in southern Sudan (along the border with South Sudan) where, as a result, the experiences of communities are likely to differ significantly from those in more economically developed regions in central and northern Sudan.

Darfur, in particular, has been in a state of humanitarian emergency since 2003 when the Sudan Liberation Movement/Army and the Justice and Equality Movement armed themselves against the government. The government played a role in the expansive ethnic cleansing of non-Arabs in the area. Since the conflict began in 2004, an estimated 200,000–300,000 people have died, and 4.7 million (of the total population of 6.2 million) have been directly affected by the conflict (UNICEF 2008). Khalid (2009, 35) describes the causes of the war as "hegemony by an omnipotent and omniscient Khartoum-based central government over the rest of Sudan."

More recently, conflict has spread to South Kurdufan and the Blue Nile states, where the Sudan Revolutionary Front, consisting of several Darfur rebel movements as well as the Sudan People's Liberation Movement–North, took up arms against the government, demanding that those states be included in Sudan rather than in South Sudan when the referendum was held in July 2011.

This political instability across regions in the south of the country was exacerbated by the secession of South Sudan in 2011, particularly affecting the border areas and contested regions, such as Abeyi. In addition, the secession and consequent loss of oil revenue for Sudan led to cuts in fiscal expenditures that may be

Map 3.1 Distribution of Monthly Household Income, State Level
Sudanese pounds

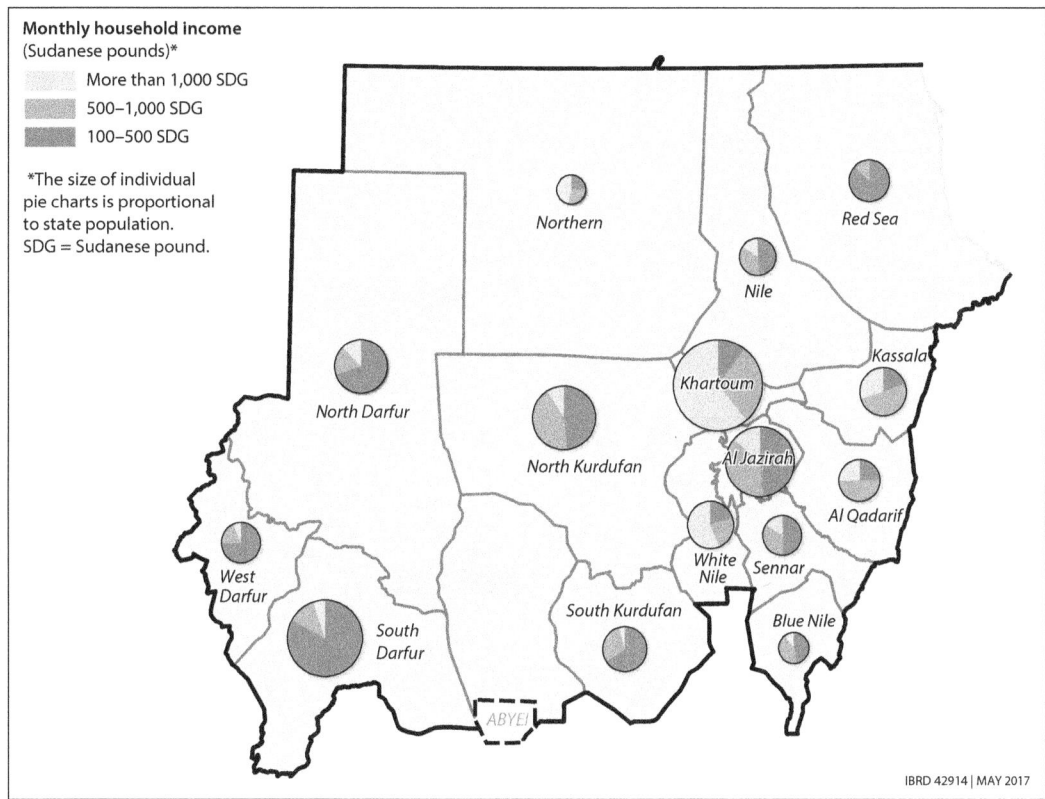

Source: Based on data from the 2013 U.K. Department for International Development Sudan household surveys.
Note: The size of individual pie charts is proportional to state population. SDG = Sudanese pound.

further marginalizing the peripheral regions of the country and increasing existing divisions. Those divisions are illustrated in map 3.1, which shows monthly income distribution by state. Darfur, North Kurdufan, South Kurdufan, and Blue Nile very clearly have a higher proportion of respondents in the lower income bracket compared with the rest of the country.

Data Limitations in Conflict Areas

Data collected in conflict areas should be treated cautiously for several reasons. First, data may not follow the intended sampling strategy (see chapter 2 of this volume). Conflict settings lead to large proportions of displaced citizens who may relocate across borders, enter refugee or internally displaced persons (IDPs) camps, or move to other areas. Therefore, capturing the transitory nature of home for these citizens is particularly challenging. Second, in areas where conflict is constantly present, whole villages and towns often can be abandoned or altogether destroyed. The high frequency at which these changes occur and

Map 3.2 Populations of Internally Displaced Persons

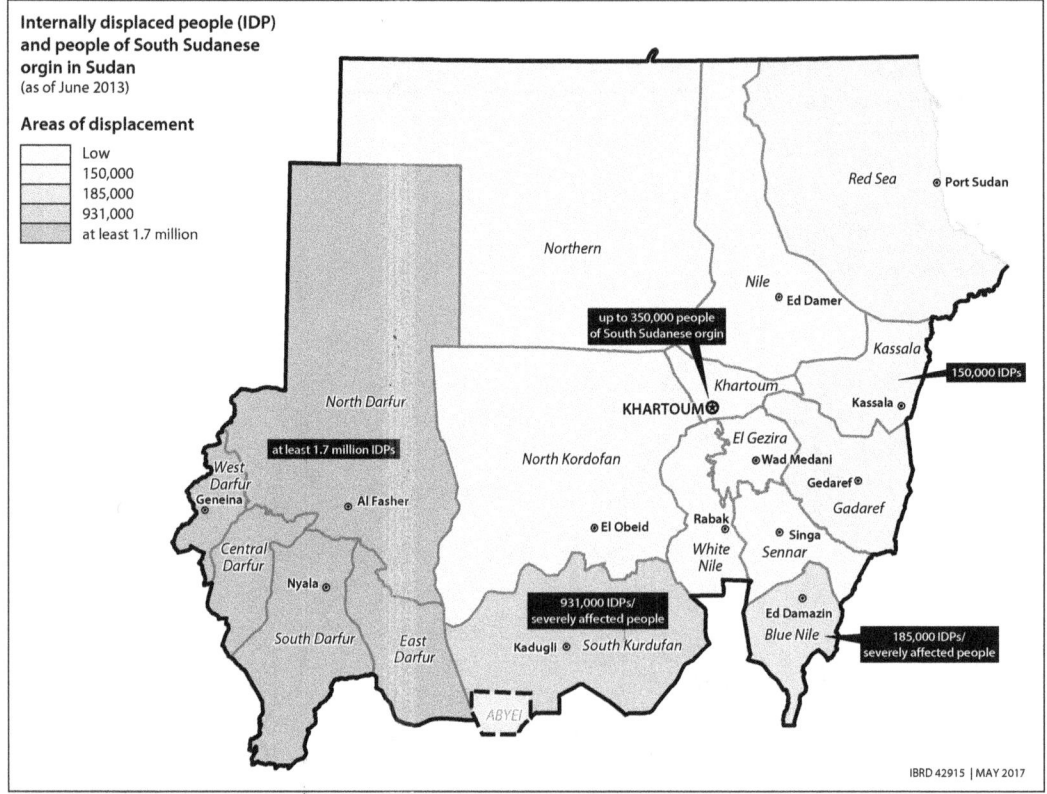

Source: Internal Displacement Monitoring Centre 2013.
Note: IDP = internally displaced person.

the paucity in spatial information available make designing a sampling strategy challenging. Third, damage to the physical infrastructure in conflict areas, particularly to roads, makes accessing these locations difficult. High insecurity can also make traveling safely to and within certain areas too dangerous for data collectors. Consequently, those who are most isolated by the dynamics of conflict are often left unrepresented by survey data.

Map 3.2 illustrates this point more clearly. It shows the estimates for the number of IDPs in the Darfur, South Kurdufan, and Blue Nile states as of June 2013. Sudan has one of the highest volumes of displaced persons in the world, with over 300,000 people displaced in Darfur in the first six months of 2013 alone.

The large numbers of displaced persons signal the difficulty in accurately reflecting the views of this population within the survey data. Furthermore, it raises the question of whether a static view of these populations is valuable, because the displacement is in and of itself one of the primary challenges for these populations and reflects their changing needs.

A further issue is the history of restrictions on the movement of international organizations in conflict-affected areas. As a result, there may be constraints on travel or delays in securing permits required to enter certain areas. This issue has proved to be particularly problematic in Darfur. Though the government largely accepts data collection as a permissible activity, it still restricts access to some urban centers and particular IDP camps that fall under its control. Data collectors for the DFID Sudan household surveys, for example, cited that they faced travel limitations within Darfur states.

In addition to the challenges associated with collecting data in regions affected by conflict, accessibility also can be constrained by negotiations between state and nonstate actors (Brück et al. 2013). These accessibility issues can be addressed by identifying and sampling communities representative of the segments of the population that are excluded from the existing sample. However, this process can be time consuming and expensive; often the best that can be done is to understand the limitations of the existing sample and the caveats that come with using it. Furthermore, these limitations are exacerbated by the existence of localized conflict; oftentimes, complex local dynamics are at play. These dynamics can be understood comprehensively only through in-depth local knowledge of the specific communities under study. For example, although rival factions at a national level can affect conflict at the local level, intercommunity tensions may occur simultaneously as a result of limited resources and increased food insecurity. Carefully designed surveys and the collection of representative samples are well placed to capture such issues, but often researchers must also rely on other qualitative research tools. In addition to in-depth interviews, such tools may include surveys at a unit of analysis that is higher than the household level.

The collection of responses to politically sensitive questions may possibly interact with the ongoing conflict. In Sudan, where conflict is linked to issues of self-determination and control, local political allegiances can contribute to the conflict's dynamics. Sensitive questions are more likely to elicit biased responses, where respondents may, for example, misrepresent their experiences because of social expectancy bias or the idea that certain responses are more likely to generate subsequent support from international organizations. If long-term residents of camps are frequently asked to respond to surveys, they may be reluctant to participate. In addition, considering the psychological effect of conflict on the population as a whole is important. That consideration introduces ethical concerns about whether conflict-affected populations should be asked about their experiences.

Using sampling methodologies specifically designed for refugee or IDP camps can mitigate some of the concerns outlined above. Because these methodologies are based on detailed maps produced by international agencies, they are therefore carefully designed to account for the unique structures of refugee or IDP camps. However, other accessibility concerns remain, and understanding the limitations of the data collected in addition to attempting to sample communities to make the data more representative are important.

Investigating Conflict in the DFID Sudan Household Survey Data

For the DFID Sudan household surveys, respondents living in the states of North, South, and West Darfur; North and South Kurdufan; and Blue Nile were asked to respond to questions on their experiences of conflict and humanitarian assistance. Respondents in the Darfur states were also asked a set of questions on the legal status of state boundaries in their own region. In this section, we revisit some of the limitations of data collected in fragile and conflict-affected states that we discussed in the previous section. Specifically, we will discuss accessibility issues encountered by the Sudan Polling and Statistics Center and the limitations of the data in providing a comprehensive understanding of conflict in Sudan.

As mentioned in chapter 2 of this volume, the Sudan Polling and Statistics Center reported security issues in both North Kurdufan and South Kurdufan and poor accessibility because of both compromised infrastructure and high proportions of displaced persons. These issues prevented data collection in accordance with the designed sampling strategy. One method to address the inaccessibility would be the use of sampling methodologies that are specifically designed for refugee or IDP camps, as discussed earlier. Sampling in refugee or IDP camps would enable researchers to survey people who had been displaced from their homes. Inaccessibility can also be addressed by selecting replacement sampling point regions as geographically proximate to the original regions as possible, with the same stratification criteria applied to the replacement points.

Additionally, we find that responses to questions in the survey are often best supplemented by nonsurvey data in a process of triangulation. Nonsurvey data may provide greater detail about why questions were answered as they were, in cases in which responses were not in-depth enough to provide a comprehensive understanding of the topic.

Map 3.3 shows the percentage of individuals who responded positively to a question of whether they personally had seen war in the previous year. The question was not asked of respondents in areas of the map shaded black. The results indicate that North Kurdufan had the lowest proportion of respondents (36 percent) having directly experienced war in the previous year. Little variation occurs in proportions across the other states, with North Darfur reporting the highest proportion at 86 percent. That factor may have been attributable to the intensification of fighting between the government of Sudan and the Sudan Revolutionary Front in North Darfur in 2012 (FEWS NET 2012). Though these figures provide a benchmark in understanding the magnitude of the conflict and its effect on residents in these states, our previous discussion suggests that we should be cautious when extrapolating results.

Respondents were also asked whether they knew of anyone else who had experienced war in the previous year, which elicited much higher proportions of positive responses. Across all states surveyed, at least 80 percent of respondents knew of someone who had seen war in the previous year. Although

Map 3.3 Experience of War at the State Level

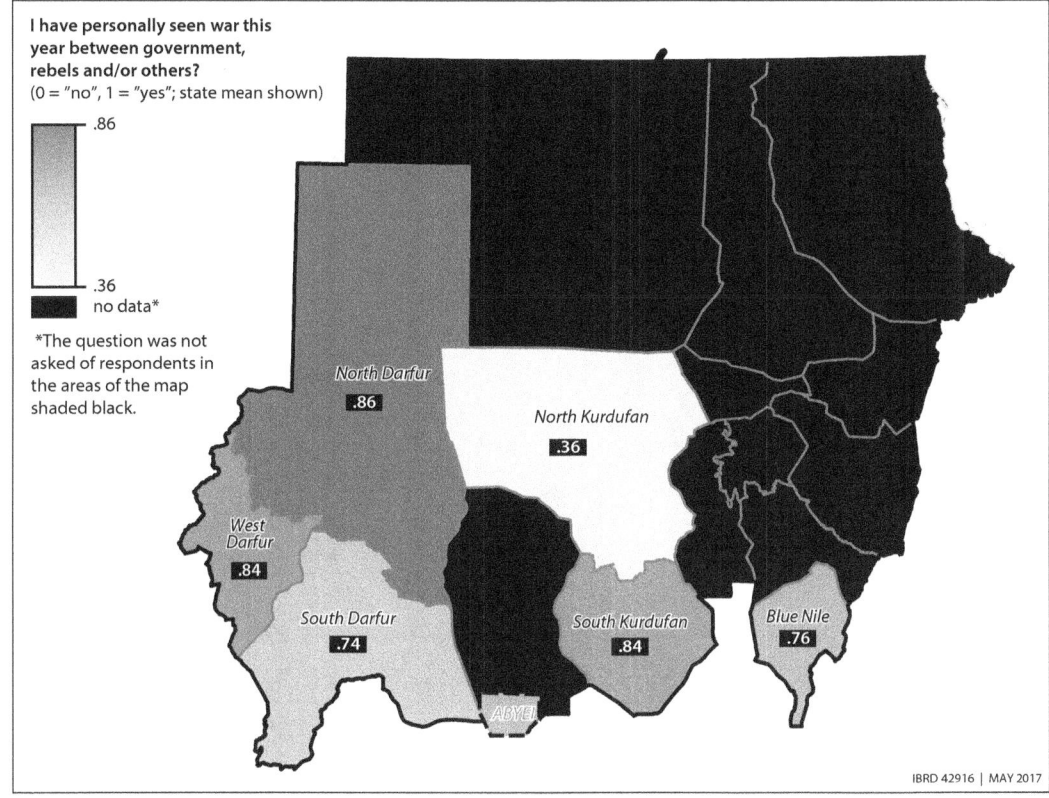

Source: Based on data from the 2013 U.K. Department for International Development Sudan household survey.
Note: The question was not asked of respondents in areas of the map shaded black.

responses to both of these questions signal that a large proportion of individuals had been in troubling proximity to conflict, noting that the word *seen* may have different interpretations in this context is important. Respondents might have experienced conflict of different intensities or types that is not captured within our data. Although the question could have been asked in a more specific manner, doing so also may have raised ethical concerns in that asking respondents to recall more specific experiences may have been more traumatic.

The DFID Sudan household surveys also asked respondents whether they had been displaced from their homes in the previous year because of safety concerns (see map 3.4).

Unlike the question on respondents' experience of war, significant variation occurs across states in the proportion of individuals reportedly displaced from their homes. Although the relatively low numbers of respondents having experienced war in North Kurdufan are accompanied by relatively low levels of displacement, we see a contrast in the percentages of people who reported having seen war in South Darfur and those in the same state that reported being displaced. The same applies to Blue Nile.

Map 3.4 Displacement at the State Level

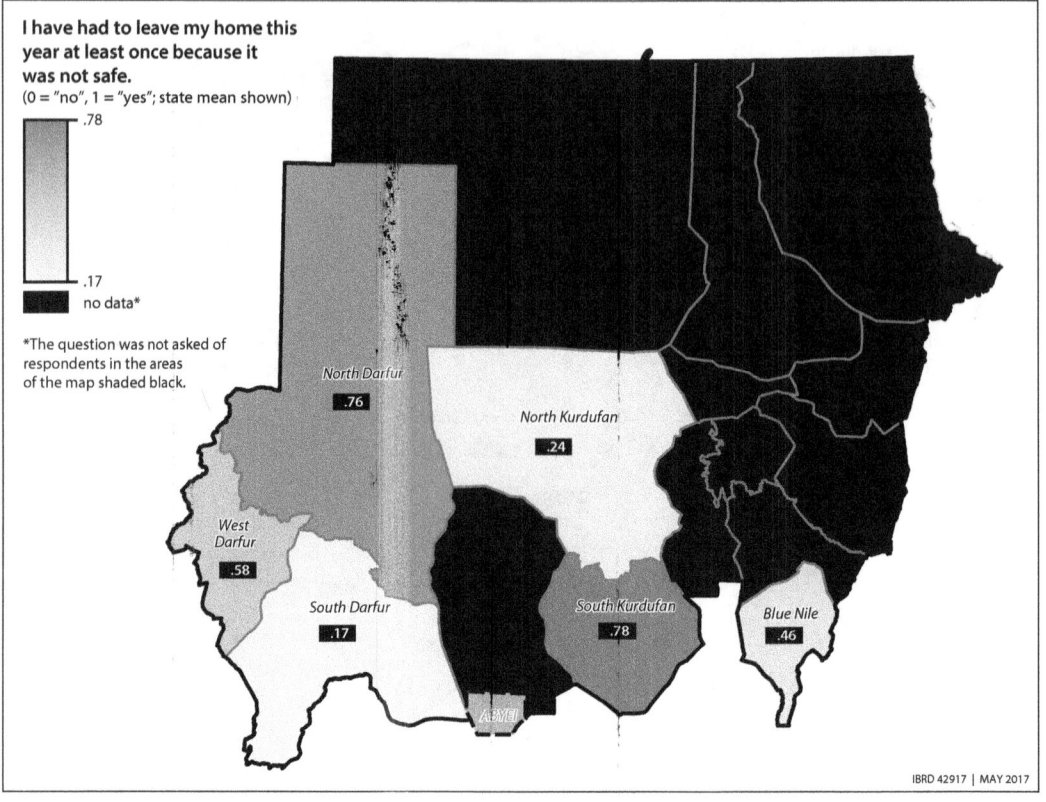

Source: Based on data from the 2013 U.K. Department for International Development Sudan household survey.
Note: The question was not asked of respondents in areas of the map shaded black.

Interestingly, the data show a relatively low level of displacement in South Darfur, with only 17 percent of respondents reporting that they had to leave their homes, compared with 76 percent in North Darfur and 58 percent in West Darfur. These levels of displacement correspond with what we know about the conflict in the second half of 2011 and the beginning of 2012: there was increased fighting in the western part of Darfur, aerial bombardments of parts of North Darfur, and a peak in the conflict in South Kurdufan. Radio stations in North Darfur revealed that militia attacks on camps caused further displacement (Reeves 2013). Reeves also claims that the figures on displaced persons released by the United Nations in 2011 and 2012 were inaccurate, suggesting that published figures may fail to account for known, significant displacement. His own conservative estimates for displacement in the Darfur region during that period are 200,000 people in 2011 and 150,000 people in 2012 (Reeves 2013).

In addition, we can analyze experiences of conflict along dimensions other than state, such as gender-based experiences of conflict. Figure 3.1 plots, by gender, the proportion of individuals who had experienced conflict in the

Figure 3.1 Experiences of Conflict in the Past Year, by Gender

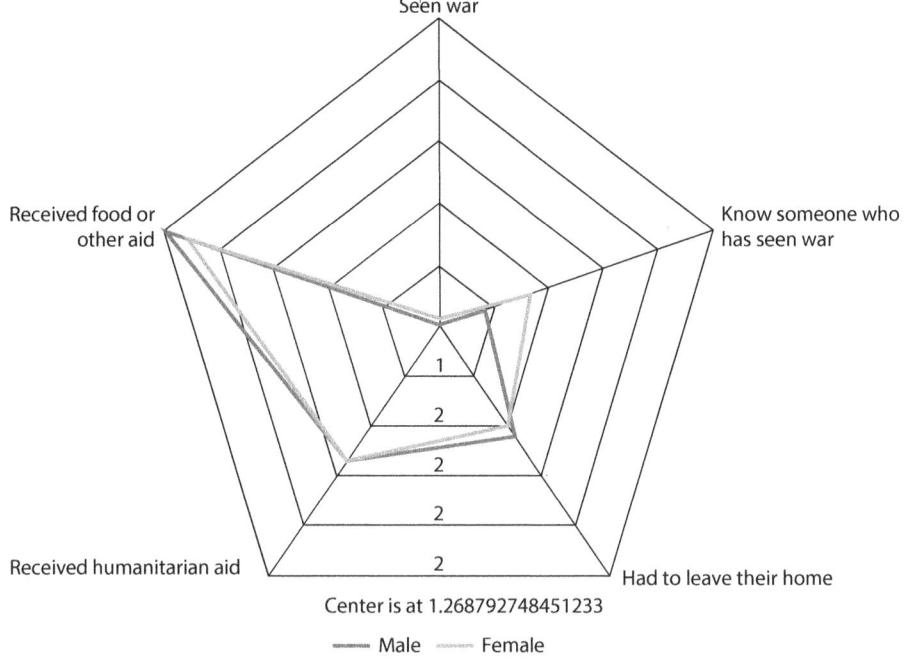

Source: Based on data from the U.K. Department for International Development Sudan household surveys.

previous year against whether they had received humanitarian aid, food, or other assistance.

We find that experiences of conflict documented in our data varied little between men and women. Additionally, the proportion of women who reported receiving aid was almost the same as the proportion of men who reported doing so. However, research has shown that vulnerable groups are often disproportionately affected by food insecurity and that women may be harder hit by the effects of conflict than men (Global Emergency Overview 2012). Therefore, the conflict could in fact have affected the Sudanese population differentially by gender, but that is not captured by our data set. It is also noteworthy that the survey does not examine the intensity with which respondents experienced the effects of conflict or food insecurity. That in and of itself may limit our understanding of the results exhibited with regard to the variation in experiences of conflict by gender, indicating that future surveys may consider delving into greater detail on the intensity and extent of conflict experienced by respondents, though as mentioned earlier, this approach comes with important ethical considerations.

As for geographic variation, map 3.5 shows levels of food insecurity across Sudan, revealing that West Darfur, North Darfur, and South Kurdufan are particularly food insecure. Not only did the conflict propagate food insecurity, it also exacerbated the problem when poor food production led to inflation and

Map 3.5 Food Insecurity in Sudan

Source: FEWS NET 2012.

higher food prices in 2011. Localized inflation in North Darfur reached 52.2 percent in 2012, which significantly reduced residents' purchasing power (FEWS NET 2012). Triangulation of the data in this manner enables us to compare findings across a variety of sources to obtain a comprehensive view of the topic.

Suggestions for Future Data Collection

To ensure that the sample from fragile and conflict-affected states is representative of the population at large, researchers must design a sampling strategy that is cognizant of conflicts in relevant regions. Although the difficulties associated with data collection in conflict zones—including displacement, accessibility, government restrictions on travel, and collection of potentially biased information—often cannot be overcome, acknowledging these issues and preparing for them with a well-designed sampling strategy can lead to the collection of more representative data.

Triangulating survey data responses with nonsurvey data enables the researcher to achieve a comprehensive understanding of a topic when the responses are not sufficiently in-depth or do not provide a complete view of the topic. This procedure supplements qualitative research methods at both the individual level and the community level, where focus groups and community-level surveys can be conducted. This approach would be particularly valuable, for example, in the case of understanding the intensity and scale of the conflict experienced by respondents in addition to the way many experienced that conflict.

Case Study: Access to Finance

Though the data problems that we have discussed are not necessarily as pronounced for data on the economy and corruption as they are for data on conflict, we consider this case study because respondents had limited experience of accessing financial services or business creation, and therefore the data were limited in scope. Furthermore, the design of the questions did not produce enough detail on the topic for researchers to use the survey data independently to inform evidence-based decision making. For example, one of the sets of questions in the DFID Sudan household surveys asks respondents whether they had access to several financial services. However, it does not ask respondents about the ease of access, the sources of access, or the obstacles to access. To inform policy in access to finance in this setting, we would want to obtain an understanding that includes the aforementioned information. We therefore examine methods of triangulating survey data with other forms of data in order to supplement the data collected.

Background

Considering data limitations in the context of Sudan's current economic situation is particularly important. One of the prominent features of this situation is the high level of differential access to economic and financial resources across the country. Inequality in resources is in part attributable to the long-standing neglect of peripheral regions in Sudan, which stems from the establishment of a centralized government during the colonial period and the subsequent concentration of economic activities by elites in the center of the country (Ateem 2007). Khalid (2009, 35) refers to this inequality as the "perpetuation of the economic development paradigm established by British rules to serve their colonial interests," and a source of the conflict in Darfur.

These inequalities have been perpetuated in part by the country's heavy dependence on the export of oil. Historically agriculture based, Sudan's economy has undergone dramatic changes over the past few decades as a result of the increased production and export of oil. In 1999, the country began exporting crude oil. As a result, Sudan experienced high levels of growth and expansion until 2011. During that decade, oil rents further contributed to the existing divide between the center and the periphery and propagated social inequalities (Musso 2015, 259). The loss of three-quarters of the oil resources in 2011 with the secession of South Sudan dealt a harsh blow to Sudan's gross domestic product (GDP) and foreign direct investment, particularly because the period of oil-driven growth shifted the economy away from value addition in other industries, including agriculture and livestock.

The secession of South Sudan is associated not only with a disruptive loss in oil revenue but also with high internal and external deficits, high inflation, and threats to the macroeconomic stability of the country (Darbo, Eltahir, and Suliman 2013). To promote fiscal consolidation, the government drastically reduced infrastructural investment and fiscal expenditure, devalued the Sudanese pound (SDG), and removed fuel subsidies worth SDG 3.6 billion. These austerity measures, particularly the latter, led to widespread and violent rioting in the capital city. These issues—in addition to U.S. sanctions and the ongoing conflicts in South Kurdufan, Blue Nile, and the Darfur states—made for a very fragile economic situation.

These economic concerns are evident in the responses from the DFID Sudan household survey data. Figure 3.2 shows the top responses, by state, to the question of what respondents felt were the biggest issues facing Sudan at the time. "Lack of job opportunities" and "Economy" were two of the top responses across all states.

Figure 3.2 Biggest Issues Facing Sudan Today at the State Level

North Darfur	
1. Lack of job opportunities	0.412
2. Economy	0.353
3. Armed robbery and criminality	0.225
4. Discrimination against people on the basis of racial and ethnic and tribal	0.225
5. Access to justice	0.216

South Darfur	
1. Economy	0.477
2. Internal conflict insurgency	0.402
3. Lack of job opportunities	0.317
4. Corruption and nepotism	0.276
5. Armed robbery and criminality	0.256

West Darfur	
1. Economy	0.550
2. Discrimination against people on the basis of racial and ethnic and tribal	0.384
3. Access to justice	
4. Corruption and nepotism	
5. Tribe	

Northern	
1. Economy	0.513
2. Lack of job opportunities	0.400
3. Corruption and nepotism	0.247
4. Relationship with southern Sudan	0.247
5. Violence against women	0.147

River Nile	
1. Lack of job opportunities	0.447
2. Corruption and nepotism	0.433
3. Economy	0.367
4. Relationship with southern Sudan	0.267
5. Internal conflict insurgency	0.140

Red Sea	
1. Economy	0.547
2. Corruption and nepotism	0.407
3. Lack of job opportunities	0.347
4. Access to clean drinking water	0.333
5. Access to health services	0.240

Kassala	
1. Internal conflict insurgency	0.436
2. Economy	0.393
3. Corruption and nepotism	0.371
4. Lack of job opportunities	0.364
5. Relationship with southern Sudan	0.264

Al Qadarif	
1. Corruption and nepotism	0.427
2. Lack of job opportunities	0.400
3. Economy	0.253
4. Internal conflict insurgency	0.233
5. Relationship with southern Sudan	0.213

Khartoum	
1. Corruption and nepotism	0.457
2. Economy	0.349
3. Lack of job opportunities	0.302
4. Internal conflict insurgency	0.298
5. Relationship with southern Sudan	0.279

"What are the biggest issues facing Sudan today?"

North Kurdufan	
1. Corruption and nepotism	0.387
2. Internal conflict insurgency	0.353
3. Relationship with southern Sudan	0.273
4. Lack of job opportunities	0.247
5. Armed robbery and criminality	0.207

South Kurdufan	
1. Internal conflict insurgency	0.636
2. Economy	0.497
3. Corruption and nepotism	0.280
4. Armed robbery and criminality	0.273
5. Relationship with southern Sudan	0.189

White Nile	
1. The development of the agriculture sector	0.380
2. Access to justice	0.360
3. Discrimination against people on the basis of racial and ethnic and tribal	0.353
4. Tribe	0.240
5. Economy	0.207

Blue Nile	
1. Lack of job opportunities	0.340
2. Economy	0.293
3. Access to justice	0.267
4. Internal conflict insurgency	0.220
5. Violence against women	0.173

Al Jazirah	
1. Lack of job opportunities	0.488
2. Corruption and nepotism	0.355
3. Economy	0.256
4. Relationship with southern Sudan	0.256
5. Internal conflict insurgency	0.233

Sennar	
1. Lack of job opportunities	0.420
2. Corruption and nepotism	0.360
3. Economy	0.333
4. Relationship with southern Sudan	0.273
5. Internal conflict insurgency	0.200

Source: Based on data from the 2013 U.K. Department for International Development Sudan household surveys.

Working with Incomplete Data Sets

To address these economic challenges, the government planned to improve its public debt management and address high levels of inflation through credit tightening and liquidity management. In addition, it partnered with nongovernmental and international organizations to promote value addition in agriculture and industry. To do so, the government planned, among other things, to address the significant obstacles faced by small and medium enterprises (SMEs), including high costs of foreign inputs and exchange rate pass-through to imported inputs, given that SMEs in the country have driven the diversification of the economy (Darbo, Eltahir, and Suliman 2013). Map 3.6 illustrates the proportion of Sudanese respondents who either had started or had considered starting a business at the time of the surveys, with almost 50 percent of respondents in the states of Northern, North Darfur, West Darfur, and Khartoum responding positively.

However, the interest in business creation does not equate to the ability of small business owners to overcome obstacles faced by SMEs in Sudan and other low-income countries. This issue is part of a much larger discourse across the development economics literature pertaining to business development.

Map 3.6 Starting a Business at the State Level

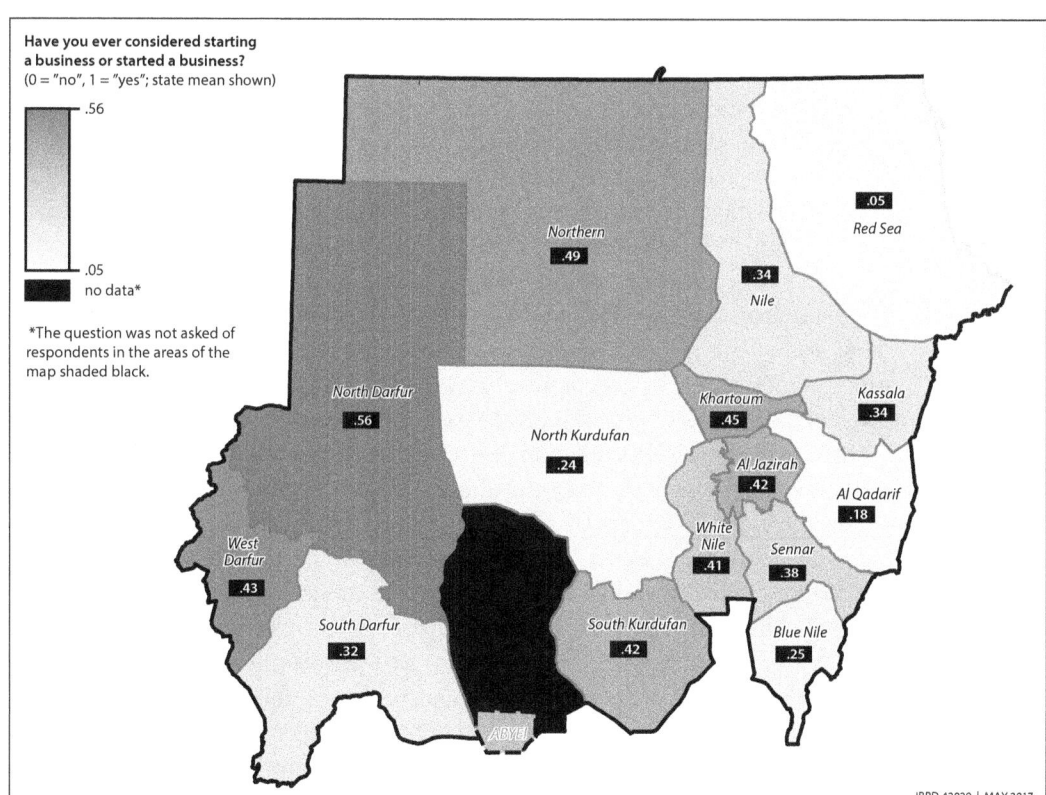

Source: Based on data from the U.K. Department for International Development Sudan household survey.
Note: The question was not asked of respondents in areas of the map shaded black.

Data-Driven Decision Making in Fragile Contexts: Evidence from Sudan
http://dx.doi.org/10.1596/978-1-4648-1064-0

In this climate of political and economic uncertainty, researchers ought to consider investigating the economic and financial behavior of respondents along with their perceptions on the economy in order to use these data to influence policy. The subsection of the DFID Sudan household survey on the economy and corruption (under the larger development issues section) attempts to garner this information from respondents, which can in turn be linked to levels of trust in public institutions, ratings of public services, geographic location, socioeconomic status, and more. The topics that we cover here are respondent access to financial services, creation or planned creation of a business, and the main constraints when doing so.

Limitations to Data on Access to Finance

The first set of questions on access to financial services seeks to determine the degree of access to financial services in Sudan and to what extent that access is distributed across geographic areas, ethnic groups, genders, income groups, and other socioeconomic and demographic categories. However, the survey does not address issues around who provides these services. In particular, it does not consider whether they are provided formally, informally, or semiformally or how easy it is to reach a service provider. We note that the survey questions on access to financial services include various services that are offered through nonbank providers—such as training to support livelihood and income increases and capital for machines and tools—and therefore indicate context-informed knowledge of the Sudanese economy, and the resources that are potentially available to low-income individuals. As figure 3.3 illustrates, access to different financial services is still dramatically correlated with demographic and socioeconomic characteristics, including that of income.

The correlation between income and access to financial services raises an important question: Why do certain individuals not have access to finance? Though respondents are asked to state the kinds of financial services to which they have access, the question does not establish why individuals do or do not have access. There are several possible obstacles to financial access, especially in low-income countries. For example, geographical obstructions may exist, including having to travel long distances to financial providers, or conflict in certain areas may prevent individuals from traveling. Individuals may also lack the financial profile to benefit from services through formal institutions, which are often a corollary of their demographic or socioeconomic characteristics. Researchers may be in a position to infer why individuals lack access, for example, noting that individuals in states affected by conflict have less access than those in states that are not. However, knowing definitively is impossible, given that respondents were not asked.

Moreover, investigating financial access in low-income countries relies on a clear understanding of the sources of finance. The method of access is often an important indicator of the conditions under which the services are provided. For example, research has indicated that informal loans in developing countries often have much higher interest rates than loans provided through formal channels, and they certainly have more variability in interest rates (Aleem 1993; Banerjee and Duflo 2011). However, loans provided formally often have stricter terms of

Figure 3.3 Access to Financial Services, by Income Group

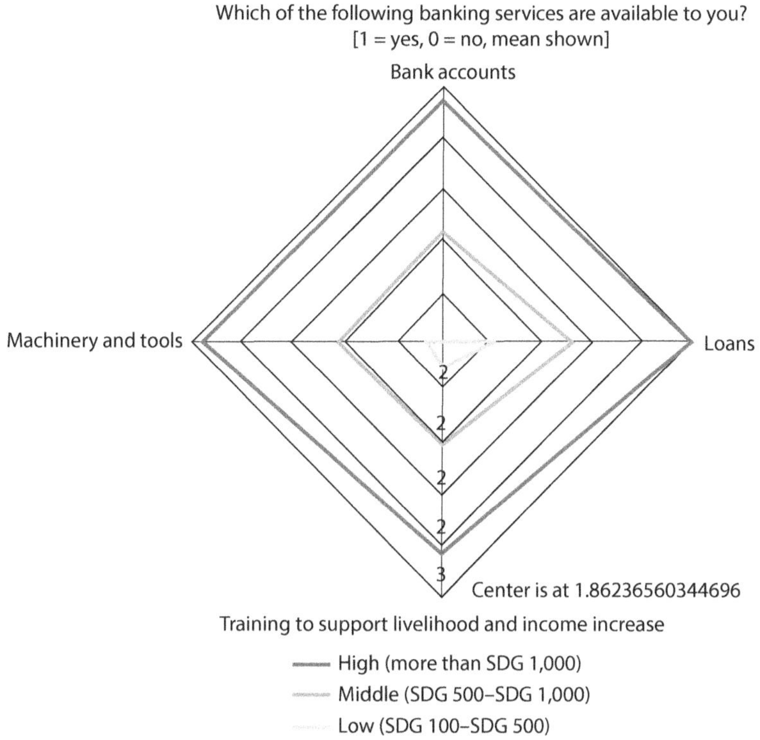

Which of the following banking services are available to you?
[1 = yes, 0 = no, mean shown]

- Bank accounts
- Loans
- Training to support livelihood and income increase
- Machinery and tools

Center is at 1.86236560344696

— High (more than SDG 1,000)
— Middle (SDG 500–SDG 1,000)
— Low (SDG 100–SDG 500)

Source: Based on data from the 2013 U.K. Department for International Development Sudan household surveys.
Note: SDG = Sudanese pound.

repayment, whereas those that are provided informally may not. Different service providers are also likely to have different incentive structures. Thus, investigating not only whether individuals have access but also what type of access they have and who provides it is important.

The questions on the topic of business formation, in contrast, do include asking what obstacles respondents faced or expected to face in starting a business, in addition to whether respondents had started a business. However, the questions did not ask respondents what type of business they had started. That subject is particularly important because different states in Sudan have dramatically different economic profiles, which may affect whether or not a state has a high level of entrepreneurship.

The questions on business formation, however, attempt to gauge (a) whether respondents had started a business or had considered starting a business and (b) what obstacles they had faced or expected to face in doing so. The questions were designed to ascertain why entrepreneurship may not be successful or considered successful in Sudan or, more specifically, in particular regions and across particular groups in society.

Furthermore, the questions on business formation do not distinguish between respondents who have merely considered starting a business and those who have already started one. Because making the leap between thinking about starting a business and actually starting one requires resources, effort, connections, and other factors, in future surveys, this distinction should be recognized in the design of survey questions.

Investigating Access to Finance in the DFID Sudan Household Surveys

We have seen that access to banking services is correlated with income, as shown clearly in figure 3.4. This inequality in access is also likely present across the center–periphery dynamic in Sudan, wherein power, elites, and wealth are concentrated in Khartoum and the northern states to the detriment of the peripheral areas.

The neglect of the periphery by the central government in Khartoum has often dictated prospects for development, both economic and social. Consecutive Sudanese governments have done little to address this centralization, established in the colonial period, and inequalities continue to exist across this dynamic. To capture those inequalities in the DFID Sudan household survey data, we created a binary variable based on the proportion of the population in each state living below the poverty line, where the poverty line was defined according to a consumption metric derived by Castro (2010). We defined the *center* as states in which less than 40 percent of the population lives below

Figure 3.4 Access to Financial Services, by Center–Periphery Dynamic

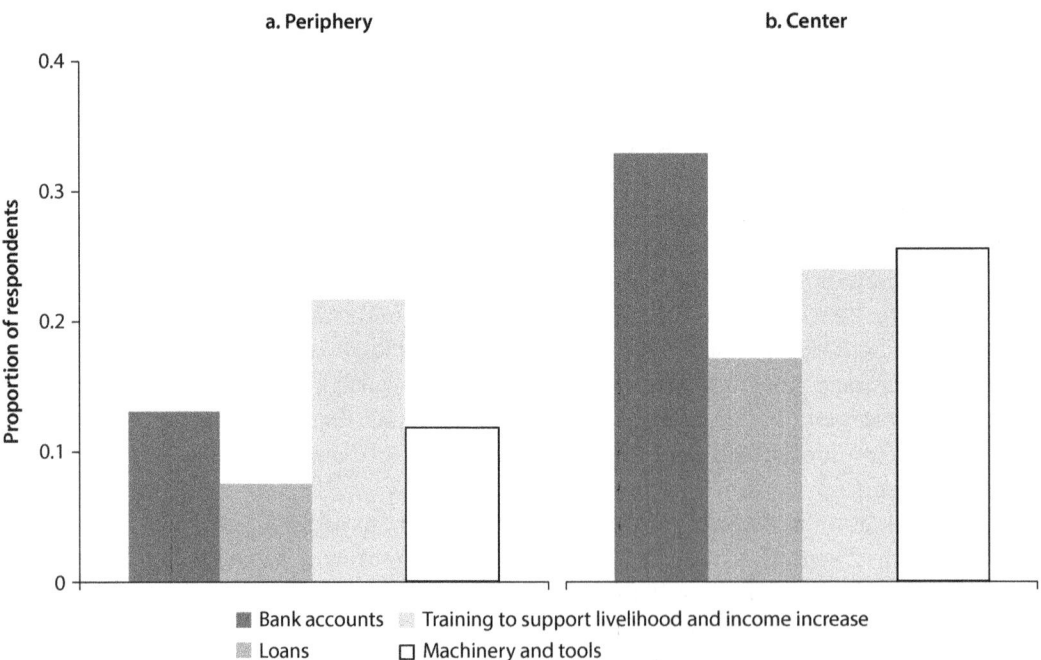

Source: Based on data from the 2013 U.K. Department for International Development Sudan household surveys.

the poverty line and the *periphery* as all other states. This income-based classification is supported by extensive context-informed literature and qualitative research (Castro 2010). This research showed the classification to be astute across a number of different sources, in the sense that the 40 percent cutoff led to a definition of periphery that was supported by other discussions in the literature regarding the marginalization of Sudanese states (Castro 2010).

The investigation into the access of banking services by the center–periphery dynamic indicated that individuals living in the center are more likely to have access to services than individuals living in the periphery. This differentiation is more pronounced in access to bank accounts, loans, and machinery than it is in access to training to support livelihood and income increases, perhaps suggesting that government or nongovernmental organizations may be effectively providing training services to individuals in the poorer states of the country. However, financial inclusion with regard to access to bank accounts and to loans has not expanded into these regions to the same extent that it has in the center states of the country.

We can similarly investigate whether the center–periphery dynamic and income as inequalities interact with each other. For example, whether individuals in the periphery have less access to banking services because of their distance from the center or because they are more likely to be poor is unclear in figure 3.4. Is access to banking services a function of the center–periphery dynamic, of income, or of both? Figure 3.5 illustrates access to financial services

Figure 3.5 Access to Financial Services, by Center–Periphery Dynamic and Income

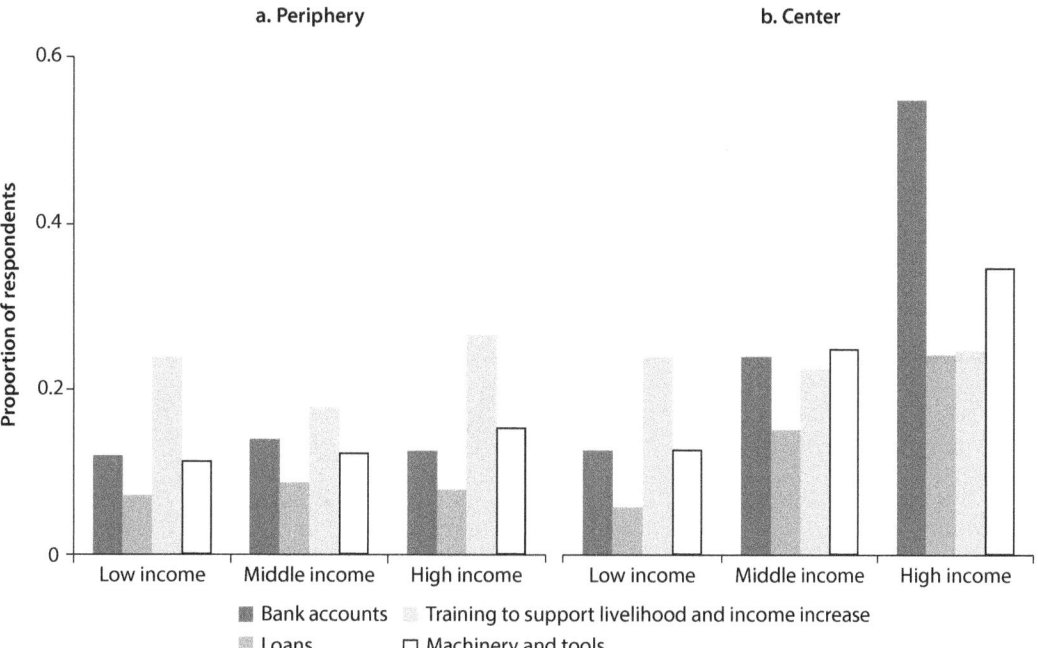

Source: Based on data from the 2013 U.K. Department for International Development Sudan household surveys.

for those in the center and those in the periphery, now shown across the three income groups within our data set.

The monthly pay for low-income earners is SDG 100–SDG 500; for middle-income earners, SDG 500–SDG 1,000; and for high-income earners, more than SDG 1,000. We can see that low-income earners have similar levels of access whether they reside in the center or in the periphery. However, middle- and high-income earners are more likely to have access to banking services if they reside in the center rather than periphery. In fact, individuals residing in the periphery have similar levels of access across all three income groups. This finding supports the idea that an individual's location—in either the center or the periphery—and the individual's income both affect his or her level of access to financial services.

We can also investigate this topic using the gender dimension. Figure 3.6 illustrates the inequality in access to financial services by gender. Inequality is greater for certain services, particularly loans and bank accounts, than it is for training, for example. In fact, we previously saw that access to training was relatively equal across all respondents living in both the center and the periphery. Further investigation into why access to training is provided more effectively to different groups in Sudan than other financial services would be interesting.

Similarly, we can look at business creation with respect to relevant socioeconomic and demographic characteristics. Individuals with higher levels of

Figure 3.6 Access to Financial Services, by Gender

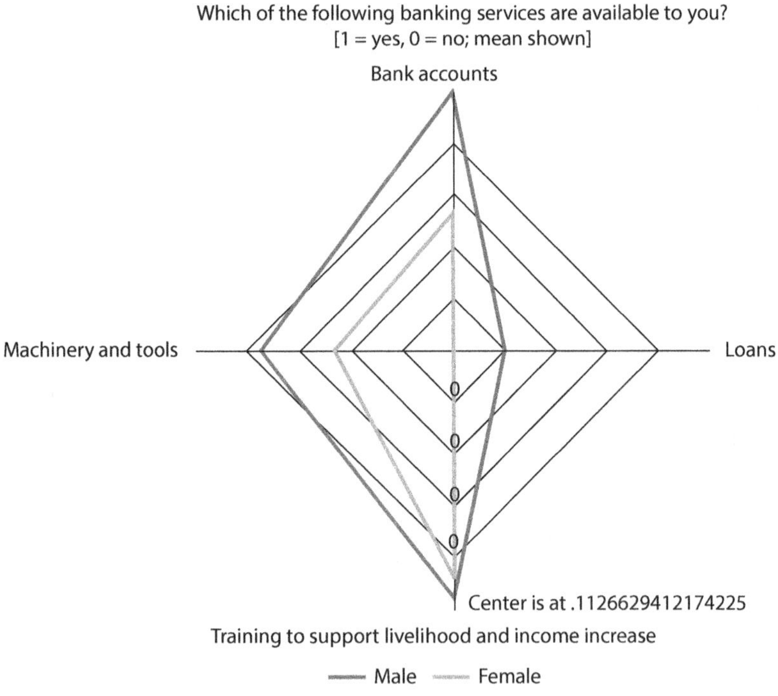

Source: Based on data from the 2013 U.K. Department for International Development Sudan household surveys.

education were more likely to have started a business, as were those individuals who had access to financial services. Over half of the individuals with access to a bank account either had created or had thought about creating a business compared with 32 percent of those with no access to a bank account.

We can address the limitations of the data by supplementing it with information from other data sources. This triangulation process has been defined in qualitative research as a method of cross-checking data from multiple sources to identify both regularities and irregularities in the data (O'Donoghue and Punch 2003). Our survey does not reveal information regarding the institutions providing respondents with loans. We now know that access to financial services is correlated with income, so by drawing from other reports, we can identify the main categories of financial service providers in Sudan and the reason those providers are not reaching the lowest income groups. In most developing countries, those providers consist of microfinance institutions, private moneylenders, and formal financial institutions, including public and private sector banks. Sources on Sudan's financial infrastructure suggest that the major providers of finance are banks and microfinance institutions that operate through branches (HORUS 2011). This factor suggests that low financial access among the poor is largely a result of low accessibility, in addition to the poor lacking the assets that are often required by formal financial institutions as prerequisites for borrowing. Low accessibility includes poor road infrastructure, low population density, and difficulties in managing cash and maintaining staff in rural areas.

We now can investigate whether, in fact, the poor live in areas with lower accessibility by analyzing the geographic distribution of low-income individuals in the DFID Sudan household survey data. Map 3.1, for example, illustrates that a much larger proportion of low-income individuals live in the Darfur states, North Kurdufan and South Kurdufan, and the Red Sea states than elsewhere. Given that these states are conflict affected, individuals in these areas very likely have low accessibility because of compromised infrastructure and roads and security concerns with traveling in areas where signs of conflict still exist.

The issue of accessibility as an obstacle to financial access can be investigated more thoroughly. In future surveys, however, asking respondents what were their obstacles to obtaining different services might be valuable.

Suggestions for Future Data Collection

In light of the data collection issues that have been outlined here, collecting data for a more in-depth understanding of the economic and financial behavior of respondents would be ideal. Such data might be collected by asking a more comprehensive set of specific questions, which would require an understanding of the subject matter at hand and the nuances that we have mentioned, including the range of different types of financial services and financial providers and the terms and conditions associated with accessing services through these different mechanisms.

Similarly, in view of the wide differences in levels of accessibility and the likely financial demands of different populations across Sudan, researchers may want to consider designing different versions of the survey, depending on respondents' location and socioeconomic status, for example, to account for the heterogeneity in economic and financial needs.

Conclusion

In this chapter, we discuss working with incomplete data sets by investigating two case studies from the DFID Sudan household survey data. The case study on the conflict data illustrates that obtaining a representative sample is challenging in fragile and conflict-affected states for a number of reasons, including displacement, accessibility, government restrictions on travel, and collection of potentially biased information. We discuss methods to address these challenges, including using sampling from IDP or refugee camps, finding replacement samples in similar geographic areas, and collecting information at a level higher than that of the individual.

In the case study on access to finance, we show that the design of survey questions did not elicit enough information from respondents to provide a comprehensive understanding of the barriers to financial access among the Sudanese population. To improve access to finance, we need to understand the barriers and the way to tackle them. We therefore discussed how to improve future surveys to obtain more and better information. In both case studies, we discuss triangulating survey data with nonsurvey data to obtain further detail and to confirm findings. Using these methods will be helpful in tackling the challenges illustrated in this chapter, as well as those outlined more broadly in chapter 2 of this volume.

Bibliography

Aleem, I. 1993. "Imperfect Information, Screening, and the Cost of Informal Lending: A Study of a Rural Credit Market in Pakistan." In *The Economics of Rural Organization: Theory, Practice, and Policy*, edited by K. Hoff, A. Breverman, and J. Stiglitz, 131–54. Oxford, U.K.: Oxford University Press.

Ateem, E. S. M. 2007. "The Root Causes of Conflicts in Sudan and the Making of the Darfur Tragedy." Paper presented at the Wilton Park Conference Policy Workshop on "Conflict Prevention and Development Co-Operation in Africa" Wilton Park, Susssex, U.K., November 8–11. http://www.operationspaix.net/DATA/DOCUMENT/5425~v~The_root_causes_of_conflicts_in_Sudan_and_the_makink_of_the_Darfur_tragedy.pdf.

Banerjee, A., and E. Duflo. 2011. "The (Not So Simple) Economics of Lending to the Poor." Massachusetts Institute of Technology, Cambridge, MA. http://www.pooreconomics.com/sites/default/files/A%20PDF%20of%20the%20lecture%20slides_0.pdf.

Brück, T., D. Esenaliev, A. Kroeger, A. Kudebayeva, B. Mirkasimov, and S, Steiner. 2013. "Household Survey Data for Research on Well-Being and Behavior in Central Asia." *Journal of Comparative Economics* 42 (3): 819–35.

Casciarri, B., M. A. M. Assal, and F. Ireton, eds. 2015. *Multidimensional Change in Sudan (1989–2011): Reshaping Livelihoods, Conflicts and Identities*. New York: Berghahn.

Castro, M. 2010. *Poverty in Northern Sudan. Estimates from the NBHS 2009*. Washington, DC: World Bank.

Darbo, S., Y. Eltahir, and K. Suliman. 2013. *Soudan*. http://www.africaneconomicoutlook.org/fileadmin/uploads/aeo/2014/PDF/CN_Long_EN/Soudan_EN.pdf.

Eck, K. 2011. "Survey Research in Conflict and Post-Conflict Societies." In *Understanding Peace Research*, edited by K. Hoglund and M. Oberg, 165–82. London: Routledge.

FEWS NET (Famine Early Warning Systems Network). 2012. "Sudan Food Security Outlook." July–December. http://www.fews.net/sites/default/files/documents/reports/Sudan_OL_2012_07_final.pdf.

Global Emergency Overview. 2012. *Country Analysis: Sudan*. http://geo.acaps.org/.

HORUS. 2011. "Study for the Establishment of Pro-Poor Branchless Banking in Sudan." HORUS Development Finance, Paris. http://www.mfu.gov.sd/sites/default/files/pro-poor_bb_sudan_final2.pdf.

Internal Displacement Monitoring Centre. 2013. "Sudan IDP Figures Analysis." http://www.internal-displacement.org/sub-saharan-africa/sudan/figures-analysis.

Khalid, M. 2009. "Darfur: A Problem within a Wider Problem." In *Darfur and the Crisis of Governance in Sudan: A Critical Reader*, edited by S. M. Hassan and C. E. Ray, 35–42. New York: Cornell University Press.

Musso, G. 2015. "The Islamic Movement and Power in Sudan: From Revolution to Absorption into the State." In *Multidimensional Change in Sudan: Reshaping Livelihoods, Conflicts and Identities (1989–2011)*, edited by B. Casciarri, M. A. M. Assal, and F. Ireton, 217–67. New York: Berghahn.

ODI (Overseas Development Institute). 2004. "Humanitarian Issues in Darfur, Sudan." Humanitarian Policy Group Briefing Note, April. http://www.odi.org/sites/odi.org.uk/files/odi-assets/publications-opinion-files/4901.pdf.

O'Donoghue, T., and K. Punch. 2003. *Qualitative Educational Research in Action: Doing and Reflecting*. London: Routledge.

Reeves, E. 2013. *Sudan: Research, Advocacy and Analysis*. http://sudanreeves.org.

UNICEF (United Nations Children's Fund). 2008. "Darfur: Overview." http://www.unicef.org/infobycountry/sudan_darfuroverview.html.

CHAPTER 4

Quantitative Analysis Using Household Survey Data

Chandni Raja, Naomi Crowther, and Ella Spencer

In this chapter, we provide a discussion of how to undertake quantitative analysis with household survey data. A section of the U.K. Department for International Development (DFID) Sudan household survey on public service provision is used throughout the chapter to illustrate each step. We focus on the public service provision data because of their quality as well as their importance as a political matter within Sudan. Furthermore, this analysis offers insight for donors and nongovernmental organizations working in the service delivery area. We use the data on perceptions of public service provision (a) to explore the data's strengths and limitations and their suitability for quantitative analysis; (b) to illustrate the descriptive analysis that can lead to identifying a research question; and (c) to demonstrate how to undertake advanced quantitative analysis, including factor analysis and structural equation modeling (SEM) techniques to explore causal relationships. Finally, we provide an overview of how results from this quantitative analysis might be used to inform evidence-based policy making.

We choose to look specifically at three public services: education, health, and water and sanitation. The focus on these particular public services reflects their importance within the international community in that their provision is prioritized by external actors working in Sudan. Thus, providing analysis on these services—services seen as fundamental for Sudan's development trajectory—becomes salient.

Case Study: Public Services

Identifying the Strengths and Limitations of the Data and Their Suitability for Quantitative Analysis

The DFID Sudan household survey data include responses to questions on 11 different public services: (a) public schools, (b) public hospitals, (c) piped water, (d) sanitation, (e) electricity, (f) courts, (g) police, (h) local committees, (i) religious courts, (j) state-level public administration, and (k) federal-level public administration. Respondents were asked to report on their perceptions of service quality for each public service and to report on any perceived gap in the service quality between Khartoum and the rest of the Sudan.

In chapter 2 of this volume, we outlined the challenges associated with sampling from populations in conflict settings. These challenges relate to issues of displacement, abandonment of cities and villages, and damage to physical infrastructure that make both sampling and accessibility difficult. That is no less true for data on public service provision. However, we argue that including these data within the analysis is critical in order to amalgamate a view of how perceptions across populations in conflict and nonconflict zones are likely to differ. We note, though, that service provision in conflict areas will often be provided by humanitarian organizations rather than governments, meaning that responses should be considered cautiously in a comparative sense.

Without qualitative data to support the findings, assessing whether respondents naturally relate the question specifically to *government* service provision is difficult. This difficulty is very much linked to the sizable body of research on the effect of conflict on public service provision. In the next section, we discuss how we might use this research, by effectively linking it to the data collected from conflict areas only, to triangulate across the survey data, and thus to build some view of perceptions of service provision within these contexts.

Encouragingly, with respect to data quality, nonresponse for the questions on public service delivery is limited, particularly for hospitals and schools. Perhaps the reason is that these questions are not as politically sensitive as, for example, questions on political affiliation or levels of trust in federal government. The nonresponse statistics are shown in table 4.1.

Although the data do not elicit information from respondents on why they were satisfied or unsatisfied with their public services nor with what aspects of the public service provision they were satisfied or unsatisfied, the overall quantitative rating of a public service provides a simple but informational metric with which to compare public services across different areas. The uniform metric allows us to compare the ratings for a single public service across respondents

Table 4.1 Nonresponse for Questions on Public Service Ratings

Rating of service quality	Score	Public schools		Public hospitals		Water and sanitation	
		n	%	n	%	n	%
Extremely poor	0	623	26.3	765	32.4	925	39.1
Poor	25	653	27.6	787	33.3	630	26.6
Suitable	50	737	31.2	545	23.0	478	20.2
Good	75	241	10.2	181	7.7	205	8.7
Excellent	100	86	3.6	60	2.5	57	2.4
Don't know	n.a.	21	0.9	20	0.9	58	2.5
Refuse to answer	n.a.	4	0.2	7	0.3	12	0.5
Total		2,365	100	2,365	100	2,365	100

Source: Based on data from the 2013 U.K. Department for International Development Sudan household surveys.
Note: n = number; n.a. = not applicable.

in the survey as well as to compare the ratings across several public services for the same respondents. Were the survey more detailed, information on specific aspects of public services could have been collected. In public hospitals, it would have been interesting to collect metrics of quality and availability of hospital staff, proximity of the hospital to the respondent's household, ease of access to the hospital, and resources and treatments available.

Additional data on public services in Sudan from other sources are relatively easily available compared with data on other topics within our survey, such as female genital mutilation and the preponderance of bribing. The availability of alternative data sources enabled triangulation of the DFID Sudan household survey to compare, confirm, or question the results found. It also allowed us to empirically test a theoretical model that includes measures of actual provision.

In the first case, data from other sources provide us with an opportunity to confirm or question estimates we obtain from the survey data; for example, how many people had to move from their homes or were displaced in the previous year, or how many people had access to a bank account. This information is particularly valuable when working with countries such as Sudan, where accurate or representative data are difficult to obtain because of conflict and government restrictions on researchers.

In the second case, we attempt to delineate the effects of actual service quality on perceptions of service quality from the effects of other factors, such as socio-economic and demographic characteristics and trust in public institutions, by including measures of actual service quality in our structural equation modeling. Number of public schools in a given state is used to investigate perceptions of education quality, and number of public hospitals is used to investigate perceptions of health service quality.

In accordance with the volume of data available, as well as the potential for triangulating these data, the limited number of nonresponses, and the option of comparing perceptions of different public services across different geographical areas using a simple but effective rating, we determine that enough evidence exists to proceed with the quantitative analysis. The following steps discuss how the data are well placed to inform evidence-based policy making on public service provision.

Identifying a Research Question through Descriptive Analysis

In exploring the data, we consider the identification and analysis of inequalities in public service provision in Sudan, along a number of different dimensions. In particular, we want to determine whether these inequalities are drivers of the variation in perceptions of public service quality. The investigation of this hypothesis will shed light on whether the actual service quality provided differs along geographic, gender, income, or other dimensions, and whether members of different groups along these dimensions rate services of the same actual quality differently. The former piece of information could help government and nonprofit organizations target service provision at specific groups, and the latter piece of information could give us a better understanding of the unique needs of one group compared with another. For example, women and men may both be provided with the same quality of health services, but the medical services provided through a public hospital may meet the needs of men better than those of women.

First, a descriptive analysis of the data is conducted to identify the existence of these inequalities in public service provision. In considering descriptive analysis, which largely consists of data visualizations, we view variations in ratings of public services, both across groups for a single public service and across public services for a single group. We distinguish between exploratory graphics and presentation graphics: multiple exploratory graphics are generated in the early stages of research in order to explore a research question and find results; presentation graphics are used in the later stages of the research to demonstrate those results (Chen, Hardle, and Unwin 2008).

Exploratory graphics produced from the DFID Sudan household survey data, illustrated in figures 4.1 and 4.2, allow us to identify the existence of inequalities in the perception of public services so as to develop our research

Figure 4.1 Perceptions of Service Quality, by Rural–Urban Location

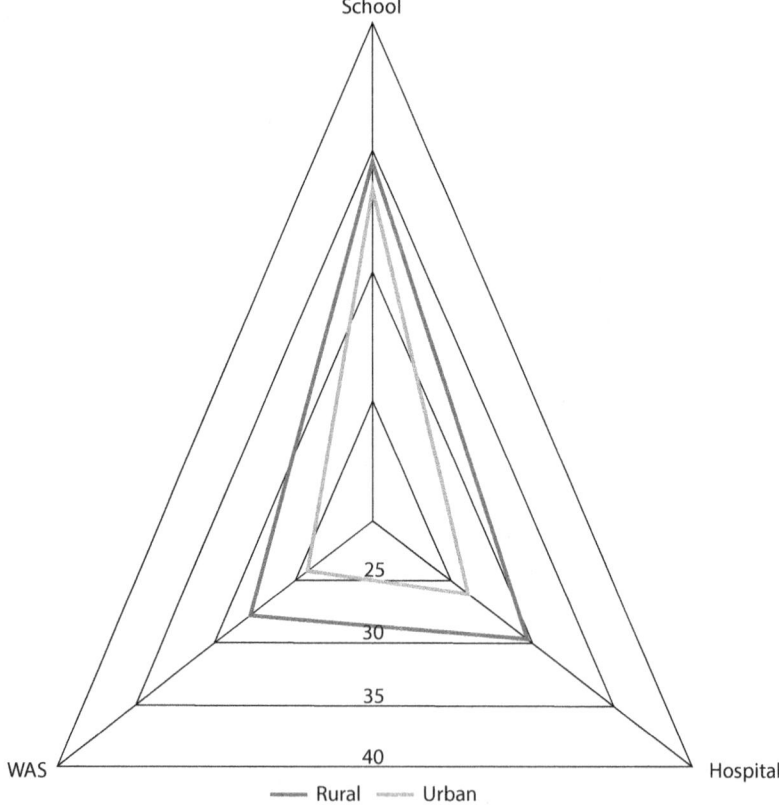

Source: Based on data from the 2013 U.K. Department for International Development Sudan household surveys.
Note: WAS = water and sanitation. The figure shows mean values.

Figure 4.2 Perceptions of Service Quality, by Income Group

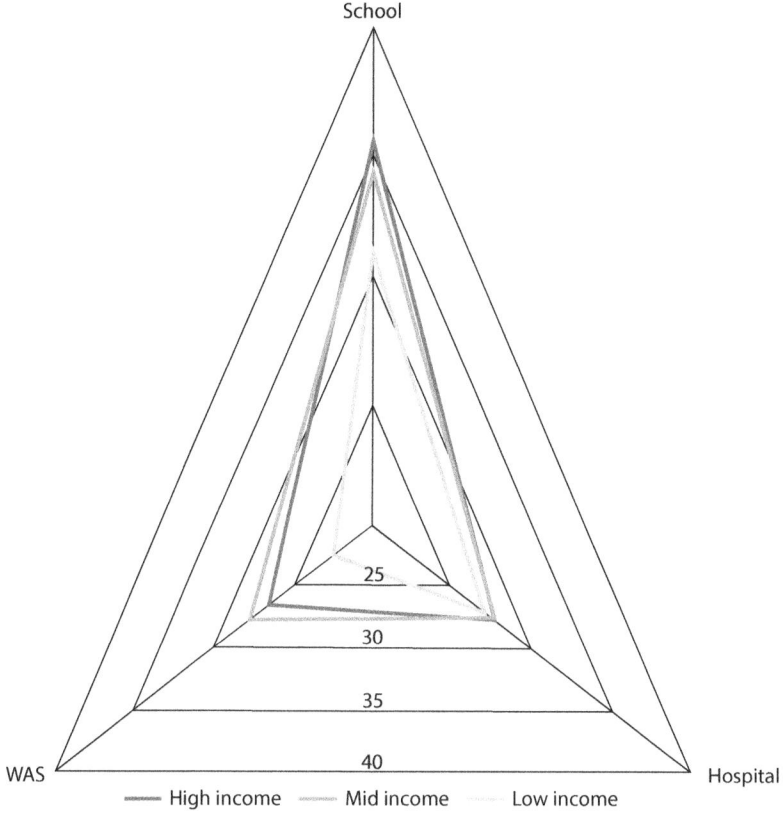

Source: Based on data from the 2013 U.K. Department for International Development Sudan household surveys.
Note: WAS = water and sanitation. The figure shows mean values.

question. The radar graph visualizations in figures 4.1 and 4.2 show variation in perceptions (a) between rural and urban areas and (b) between different income groups, respectively. Figure 4.1 shows the variation in perceptions across three services for both rural and urban groups and illustrates inequalities in perceptions between rural and urban groups for each of the services. This latter inequality is particularly pronounced for public hospitals and water and sanitation.

The rural–urban dimension is an example of a horizontal inequality, which is a group-level inequality "conceived of as inherently multidimensional… encompass[ing] economic, social, cultural status and political dimensions" (Stewart, Brown, and Mancini 2005, 3). It is distinct from vertical inequalities that are defined not at the group level but at the individual level. Income, for instance, is an example of a vertical inequality. Figure 4.2 illustrates perceptions of service quality by income.

We note, however, that inequalities can interact with one another. For example, incomes can and do differ widely across states. Figure 4.3 illustrates a way

Figure 4.3 Monthly Household Income, by Gender and Center–Periphery Location

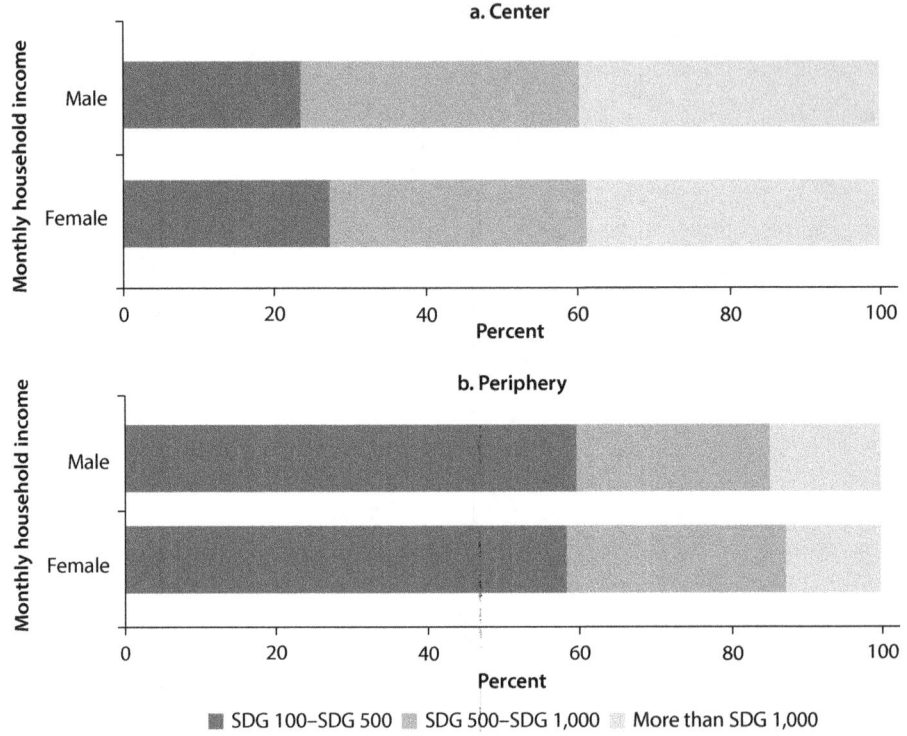

Source: Based on data from the 2013 U.K. Department for International Development Sudan household surveys.
Note: SDG = Sudanese pound.

to visualize inequalities across two dimensions. Though it is a simple bar graph, it lets us see the variation in a single outcome variable (income) across both the center–periphery and gender dimensions. We created the center–periphery variable for the average income of the state in which the respondent resides (see chapter 3 of this volume for a detailed explanation).

Our use of the center–periphery variable is an example of creating variables within the existing data set by using an interpretation of the sociopolitical context relevant to Sudan. Though we already had a rural–urban variable in the data set, whereby *urban* refers to respondents living in capital cities of each state and *rural* refers to all other respondents, we wanted to capture the variation in public service ratings across a geographic dimension, which would be more informative than whether the respondent lived in Khartoum. Indeed, much of the literature discusses a concentration of wealth in Khartoum and the northern states of Sudan, and a neglect of the periphery areas by the central Khartoum government (Johnson 2003).

Furthermore, although the center–periphery divide is wealth based, it also cuts across other socioeconomic and demographic characteristics, including ethnicity and exposure to conflict. Indicators of ethnicity and other forms of identity (Arab, Muslim, and nomadic) are often geographically concentrated; therefore, inequalities that we characterize as center–periphery may be proxies for inequalities based on ethnicity and other forms of identity. They may also reflect inequality in exposure to conflict, where conflict is acutely linked to the peripheral areas of Sudan. As such to a certain extent, horizontal inequalities, by way of center–periphery, can proxy for identity and conflict.

Developing a Theoretical Model

Having identified that exploring inequalities in perceptions of public service provision is an important research issue, we develop a theoretical model that will be investigated empirically using the DFID Sudan household survey data. This theoretical model is informed by the descriptive analysis outlined in the previous section as well as an extensive literature review.

The descriptive analysis indicated both that public service ratings were a function of actual provision of public services and that other factors play a role in perceptions. See, for example, figure 4.4, which illustrates ratings of public services across three states: Khartoum, North Darfur, and West Darfur. It shows not

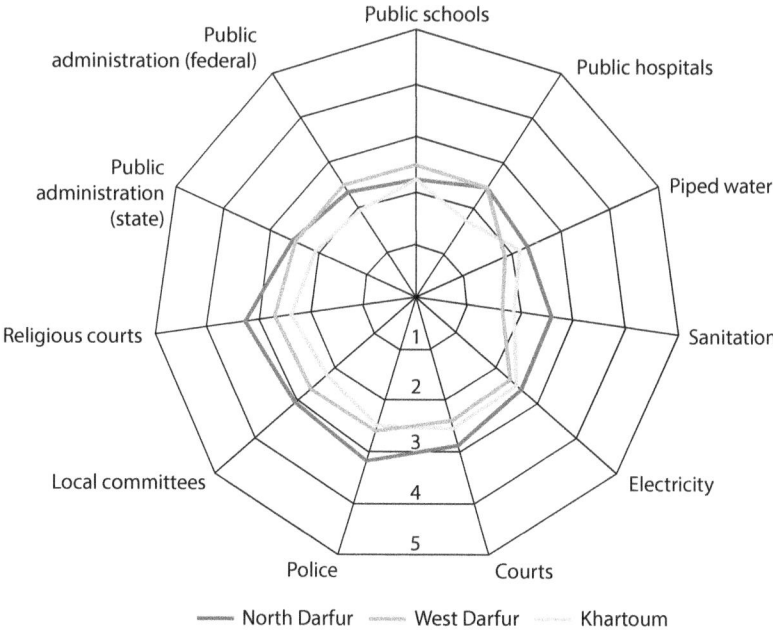

Figure 4.4 Ratings of Public Services for Three States

How would you rate the overall quality of the service...

[1 = very low, 2 = low, 3 = suitable, 4 = good, 5 = excellent]

Source: Based on data from the 2013 U.K. Department for International Development Sudan household surveys.

only variation in ratings across the services in a single state but also variation in the ratings for a single service across the states. We also notice that ratings in Khartoum were lower than ratings in the Darfur states for most services. However, factors other than actual provision are likely causally related to perceptions of public services, where actual provision refers to the realized form of service provision that each individual receives. Indeed, if the unique factor influencing perceptions of service quality were actual provision, respondents in Khartoum, which receives a more complete and sustained service, would report higher ratings than would respondents in Darfur.

The expectations of different respondents, with regard to the quality of service provision, likely will vary geographically. This factor, along with others that may influence expectation such as income and gender, likely entails that variation in perceptions across different service areas is influenced by multiple factors.

This hypothesis emerging from the data is confirmed by existing literature on perceptions of service quality.

Bouckaert and Van de Walle (2003, 330) state that attempts to measure actual provision using perceptions "are misleading if they claim to be measuring good governance; as [perceptions are] difficult to measure and very service-specific."

Maister (1995) notes that research has also shown that service quality ratings are a function of the respondent's perception of a service outcome and an expectation of that service. Therefore, we posit that a theoretical model should include socioeconomic and demographic characteristics that are proxies for predisposition and expectations of service quality. These factors may include the dimensions along which we investigated inequalities, including gender, residency in a rural or an urban area, residency in the center or in the periphery, and income.

Our literature review on the factors determining perceptions uncovered another important component of the model: trust in public institutions. Researchers have theorized that citizens' trust in government could be a proxy for a positive or negative predisposition that biases ratings of service quality (Kampen, Van de Walle, and G. Bouckaert 2006). Harding (2013) provides the empirical backing to this theory, showing that higher levels of trust in government are correlated with higher ratings of public services. Furthermore, Harding (2013) and Sztompka (2001) suggest that trust is developed over time and is closely linked to an individual's broader belief system. Following our literature review, we included trust in our theoretical model and investigated its role in determining perceptions.

Figure 4.5 illustrates the correlation between overall level of trust and overall perception of quality, as reported in the DFID Sudan household survey data. It confirms the existence of a correlation, as would be expected on the basis of the literature.

Drawing from the literature, we also postulate that trust as a factor may take on multiple forms, given that people interact to a greater or lesser degree with representatives of certain public institutions. Ordinarily, members of

Figure 4.5 Average Overall Perception of Quality versus Average Overall Level of Trust, at the Individual Level

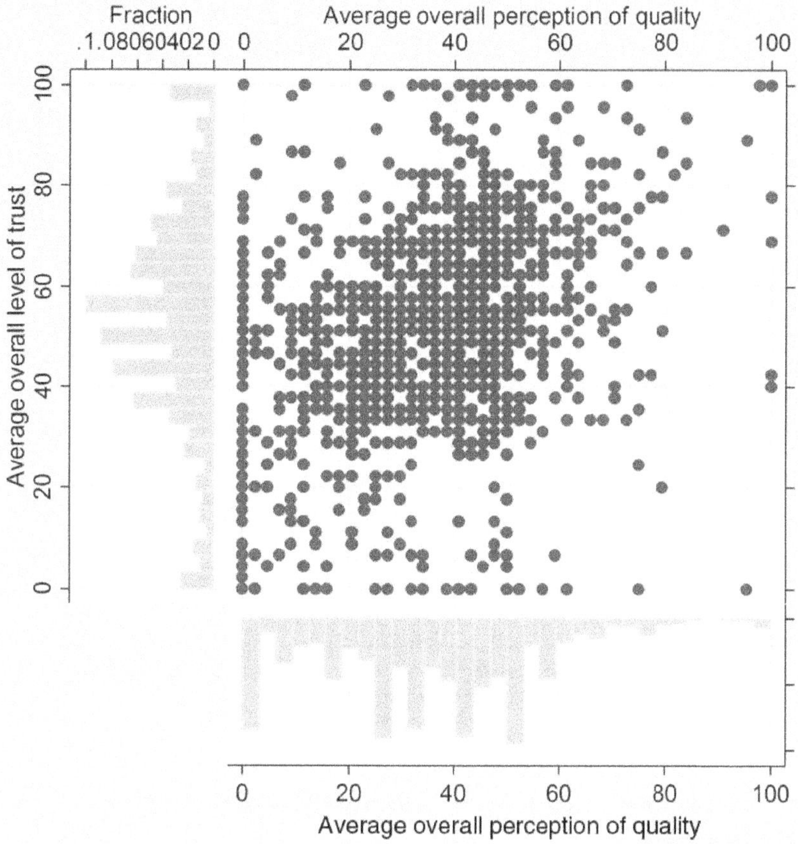

Source: Based on data from the 2013 U.K. Department for International Development Sudan household surveys.

the public are more likely to have sustained interaction with public service providers in areas such as health, education, and water and sanitation services than with other government officials. In our factor analysis, we distinguished between public services with which the population has sustained contact—factor 1, "trust in public services"—and services with which people do not interact often—factor 2, "trust in government." The idea behind this distinction is that the ratings of the public services with which people have little interaction were based less on actual provision and more on the other factors already discussed, such as expectation of both the service and the service providers and a predisposition to positivity or negativity. We discuss the multiple factors that may inform trust in the next section. Figure 4.6 provides a visual representation of our theoretical model, showing a framework for the way in which different factors may inform a person's perception of service quality.

Figure 4.6 Theoretical Framework for the Determinants of Service Quality

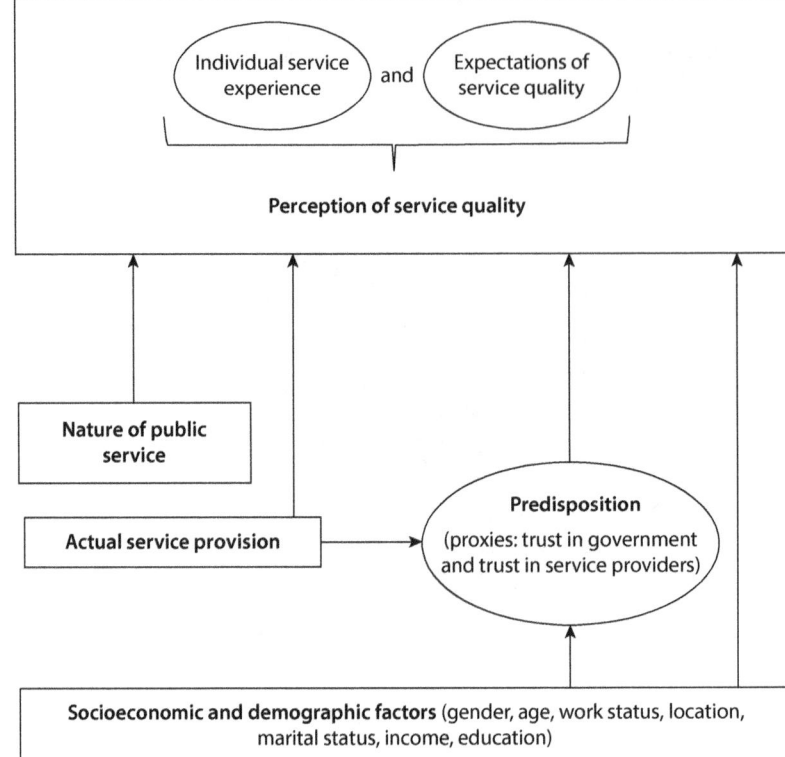

Advanced Quantitative Analysis–Factor Analysis and Structural Equation Modeling

Using Factor Analysis to Obtain Latent Factors from Observable Variables

In surveys that ask a number of questions on a related topic, using exact wording apart from the object of the question, the responses tend to be correlated with one another. As a result, in the DFID Sudan household survey—which asked for levels of trust in 15 public institutions using the same wording—we expected the questions to produce intercorrelated responses. As discussed previously, we expected two underlying trust "factors": a trust in government and a trust in public service providers. Consequently, we conducted exploratory factor analysis (EFA), a statistical technique used to reduce a number of observable variables into a smaller number of factors.

Our methodology consisted of the following steps: (a) we determined whether a sufficient level of intercorrelation existed between the observable variables in which we were interested; (b) we specified the number of expected latent factors in these observable variables, based on our theoretical and contextual understanding; and (c) once we obtained a resulting pattern matrix that identified the variables that made up each of these factors, we used them to empirically investigate our theoretical model.

In the first step, we examined a correlation matrix of the observable variables we were interested in from our data set, which were all 15 of the variables on trust in public institutions (see the correlation matrix in table 4.2).

Using this correlation matrix, we needed to determine whether the level of intercorrelation between these trust variables was high enough to claim that certain latent factors determine these variables, which is the underlying assumption for EFA. That determination can be done using two indicators: (a) Bartlett's sphericity test, which provides the statistical probability that the matrix has significant correlations among at least some variables in the matrix; and (b) the Kaiser-Meyer-Olkin (KMO) index for sampling adequacy. We describe each of these indicators in turn.

Bartlett's sphericity test examines the null hypothesis that the correlation matrix is an identity matrix, where all diagonal elements of the matrix are 1 and off-diagonal elements are 0, meaning all the elements are uncorrelated. If we reject this null hypothesis, we can conclude that all elements of the matrix are not uncorrelated and that the variables in the matrix are suitable for EFA. The results from Bartlett's test for the matrix shown in table 4.2 indicate that we can reject the null hypothesis at a 0.1 percent significance level and that the variables in the matrix are suitable for EFA.

The KMO index is a measure of the sampling adequacy of the data and uses correlation and partial correlation to determine whether the data will factor well. Rather than test the significance of a null hypothesis of no correlation, the KMO index categorizes the common part of the matrix that is predictable by regressing each variable on all other variables into categories: 0.00–0.49 as "unacceptable" for factor analysis; 0.50–0.59 as "miserable"; 0.60–0.69 as "mediocre"; 0.70–0.79 as "middling"; 0.80–0.89 as "meritorious"; and 0.90–1.00 as "marvelous" (Kaiser 1974; Trujillo-Ortiz 2006). A higher proportion reflects a larger common part of the matrix, or a part of the matrix that is explained by the other variables in the matrix. The KMO index for the matrix shown in table 4.3 is 0.93, indicating that it is "marvelous" for EFA.

Now that we have determined that our observable variables are suitable for factor analysis, the second step is to conduct EFA based on our theoretical and contextual understanding that two latent factors are driving the responses to the trust in public institutions questions. Using the EFA results in a pattern matrix (shown in table 4.3), we see that these two latent factors account for 54 percent of the total variation in the responses to the trust in public institutions questions. In other words, the responses varied in the same way across the different questions on trust in public institutions 54 percent of the time and therefore were driving the variation we see across respondents.

The pattern matrix also shows that the two factors are delineated conceptually into those variables reflecting central government institutions and those related to public service providers, as well as private companies. This result is in line with the theoretical literature, which suggests that there is only "one opinion of trust in [central] government because people do not make distinctions" between government institutions (Bouckaert and Van de Walle 2003). The grouping of private companies with public service providers is also in line with

Table 4.2 Correlation Matrix of Trust in Public Institutions
Percent

	Variable	Mean	SD	% DK	% NR	t1	t2	t3	t4	t5	t6	t7	t8	t9	t10	t11	t12	t13	t14	t15
t1	National parliament	2.3	1.0	8.8	1.2	1.00														
t2	Judiciary	2.7	1.0	5.8	1.0	0.63	1.00													
t3	Political parties	1.9	1.0	7.7	1.3	0.50	0.34	1.00												
t4	Armed forces	3.0	1.1	3.9	0.9	0.48	0.61	0.25	1.00											
t5	Public adm. (federal)	2.3	1.0	11.0	1.4	0.52	0.49	0.43	0.48	1.00										
t6	Local government	2.2	1.0	6.6	1.3	0.56	0.48	0.44	0.43	0.62	1.00									
t7	The Imam of my mosque	3.3	1.0	5.5	1.3	0.31	0.48	0.19	0.53	0.44	0.39	1.00								
t8	Local hospital	2.4	1.0	3.5	1.0	0.44	0.38	0.42	0.33	0.50	0.50	0.38	1.00							
t9	Local school	2.8	1.0	3.8	0.9	0.42	0.44	0.32	0.39	0.47	0.44	0.50	0.68	1.00						
t10	Electricity company	2.6	1.0	4.7	0.9	0.40	0.45	0.24	0.40	0.39	0.36	0.36	0.45	0.53	1.00					
t11	Federal government	2.3	1.0	9.7	1.8	0.58	0.54	0.36	0.49	0.58	0.56	0.38	0.46	0.47	0.52	1.00				
t12	Police	2.6	1.0	4.5	0.9	0.52	0.56	0.35	0.54	0.50	0.50	0.47	0.46	0.49	0.46	0.62	1.00			
t13	Journalists	2.3	1.0	11.1	1.2	0.32	0.36	0.43	0.29	0.40	0.43	0.32	0.43	0.40	0.43	0.43	0.43	1.00		
t14	Private companies	2.5	1.0	10.8	1.2	0.28	0.33	0.31	0.22	0.33	0.32	0.27	0.37	0.36	0.40	0.32	0.31	0.48	1.00	
t15	My local tribal chief	2.8	1.1	12.1	2.8	0.35	0.34	0.29	0.35	0.30	0.33	0.38	0.42	0.38	0.33	0.35	0.34	0.37	0.38	1.00

Source: Based on data from the 2013 U.K. Department for International Development Sudan household surveys.
Note: adm. = administration; DK = don't know; NR = no response; SD = standard deviation.

Table 4.3 Factor Analysis of Trust in Public Institutions

	Variable	Rotated factor loadings			Coefficients		KMO
		Factor 1	Factor 2	Uniqueness	Factor 1	Factor 2	Overall = 0.9
t1	National parliament	0.697	0.294	0.428	0.188	−0.069	0.91
t2	Judiciary	0.784	0.200	0.346	0.257	−0.153	0.92
t3	Political parties	0.285	0.556	**0.610**	−0.072	0.222	0.90
t4	Armed forces	0.809	0.060	0.342	0.315	−0.241	0.93
t5	Public administrations (federal)	0.647	0.376	0.440	0.140	−0.005	0.94
t6	Local government	0.609	0.408	0.463	0.113	0.027	0.95
t7	The Imam of the mosque	0.627	0.218	**0.559**	0.186	−0.089	0.91
t8	Local hospital	0.378	0.667	0.413	−0.071	0.254	0.91
t9	Local school	0.467	0.570	0.457	−0.001	0.168	0.90
t10	Electricity company	0.447	0.498	**0.552**	0.016	0.133	0.94
t11	Federal government	0.694	0.356	0.392	0.167	−0.033	0.94
t12	Police	0.716	0.309	0.392	0.191	−0.067	0.96
t13	Journalists	0.232	0.721	0.427	−0.149	0.334	0.92
t14	Private companies	0.099	0.742	0.440	−0.212	0.392	0.92
t15	My local tribal chief	0.284	0.552	**0.615**	−0.071	0.220	0.94

Source: Based on data from the 2013 U.K. Department for International Development Sudan household surveys.
Note: KMO = Kaiser-Meyer-Olkin index.

contextual information. In Sudan, private firms or nongovernmental organizations increasingly provide many public services (Crowther et al. 2014). We can therefore take these two factors and use them in our regression analysis.

The Path to Structural Equation Modeling
Individual-Level Regressions

Based on our theoretical model, we decided to test the following empirical model, including socioeconomic and demographic characteristics as well as trust factors, as determinants of perceptions of quality of public services.

In the path diagram (see figure 4.7), we see that the socioeconomic and demographic factors are expected to have a causal relationship not only with perception of service quality but also with trust in public institutions. We tested this model at both the individual and the state level. At the state level, we included in our model the average values for each of these variables; our sample size was the 15 states that were included in the data set.

Before selecting this empirical model, however, we considered two other empirical models that look at the determinants of quality of public services. These empirical models acted as stepping-stones to building a broader narrative. The first model (figure 4.8) does not include the trust factors. The second model (figure 4.9) does not include the trust factors as mediators in the form of a structural equation model. Rather, the socioeconomic and demographic characteristics and the trust factors are determinants of service quality ratings, but the former do not act as determinants of the latter.

We determine that the model presented in figure 4.7 is the most accurate empirical test of the theoretical model developed within this chapter.

Figure 4.7 Regression of Service Quality Rating on Demographics and Trust Factors, with Trust Factors as "Mediators"

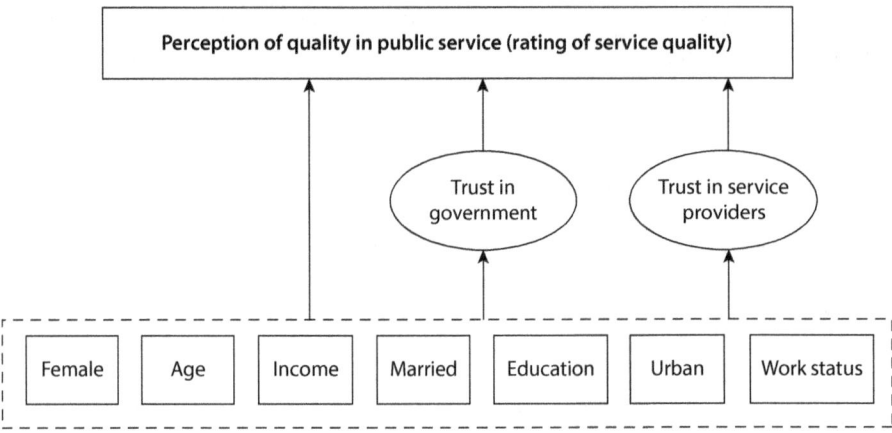

Source: Based on data from the 2013 U.K. Department for International Development Sudan household surveys.

Figure 4.8 Regression of Service Quality Rating on Socioeconomic and Demographic Variables

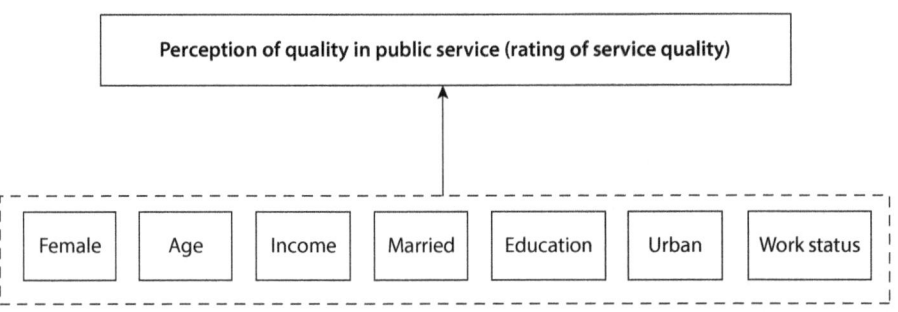

Source: Based on data from the 2013 U.K. Department for International Development Sudan household surveys.

Figure 4.9 Regression of Service Quality Rating on Socioeconomic and Demographic Variables and Trust Factors

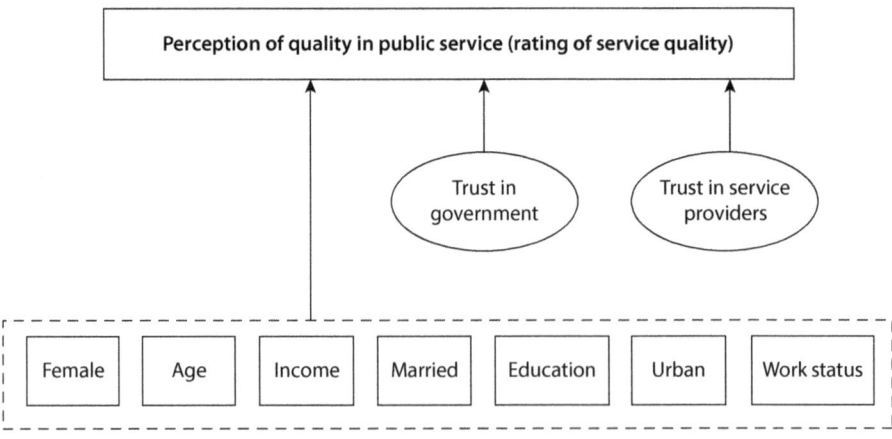

Source: Based on data from the 2013 U.K. Department for International Development Sudan household surveys.

We next use a statistical technique known as structural equation modeling to test this model. SEM is an extension of multiple regression analysis, but it allows a variable to serve as both a source variable (independent variable) and a result variable (dependent variable) in a chain of causal hypotheses. This kind of variable is called a mediator (Lei and Wu 2007). In our model, we can empirically test the determinants of public service quality using trust as a mediator, because (a) it is determined by socioeconomic and demographic characteristics, and (b) it determines the public service quality rating.

To use SEM, we note the following:

> SEM is a multi-equation technique that enables simultaneous estimation of all direct and indirect interrelationships and multiple regression equations in a single framework. It is also a confirmatory procedure, where a complete structure of the model, known as a path-diagram, must be specified in advance of statistical analyses. Data is used within SEM to examine how closely the analysis fits the expectations from the theoretical model. (Crowther et al. 2014, 38)

Results from our SEM analysis for the rating of public schools are shown in the third column, titled, "Ordered logit + mediation," in table 4.4. The other two

Table 4.4 Regression Results for Rating Public Schools

Dependent variable: perception of quality in public schools	(I) Ordered logit	(II) Ordered logit	(III) Ordered logit + mediation	Mediators in (III)	
				Trust in government	Trust in service provider
female (=1 if female, =0 if male)	−0.0349 (−0.34)	0.0178 (0.14)	0.0311 (0.27)	2.915 (1.52)	5.239** (2.63)
age (min:18, max:87)	−0.00884 (−1.94)	−0.00386 (−0.67)	−0.00148 (−0.28)	−0.0649 (−0.74)	0.110 (1.21)
income (1 = SDG 100–SDG 500, 2 = SDG 500–SDG 1,000, 3 = > SDG 1,000)	0.127 (1.78)	0.179* (2.04)	0.198* (2.49)	0.769 (0.59)	0.894 (0.66)
married (=1 if married, =0 otherwise)	−0.0387 (−0.35)	−0.0368 (−0.26)	0.0116 (0.09)	1.681 (0.79)	−0.960 (−0.43)
education (1–8)	−0.123*** (−4.05)	−0.0555 (−1.45)	−0.0416 (−1.19)	0.264 (0.46)	−1.699** (−2.84)
urban (=1 if urban, =0 if rural)	0.0894 (0.95)	0.111 (0.95)	0.0798 (0.68)	3.401 (1.72)	−6.022** (−2.94)
Work status (=1 if in work, =0 if not in work)	−0.0473 (−0.45)	0.0271 (0.20)	−0.0259 (−0.21)	3.883 (1.91)	2.510 (1.19)
(14 state dummies are omitted from display)					
Trust in government		0.0169*** (8.60)	0.0185*** (10.47)		
Trust in service provider		0.00799*** (4.14)	0.00812*** (4.92)		
N	2,002	1,312	1,320		

Source: Based on data from the 2013 U.K. Department for International Development Sudan household surveys.
Note: *t*-statistics in parentheses; SDG = Sudanese pound. Complete information, including all state dummies, is provided in appendix 3 of 2013 U.K. surveys.
*$p < 0.05$, **$p < 0.01$, ***$p < 0.001$.

columns reference the models in figures 4.8 and 4.9, and analysis of the results of these columns confirms the decisions to rely on the third model as the basis for our quantitative analysis. Namely, comparison of the first model with the second illustrates that education is no longer a significant determinant of ratings, and the R^2 values for each of these models illustrate that the second model explains the determinants of ratings much better than the first.

These results are from an ordered logit regression model that means a coefficient of –0.123 for education implies that a one "unit" increase in the education level of the individual leads to a 0.12 decrease in the ordered log—odds of having a higher level of perception of quality, holding all else constant. In other words, a one "unit" increase in the education level of the individual leads to 0.88 times greater odds of having a higher level of perception of quality.

These results indicate that gender, education, and rural–urban location are statistically significant determinants of trust in service providers. Education is negatively related with trust in service providers and affects the ratings of public schools through this mediator rather than independently. We find that being male is also negatively related to trust in service providers. Living in an urban area, however, is positively related. We find that the relationships between these characteristics and trust in service providers are consistent across the three public services. This result is critical to our understanding of the role of horizontal inequalities in determining perceptions of public services.

Furthermore, we can see that income is a direct determinant of ratings. Income is positively related to the rating of public schools. This result creates a differential that suggests that an individual with higher income is more likely to rate public schools higher than an individual with lower income, holding all other variables constant. This rating may be influenced by whether an individual sends his or her child to a private or public school. Those with a higher level of income are more likely to have the resources to send their children to private schools and thus may have a divergent perception of state schools. Alternatively, the level of income may determine the quality of public school to which a person has access, simply linked to the location of that person's home within a particular region.

State-Level Regressions

When we test the model at the state level, it has two main differences. First, we can include our indicators of actual service provision, which we could not do in the individual-level regressions because data on actual service provision was not available at this granular level. For example, we know the number of public schools per capita in the state of Blue Nile, but we do not know the number of public schools per capita in each of the units within the state. Additionally, we cannot use SEM because it requires a larger number of observations than the number of states. SEM is a large-sample technique that generally requires n to exceed 200 observations, so we can no longer consider trust as a mediator in the model. Therefore, we cannot explore the relationships between the socioeconomic and demographic characteristics and trust at the state levels.

Table 4.5 State-Level Regression Results for Rating Public Schools

Perception of quality in public schools	Model 1	Model 2	Model 3	Model 4	Model 5	Model 6
Trust in government	0.647	0.718	0.714	0.816	1.371*	1.319***
	(0.389)	(0.440)	(0.347)	(0.433)	(0.283)	(0.193)
Trust in service provider	0.420	0.400	0.606	0.573	1.820	1.313***
	(0.381)	(0.427)	(0.474)	(0.308)	(0.485)	(0.211)
age	−1.593	−0.912	−2.314	−0.629	−1.700	
(min: 29.9, max: 37.9)	(2.222)	(4.167)	(2.620)	(3.419)	(2.120)	
income	1.794	3.235	−0.0728	1.783	−10.20	
(min:1.1, max: 2.5)	(9.718)	(12.80)	(9.364)	(10.53)	(9.057)	
married	29.78	16.96	40.34	17.20	53.38	
(min: 45%, max: 75%)	(63.96)	(92.76)	(79.57)	(71.19)	(59.05)	
education	0.0180	−1.069	0.834	−1.817	−2.267	−5.212**
(min: 2.8, max: 5.1)	(6.404)	(7.910)	(8.036)	(6.197)	(5.216)	(1.240)
urban	−17.29	−18.78	−22.06	−24.68	−61.81	−54.19***
(min: 20%, max: 81%)	(15.46)	(17.87)	(16.85)	(19.45)	(18.49)	(6.142)
center[a]	10.43	9.858	12.74	16.44	51.21	33.40***
	(11.46)	(14.05)	(10.88)	(11.03)	(18.44)	(4.556)
Work status	−10.27	−6.936	−9.691	−8.329	−14.72	
(min: 34%, max: 64%)	(52.93)	(56.75)	(54.75)	(49.92)	(26.50)	
Student–teacher ratio[b]		0.134			−0.652	
		(0.405)			(0.639)	
No. of public schools per capita[b]			−4.481		−11.78*	−11.88***
			(4.091)		(2.242)	(1.408)
Per-student education spending[b]				−0.0448	−0.238	−0.144***
				(0.0673)	(0.0990)	(0.0263)
_cons	14.86	−7.866	28.81	−9.402	33.73	−22.11
	(50.19)	(104.8)	(50.87)	(77.55)	(76.99)	(16.91)
N	15	15	15	15	15	15
adj. R^2	0.245	0.079	0.206	0.156	0.732	0.866

Source: Based on data from the 2013 U.K. Department for International Development Sudan Household Health Surveys.
Note: Standard errors in parentheses. No. = number.
a. Dummy variable is 1 if the state is classified as "center" and 0 otherwise, see chapter 3 for the definition of "center/periphery."
b. See table 1 in chapter 3 for the description of the variable from nonsurvey data.
*$p < 0.05$, **$p < 0.01$, ***$p < 0.001$.

However, we hope that by running these two types of regression models, we can confirm and corroborate the results.

The results of the state-level regressions for the rating of public schools are shown in table 4.5. We find that model 6 best explains the variation in ratings based on the R^2 value and that our trust factors and education, rural–urban location, and center–periphery location, along with the indicators of actual provision, are all statistically significant in determining the rating of public schools.

Deriving Policy Implications

Now that we have produced results from the quantitative analysis, we attempt to derive policy implications from these results. We confirm the existence of inequalities, both horizontal and vertical, in perceptions of public service quality. Therefore, addressing these inequalities in public service provision and recognizing that these inequalities are likely a function of differences not only in actual provision along these dimensions but also in other factors that mediate the relationship between socioeconomic and demographic characteristics and perceptions of public services, the notable example being trust, is important.

Since inequality in service provision—both in terms of the quality and access to provision and in terms of perceptions—can be seen as an important source of potential instability, addressing these issues using evidence-based policy initiatives, leveraging these findings, appears to be a sensible approach.

Deriving policy implications within the Sudanese context is relevant in two ways. On the one hand, central and localized governments may deem the findings pertinent for policy development. On the other hand, humanitarian organizations that provide services may want to consider what these results mean for their in-country programming, particularly organizations working in camps for refugees and internally displaced persons. Though a political economy approach remains important, we are also aware that the level of marginalization across states means that the central government does not always have an incentive to improve service delivery. This perspective also points toward the need for more advocacy from international actors with regard to quality service provision for ostracized members of the population.

Fundamentally, policy recommendations clearly can come both in a number of forms and from an array of actors working across service delivery within Sudan. Perhaps most interesting, and beyond the regular outcome-based indicators used by most implementing partners, understanding the perception of service quality—and using an indicator to assess it—may be seen to play an important role in actively reducing inequalities. For example, we may consider the average perception of service quality for specific groups who have been identified as having unequal access and consider, across this group, the average perception of quality. Policy makers might then look to increase the average for this particular group.

This indicator in isolation is clearly relatively malleable and subject to interference. As such, a complementary indicator could be introduced measuring the gap between two groups. As an example, we might consider taking the ratio of perception of school quality for men and women to measure gender inequality in the perception of service delivery with respect to public schools. The objective then would be for the implementing body to contribute to a decrease in this indicator over time.

Several advantages result from using these two indicators to measure the effectiveness of public service provision policies, specifically with respect to inequalities. Because data already are collected with respect to the nationwide survey discussed within this chapter, organizations focused on these indicators would have the means necessary to calculate the indicators regularly. Doing so would also contribute to a broader analysis of these longer-term trends.

Collecting similar data in other countries to conduct comparisons of perceptions of public services across different contexts might also be possible. Additionally, though this analysis proves useful along specified dimensions, it also encourages the collection of more accurate and expansive data on service provision.

Understanding the Situational Context

To use the findings from our quantitative analysis to inform evidence-based policy making, we must place the analysis in the situational context, by understanding the way in which the state is set up to deliver public services in Sudan, for example. Public service provision in Sudan is devolved to state and local levels according to its decentralized system of governance. The federal level is responsible primarily for policy, planning, coordination, formation of international partnerships, and monitoring and evaluation of services. The state government focuses on local programming and project development and the local government on policy implementation and service delivery.

Figure 4.10 illustrates the structure of governance and flows of public resources in the education sector in Sudan. This structure is similar for other public services. For all public services, the federal government provides transfers to state ministries—some of which are earmarked for specific public services, and some are at the discretion of the state government. In addition to these transfers, states can generate their own income by collecting local taxes,[1] though the

Figure 4.10 Structure of Governance and Public Resource Flows in the Education Sector

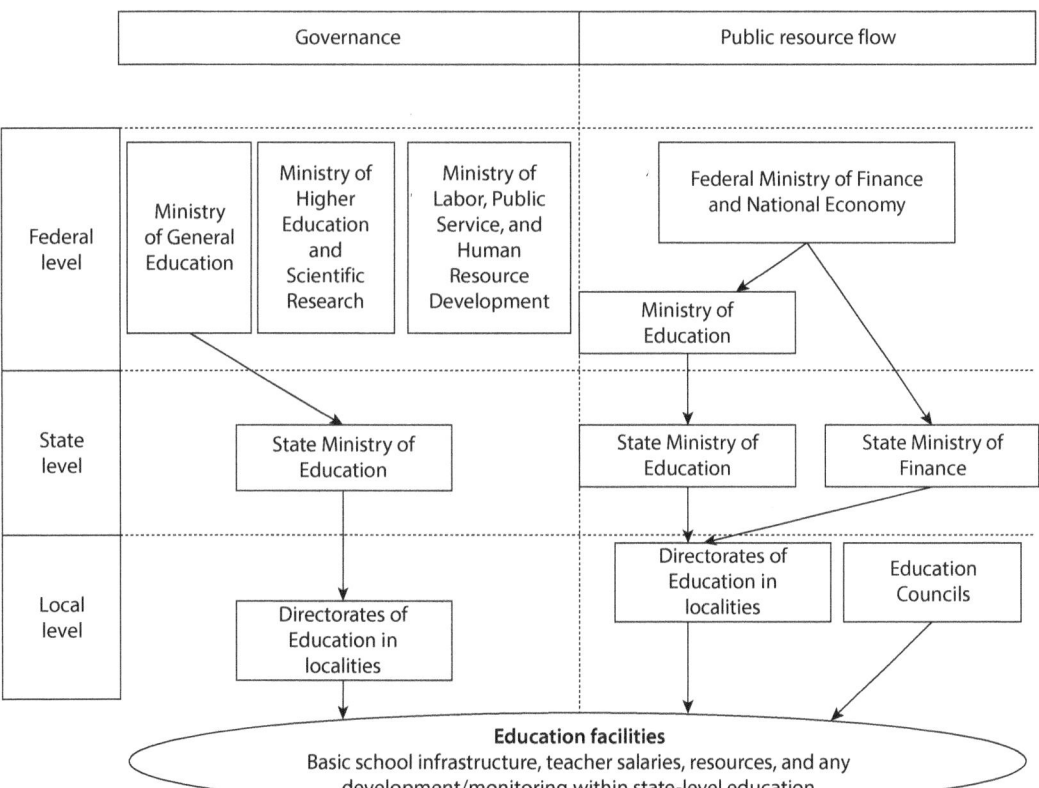

Source: Based on World Bank 2012.

capacity of a specific state to raise finances in this way depends on local administrative infrastructure and the resource levels of local populations, as well as other external factors. Ultimately, many states rely on federal transfers and have limited state-level tax revenue with which to enhance budgets for public service provision.

An interesting facet of the education system in Sudan is the locally elected education councils at the school level.[2] These councils often provide additional funding from the community for resources, teacher accommodation, and more. In some locations, the education councils are more influential than the directorates of education in the localities.[3]

Although decentralization, and fiscal federalism in particular, have been lauded for their effects on "political stability, public service performance, equity, and macroeconomic stability" (World Bank 2012), the decentralized structure of public services is often cited as contributing to several governance issues because it relies on limited local human resource capacity and is associated with significant financial leakages in the budgeting systems (World Bank 2011). In education, the majority of the budget is spent on teachers' salaries, leaving little for infrastructure, resources, training, or monitoring (World Bank 2012).

Conclusion

This chapter uses data from the DFID Sudan household survey as a practical illustration of the steps used to explore the limitations of a data set, ascertain the suitability for quantitative analysis, identify a research question, triangulate the data, and perform advanced quantitative analysis.

Our data set had several limitations, including a lack of actual service provision data and explanations of the rating assigned for a given service. However, given the scope for triangulation—which is crucial in conflict environments because they are particularly prone to incomplete data, as discussed in previous chapters—and the poignancy of information on public service provision in conflict states, we chose to explore these data.

Through data visualizations, we explore the existence of inequalities across ratings of public services and across groups for a given service. Radar graphs enable us to identify horizontal and vertical inequalities across income groups and center–periphery divides. Drawing on the literature, we model the variation in ratings across and within public services. The theory highlights expectation of service provision and quality, as well as predisposition to positivity or negativity as key determinants of ratings. As such, we explore ways either to include or to provide a proxy for these elements in the model. Socioeconomic variables along with demographic variables emerge as key players in the literature. Trust in public service providers also appears as a key determinant of ratings in the literature. However, a distinction exists between services with which individuals have sustained contact (for example, schools and hospitals) and services with which they hardly ever have contact (for example, national parliament). The latter can serve as a proxy for predisposition toward rating a public service positively or not. As such, we create two factor variables: factor 1, "trust in public services," and factor 2, "trust in the government."

We conduct several statistical tests to ascertain the relevance of factor modeling, including Bartlett's test, the KMO index, and EFA, which yielded supportive results. We then undertake quantitative modeling to provide the most comprehensive understanding of the service ratings as data would allow. After testing regression outputs from increasingly complete models, the model using trust as a mediator returns the most convincing results and corroborates the literature. After running the models on the three public services under analysis, and having undertaken individual-level and state-level analysis, our results are found to be consistent, giving us the certainty necessary to propose evidence-based policy recommendations.

Notes

1. These local taxes include income taxes; taxes on locally manufactured products; and taxes on income from investments, rents, licenses, and permits (Hamid 2002).
2. The system in Sudan allows for 13 years of education, including 2 years of preschool, 8 years of basic education, and 3 years of secondary school. These three education levels are coordinated by the Ministry of Higher Education and Scientific Research. Higher education and vocational education come under different federal agencies.
3. For example, in Darfur, the undercapacity directorates in the localities are often bypassed, meaning that education councils coordinate directly with state ministries of education.

Bibliography

Bouckaert, G., and S. Van de Walle. 2003. "Comparing Measures of Citizen Trust and User Satisfaction as Indicators of 'Good Governance': Difficulties in Linking Trust and Satisfaction Indicators." *International Review of Administrative Sciences* 69 (3): 329–43.

Bryman, A. 2011. "Triangulation." In *The SAGE Encyclopedia of Social Science Research Methods*, edited by M. S. Lewis-Beck, A. Bryman, and T. F. Liao. Thousand Oaks, CA: SAGE.

Chen, C., W. Hardle, and A. Unwin, eds. 2008. *Handbook of Data Visualization*. Berlin: Springer-Verlag.

Crowther, N., K. Okamura, C. Raja, D. Rinnert, and E. Spencer. 2014. "Inequalities in Public Services in the Sudan: Using a Perceptions-Informed View to Drive Policy in Education, Health and Water Provision." LSE Master of Public Administration (MPA) Capstone Report, London School of Economics and Political Science. http://r4d.dfid.gov.uk/Output/195649/Default.aspx.

Hamid, G. 2002. *Localizing the Local: Reflections on the Experience of Local Authorities in Sudan*. Riyadh: Arab Urban Development Institute.

Harding, L. 2013. "Service Satisfaction, Competence and Caring: Examining the Influence of Experience with the Public Bureaucracy on Citizen Attitudes of Trust in Government." PhD dissertation, University of Tennessee. http://trace.tennessee.edu/cgi/viewcontent.cgi?article=3100&context=utk_graddiss.

Johnson, D. H. 2003. *The Root Causes of Sudan's Civil Wars*. Bloomington: Indiana University Press; Kampala: Fountain Publishers.

Kaiser, H. F. 1974. "An Index of Factorial Simplicity." *Psychometrika* 39 (1): 31–36.

Kampen, J. K., S. Van de Walle, and G. Bouckaert. 2006. "Assessing the Relation between Satisfaction with Public Service Delivery and Trust in Government: The Impact of the Predisposition of Citizens toward Government on Evaluations of Its Performance." *Public Performance and Management Review* 29 (4): 387–404.

Lei, P. W., and Q. Wu. 2007. "An NCME Instructional Module on Introduction to Structural Equation Modeling: Issues and Practical Considerations, Educational Measurement." *Issues and Practice* 26 (3): 33–44.

Maister, D. 1995. "The Psychology of Waiting Lines." In *The Service Encounter: Managing Employee/Customer Interaction in Service Business*, edited by J. Czepiel, M. Solomon, and C. Surprenant, 113–23. Lexington, MA: Lexington Books.

Stewart, F., G. Brown, and L. Mancini. 2005. "Why Horizontal Inequalities Matter: Some Implications for Measurement." CRISE Working Paper 19, Centre for Research on Inequality, Human Security and Ethnicity, Oxford, U.K. http://r4d.dfid.gov.uk/pdf/outputs/inequality/wp19.pdf.

Sztompka, P. 2001. "Trust: Cultural Concerns." In *International Encyclopedia of the Social & Behavioral Sciences*, edited by N. J. Smelser and P. B. Baltes, 23: 15913. Oxford, U.K.: Elsevier Science.

Trujillo-Ortiz, A. 2006. "Kaiser–Meyer–Olkin Measure of Sampling Adequacy." http://www.mathworks.com/matlabcentral/fileexchange/12736-kmo.

University of Texas. 1995. "Factor Analysis Using SAS PROC FACTOR." Austin: University of Texas. http://www.ats.ucla.edu/stat/sas/library/factor_ut.htm.

———. n.d. "Measures of Appropriateness of Factor Analysis." Austin: University of Texas. http://www.utexas.edu/courses/schwab/sw388r7/Tutorials/PrincipalComponentsAnalysisintheLiterature_doc_html/027_Measures_of_Appropriateness_of_Factor_Analysis.html.

World Bank. 2011. *Sudan: Issues in Urban Development. Phase 1—Overview of the Urban Landscape*. Khartoum: World Bank Office Sudan.

———. 2012. *The Status of the Education Sector in Sudan*. Washington, DC: World Bank.

PART 2

Detailed Analysis of the Survey's Modules

CHAPTER 5

Using Survey Data from Sudan for Policy Making: The Determinants of Trust and the Perceived Effect on Gender of Decisions by the Tribal Leader

Alexander Hamilton and John Hudson

This chapter discusses the U.K. Department for International Development (DFID) household survey data on Sudan, collected over several years. We focus on the latest two years of data, collected in 2013 and 2014, because these contain the most comprehensive set of questions. We illustrate how the data can be used in an econometric analysis on a very specific set of issues: examining people's perceptions of fairness in tribal leadership decisions and whether or not these decisions favor women. In doing so, the chapter fills something of a gap in the literature because there has been very little empirical work on evaluating leaders in developing countries. In addition, we examine how these perceptions feed into levels of trust in the tribal leader. Survey data of this kind are invaluable for providing information on people's lives, attitudes, needs, hopes, fears, and priorities. When used in econometric analysis, such data also can provide insights into these aspects and, in particular, the way they link with socioeconomic characteristics such as age, education, and locational variables. Locational variables relate to the characteristics of where an individual lives. In the case of the DFID Sudan household surveys, the variables are derived from the survey responses themselves. This approach has been used before when analyzing survey data (Gaviria and Raphael 2001), but not as much as it might have been. Perhaps locational data have not

---

Authors' Note: This chapter is a nontechnical summary of our 2014 paper, "Bribery and Identification: Evidence from Sudan," University of Bath Working Paper 30/14. Copyrights of this paper remain with the U.K. Department for International Development, which gave permission for use of the above-noted material.

been used much because to make use of them, one first must calculate them, a process that is not totally straightforward (annex 5A). In this chapter, we discuss locational variables and demonstrate how they can be calculated within the context of the econometrics program Stata. The results illustrate that, along with individual characteristics, locational variables are an important determinant of people's attitudes and beliefs.

The chapter is divided into two parts: (a) the methodology of the DFID Sudan household surveys is described in greater detail than in chapters 2, 3, and 4 of this volume to include a discussion of the data set and (b) this methodology is used to analyze attitudes toward tribal leaders' decisions and the effect of such attitudes on trust in the tribal leader. This analysis is an interesting issue, not least because it parallels literature that examines the perceived fairness of a leader's decisions and overall evaluations of leaders, albeit in the context of developed countries. The chapter thus proceeds as follows. In the first section, we discuss the data in general terms. The second section features a background to the analysis in a discussion of Sudan's current situation. We then review various streams of the relevant literature. Later, we present the data set specifically as it relates to the issues we are analyzing and then analyze this data. Finally, we conclude the chapter. Much of the material in the latter parts of the chapter provides a nontechnical summary of the material in Hamilton and Hudson (2014b). One of the main conclusions to emerge from the analysis is the importance of both individual characteristics and the characteristics of the location in which the individual lives. Along both dimensions, a particularly important factor is the level of education.

The Data Set

Although referred to in chapters 2, 3, and 4 of this volume, the DFID Sudan household surveys are described here in some detail. We are concerned with data sets collected by the Sudan Polling and Statistics Center in collaboration with DFID on July 11–21, 2013, and June 3–5, 2014.[1] The sampling process entailed three stages: (a) one cluster was randomly selected from equally sized (for population) areas of every state (the probability that any given locality was selected was proportional to size); (b) households in the locality were randomly selected with a replacement sampling strategy; and (c) an individual age 18 years or older from within each household was selected to respond to the surveys using the Kish Table method for selection (see chapters 3 and 4 of this volume for additional information). Field interviewers were allocated to their own hometown or countryside to facilitate a greater capacity to understand cultural, social, and political conditions. However, the surveys were carried out in less than ideal conditions: security issues in South Kurdufan and North Kurdufan hindered, though did not prevent, work in these states. Indeed, such problems added to the value of the survey data collected, simply because hard data on these areas are more difficult to find. Poor accessibility caused both by compromised infrastructure and by high proportions of displaced people as a result of conflict also deterred survey efforts. Similar concerns were reflected by Alexander Hamilton, the statistics adviser in DFID Sudan, who commented on these difficulties in 2013 (Hamilton 2013b). As Crowther et al. (2014) observe, such issues pose problems for data collection in terms of constructing a sampling framework and in terms of finding individuals in specified regions. Devising sampling frames is particularly difficult when villages and roads listed in official documents no longer exist because of conflict, or indeed other reasons such as damage linked to weather events. As Crowther et al. (2014) also point out, respondents may perceive some questions as sensitive and may feel pressured to provide certain answers. However, as we note elsewhere in this chapter, some of those issues relating to biased samples are of less concern when doing regression analysis aimed at understanding the determinants of attitudes than when attempting to provide a snapshot of those attitudes.

Question Coverage

Both surveys follow a similar format in terms of the questions asked. A number of questions establish the background of the individuals, such as their age, gender, marital status, the place where they live (urban or rural), their income, their income relative to their needs, and whether they receive overseas remittances. Many of the other questions relate to subjective issues that come under several headings and are summarized in box 5.1. A substantial proportion of the survey

---

Box 5.1 Questionnaire Structure

Individual socioeconomic variables:
    Age, gender, marital status, recipient of remittances, occupation, income, income relative to needs

Subjective background variables:
    Interest in politics, information sources
    Individual experience with war and conflict
    Individual experience with bribery

Attitudinal questions:
    Perceptions on the current state of the nation and the way it should proceed together with major priorities
    Trust in major institutions
    Identity
    Service provision: priorities, quality of service provision, perceptions of provision in other locations within Sudan
    The police: a series of questions relating to the way they perform their job and the individual's interaction with the police
    Access to banking and entrepreneurship
    Individual experience with war and conflict
    Female circumcision

is concerned with capturing perceptions of service provision, both within Khartoum as perceived by people outside Khartoum and vice versa. Many of the questions are similar to those found in other surveys, such as Eurobarometer in the European Union (EU), but some derive from the local context in Sudan relating to conflict, war, and female genital mutilation. Not all the questions were asked of everyone, though. Questions of perceptions of service delivery in Khartoum by those outside Khartoum were necessarily asked only of those not residing in Khartoum. Questions relating to the conflict in Darfur, and whether respondents had heard of the Doha Agreement relating to peace in the region, were asked only of those living in North Darfur, South Darfur, and West Darfur. Similarly, only respondents in the states of Blue Nile, North Darfur, North Kurdufan, South Darfur, South Kurdufan, and West Darfur were asked whether the conflict linked with government rebels had forced them to leave their homes. Although the responses provide useful statistical data on the effect of the conflict in these states, econometric analysis that uses these variables on the whole of the country is not really possible because we cannot assume that people in other states had not moved from the affected regions. The inability to use such data is a pity because using those variables would have been most illuminating in providing insights into how the experience of conflict affected people's attitudes on a range of issues.

Background to the Analysis: Sudan

The concept of the tribe remains critical for many African countries.[2] In Sudan, as in other countries (Hall 2002)—in many areas, particularly rural ones—an individual has multiple loyalties to the family and then the tribe and upward to the state and the nation. The potential for conflict exists on several dimensions, but to a large extent, family and tribal loyalties support each other relatively harmoniously. Wallerstein (1960) argued 50 years ago that this was true, and there is evidence (Hamilton and Hudson 2014a) that it is still the case today, despite many more pressures being placed on both the tribe and the family than in 1960. Tribal loyalties possibly can still compete with national loyalties to the detriment of the latter (Miguel 2004), but to a large extent the bigger conflicts are between tribes.

Substantial differences exist among more than 400 separate ethnic and cultural communities, which may be called tribes, in both lifestyles and governance structures. For example, tribes differ according to whether they have a chief, a hierarchy among chiefs, or indeed some other structure. The Amarar, Toposa, Turkana, and Nuer are less hierarchical than many other tribes and are "chiefless" (Nugent and Sanchez 1999). In contrast, the Zande and Shilluk are highly stratified; a king or noble chief yields considerable independent power. Substantial differences, too, exist in terms of the level of inequality among various groups within the tribe and the relative power of the central authority. All of this is likely to affect people's attitudes toward, and perceptions and understanding of, the tribal chief. Nonetheless, the tribe in its various forms is a central part of the governance structure in Sudan. Indeed, Zain (1996) has argued that the state has played little role at the local level, other than administration, allowing a greater role for the tribal elites. This role includes mobilizing for collective defense on a tribal basis, and both the army and the government have chosen to exert influence over citizens by working with the tribes. But the central government does try to influence tribal affairs, for example, to ensure a leadership that it finds amenable.

Each tribe also has its own different and differing institutions. Their economies, which in most areas are predominantly agricultural, also differ substantially, in part because of substantial climatic differences across Sudan (Nugent and Sanchez 1999). Most of the land is divided into a number of exclusive tribal areas called *dars*. Each dar retains its own, and somewhat differing, property rights. These rights may be limited to just land use, but as with the Fur, Nuba, Shilluk, and Zande tribes, they may also include the right to sell and to rent. Access to property rights also may effectively differ between men and women. Many of the differences have their roots in whether the society is predominantly based on either agriculture or herding. The Bisharin, Hadendowa, Kababish, and Turkana are nomadic tribes, with the right to take animals almost anywhere within the tribal dar, though, reasonably enough, exceptions exist to protect unharvested crops. Until recently, these tribal land areas and institutions have experienced relative stability. However, in recent years, that stability has changed to a degree because of the large flows of people following conflict both with South Sudan and also in other areas such as Darfur.[3] This change potentially has an effect on attitudes toward both the tribe and the family.

This previous stability stemmed, and to an extent still does so, from a number of factors. Some factors relate to colonial times, and the generally slow rate of economic growth and social change has tended to lead to institutional stability. However, the issue is how long this can persist. Technological developments, changing climate, and political factors, some external to the country, all tend to put the established order under pressure. In this chapter, we analyze individual attitudes toward tribes and tribal leaders, with a particular focus on the perceived fairness of tribal decisions. The analysis follows two dimensions: the decisions over all and any perceived bias in such decisions toward men. Institutional trust is important for good governance, but often it is analyzed as trust per se. Focusing on possible bias toward men enables us to analyze a subcomponent of overall trust. We also analyze the trust placed in tribes and the effect of perceived fairness on that trust. A literature on leadership, mainly in developing countries, argues that perceived fairness is an important—possibly the most important—factor determining people's overall leadership evaluations (Tyler 1986). We use trust in leadership as a proxy for an overall leadership evaluation and ask whether the relationship between this and perceived fairness in Sudan is similar to the relationship that has been analyzed in other countries. The analysis is based on the two DFID Sudan household surveys carried out in 2013 and 2014 of more than 4,700 people across the whole of Sudan. Different people were interviewed in the two samples.

Sunni Islam is the dominant religion in Sudan, although there is a small Christian minority; 70 percent of the population is classified as Sudanese Arabs.

A further dominant feature of Sudanese life lies in the conflicts that have characterized the country in recent decades, indeed dating almost to independence from the United Kingdom in 1956. Military regimes often have been in power, and they, and other regimes, have tended to favor the north and the center of the country as hubs of power and of economic development. In addition, since 1984, those regimes have been Islamic oriented. This, together with the conflicts, resulted in the establishment of the Sudan People's Liberation Movement, whose goal was to fight Islamist imposition (Johnson 2003). In 2005, the Comprehensive Peace Agreement eventually led in 2011 to the creation of an independent state of South Sudan, thus ending a civil war in which, since 1989 alone, more than two million people had died. However, all conflict within the country did not end. Until 2006, Sudan had been fighting rebels in the East, as well as the Sudan People's Liberation Movement–North in South Kurdufan and Blue Nile. A separate conflict in the western region of Darfur began in 2003 and, according to the CIA's *World Factbook* (CIA 2012), has caused an estimated 200,000–400,000 deaths, displacing nearly two million people. In addition, as we have mentioned, substantial hostility exists between the different tribes. In attempting to deal with all these problems, the army occasionally has armed tribal militias, which has sometimes exacerbated intertribal conflict (Bassil 2014).

The role of tribal identity in the escalation of the violence has been emphasized by several researchers (see Assal 2009). De Waal (2005) also argues that the "polarization of 'Arab' and 'African' identities" has adversely influenced the level of conflict. According to Madibbo (2012), the northern ruling elites are seeking to impose an Arab identity as a basis on which to define Sudan's national identity. The use of the Arabic language as the medium of education and public communication and the adoption of Islam as a state religion reflect this development. The secession of South Sudan from the rest of the country may diffuse this problem, but there is still a Christian minority in Sudan, and Sudanese Arabs comprise no more than 70 percent of the population (CIA 2012). The promoting of an Arab identity also has been, at least partially, the cause of the other conflicts already mentioned. It also may have led to increased friction between some tribes and the central authorities. In turn, in some circumstances, this effort may have affected the individual relationship between tribe member and tribal leader. The conflicts are an important backdrop to our analysis, although they are not our major concern per se. Nonetheless, the considerable work on the relationship between ethnolinguistic fractionalization and conflict (Collier and Hoeffler 2004) helps us understand both the nature of these conflicts and the intertribal relationships.

Literature

The Tribe

The concept of a tribe itself is, in fact, not that clear. There is debate over even the definition of a tribe (Fried 1975) and whether it is a more relevant concept than alternative terms, such as community, speakers of the same language, or cultural unit. These considerations are likely to be as relevant within countries as between them, and certainly within Sudan, as we have already suggested, there are substantial differences between tribes. Thus, differences also exist in what tribes and tribal leaders mean to individual members of the tribe. One particularly important distinction is likely to be that between those who live in rural, rather than urban, areas. New sources of power and prestige exist within the cities that, for many people, offer more rewards than from the traditional tribal governance structure (Wallerstein 1960). The tribe's methods of government are different, and its role in the national social structure is different. However, urban tribes arguably bear sufficient resemblance to the rural, traditional tribe for which the same term frequently is used (Wallerstein 1960). Thus, Wallerstein (1960) argues that the tribe still may be important to people in urban areas,[4] but the exact meaning they attach to the term may be slightly different to that used in rural areas, and it may be linked more to ethnic groupings. Given this, the role of and respect for the authority of the chief also may be different in the two areas.

Tribal courts are the source of much of the tribal leader's power. They are part of a complex judicial system in Sudan that is both slightly vague and also in a state of some flux. There are the people's local courts, which consist of a president, vice president, and members selected by the chief justice. At higher levels, most of the judges, such as the president and vice president, are hereditary leaders. Their legitimacy stems from this hereditary position rather than from appointment by the government. In the North, appeals can be made to higher courts, and lower courts are supervised by the chief justice. The People's Court administers *the custom* within its jurisdiction, with the proviso that the custom is not contrary to justice, morals, or public order. It may also administer any other law over which it is given the authority by the chief justice. Thus, custom is an important basis for the law and its administration. But the proviso suggests that it may be secondary to statutory law or Islamic law. Given that the judges with the ultimate control over the people's courts reside in the North, there is potential for conflict. However, evidence exists that the authorities wish to avoid embarrassing or undermining the chiefs and thus usually will allow their judgments to stand (Deng 2009). But this is not the only factor affecting the people's courts. Muslim judges have tended to argue that custom law cannot be applied to Islamic law, because Islamic law is above this, and the attempts to extend Sharia law across the country have caused problems. Political instability, too, has had an effect, and one of the consequences of the Darfur crisis, for example, is that local-level settlement of disputes has substantially diminished (Deng 2009).

Fairness

In a general context, much of the research that has been done on this topic focuses on the fairness of outcomes. Thus, for example, Rawls (1971) argues that a perfectly equal distribution is not necessarily fair if it is not to the benefit of the least advantaged. However, such contributions do not specifically relate to the fairness of decisions made by leaders. In addition, they tend to veer to the philosophical side, focusing on what is, or should be, fairness rather than what people perceive as being fair. However, some empirical research has been done on fairness, including research that evaluates the perceived fairness of leaders. Much of that research has been done within a very different context to tribal leadership in Sudan, and indeed most of the research relates to leaders in developed countries. Leventhal, Karuza, and Fry (1980) suggest that the major determinant of how satisfied citizens are with the social system and its leaders is the outcome of the process; that is, it is results focused. Tyler and Caine (1981) find both outcomes and procedures to be important, although predominantly the latter. Their study focused on teachers as leaders, as well as citizens' evaluation of political leaders. The latter is closer to the issues we are analyzing, although it is still within the context of political leadership in a democratic, developed country where leaders are elected, which is far removed from the realities of tribal leadership in Sudan.

Perhaps surprisingly, there is little empirical work on the concept of fairness as applied to leadership decisions in developing countries. Much of the literature pertains to fairness in areas such as employment tribunals or working conditions and mostly in developed countries. Thus, Korsgaard, Schweiger, and Sapienza (1995) found in the context of management teams in a Fortune 500 company that a member's input into and influence on a decision affect perceptions of procedural fairness and, as a result, commitment to the decision, attachment to the group, and *trust in its leader*. In emphasizing individual involvement and process, work by Korsgaard, Schweiger, and Sapienza (1995) reflects much of the literature in this area, which focuses on the importance of individuals having a voice in the process (Lind, Kanfer, and Earley 1990) and being made to feel valuable members of the group (Lind and Tyler 1988). These insights also may have some relevance to our issue of perceived fairness of tribal leadership decisions in Sudan.

Research also has looked at the potential effect of perceived leadership fairness. Overall leadership evaluations, from a traditional psychological perspective, have been viewed as being based on a leader's performance, skill in providing group benefits, or ability to solve group problems (Hollander and Julian 1970); once again, this is results oriented. In passing, we note that in Sudan, leaders may be evaluated not only on what they control but also on what they cannot, such as the weather. However, process also may be important. In support of this, Tyler (1986) argues that concerns over fairness are also an important factor in leadership evaluation.[5]

Concepts of Trust

As with fairness, trust has been analyzed along several dimensions: theoretical, empirical, and pertaining to real-life situations. Hardin (1993) emphasizes that trust is fully explicable as a product of rational behavior. It has a game theoretical aspect, whereby Hardin (1993) argues that people may be trustworthy because being trustworthy is in their own self-interest. That aspect tends to focus, as much of the literature does, on interpersonal trust, whereas the focus of this research study is more related to institutional trust, where the institution is the tribe along with the tribal leader. Cultural theories argue that institutional trust is exogenous (Inglehart 1997) and as such can be viewed as being learned early in life. Institutional theories, in contrast, argue that it is endogenous (Hetherington 1998; North 1990) and influenced by institutional performance—in our case, the performance of the tribal chief. In the context of our study, both may have elements of truth, with the former being more relevant when people are young and the latter as they age; that is, trust begins as being mainly determined by an individual's background, but as individuals grow older, their views are determined more by their own experiences. An important part of the literature deals with experienced trust—that is, trust based on people's experiences (Glaeser et al. 2000; Hardin 2002). Uslaner (2002) adds to this thinking the concept of "moralistic trust," which is learned early in life. Moralistic trust arises when a community has a common set of moral values that lead to expectations of honest behavior.

Direct experience of the tribal leadership is likely to vary among people in a systematic manner because people of different backgrounds may have different experiences, and the leadership possibly may give more respect to rich, successful, and educated citizens. This has echoes of the observation by Putnam (2000) that in all societies the "have-nots" are less trusting than the "haves." Some people also possibly may come into contact with tribal leadership decisions more than others, in connection with property rights for example, which may be the case when people divorce or become widowed. This theory reflects the hypothesis that attitudes toward institutions depend on knowledge of that institution. More knowledgeable people are more likely both to have an opinion and to have an opinion that is closer to reality, or at least reality as they have experienced it. Hence, we would expect their perceptions of institutions to differ from those of others, but the exact nature of the effect may vary from society to society. Knowledge can, of course, be gained in ways other than from direct experience. The most obvious variable to reflect knowledge is education, but age also may be relevant if people learn from others as well as from direct experience. However, age may reflect other lifestyle differences. Brewer et al. (2004) argue that social trust affects political trust. If both of these arguments are true, then more educated, and indeed wealthier, people should exhibit greater degrees of institutional trust. People also can gain knowledge from those around them, people they mix with in both a social and a work context. Hence, the characteristics of others in the individual's locality also are likely to influence an individual's perceptions of, in the context of our analysis, the tribal leader.

We can draw on some empirical work, although again much relates to developed countries. Hudson (2006) has analyzed institutional trust in EU countries, finding it to be lower for the unemployed and to increase with income and education—thus reflecting Putnam's (2000) observation relating to the have-nots. Hudson's work found a nonlinear effect of age: in general, trust declined with age, but for several institutions, trust first declined with age and then increased, with the turning point being between 44 and 56 years. He also found trust to be lower for divorced women in institutions that affect the divorce process: the law and the national government. Schweer's (1997) research focused on the determinants of young adults' institutional trust and concluded that the perceived attributes of an institution are relevant for the degree of trust. Mishler and Rose (2001) analyze institutional trust in Central and Eastern Europe in several contexts, including parliament, trade unions, the police, the courts, and the media. Their results show only a weak significance for socioeconomic variables, with trust increasing with age and being greater for those in smaller towns and villages. In contrast, perceptions of factors such as corruption and economic performance were much more significant.

A specific part of the literature has looked at the effect of corruption on attitudes toward a country's institutions. This is of relevance to our study because a key variable is whether individuals have been asked to pay bribes. Using national sample survey data from four Latin American countries, Seligson (2002) finds that exposure to corruption erodes belief in the political system, quite independently of socioeconomic and demographic variables. This finding is supported by other research. For example, Sun and Wang (2012) found that negative actions by the government, including corruption and the abuse of privilege, significantly reduce trust in government. In later research, Seligson (2006) found that those who experience corruption—being asked for a bribe is a component—are less likely to believe in the legitimacy of their political system. Even in high-income democracies, bribery and corruption have been found to be associated with large and more complex public sectors that are less susceptible to political, and hence electoral, oversight (Hamilton 2013a), and this also may be linked to trust.

Theory: Perceived Fairness and Trust

Given those observations, we assume that perceived fairness is linked to the distance between the individual's perception of what is right and the decision laid down by the tribal leader. The latter will depend on tribal custom. However, individual perceptions about what is right also will be determined by tribal custom, which in turn may differ between tribes. Because both leadership decisions and individual perceptions of what is right are linked to tribal custom, an alignment between the two is likely, provided the tribal leader's decisions do not deviate too far from tribal custom. Nonetheless, as indicated in the literature, individual perceptions of what is right can move away from tribal customs for a number of reasons. First, education may expose an individual to new ideas to suggest a norm of behavior different from that of tribal custom (Deng 2009). Second, apart from their own education, individuals also may be influenced by the opinions of others in their locality. Thus the characteristics of those in the neighborhood, including their average level of education, may also affect individual perceptions of what is right. Third, people may respond more quickly to a changed socioeconomic environment than do the tribal norm or tribal customs,[6] with change thus driving a wedge between individual perceptions of what is right and the tribal leader's decisions.

However, individuals also are likely to be influenced on perceptions of fairness by what is in their own self-interest and by the extent to which they are rewarded by the tribal leader. For many, the dependence on the tribe stems from limited opportunities to gain access to other types of institutions. Once an individual's opportunities expand, we would expect dependence on the tribal leadership to diminish and people to become more capable of taking a critical stance. Hence, being in paid employment, particularly in the private sector, may well result in a growing gap between the individual's perceptions of what is right and both tribal customs and the leader's decisions. This is consistent with Deng's (2009) observation that opportunities for employment pave the way for new sources of income, which inevitably affect traditional obligations and dependencies. Finally, the greater the gap between the leader's decisions and tribal custom, the more an individual will tend to question leadership decisions. We will include two variables to provide a proxy for this. The first is the extent to which people have access to the courts because delivering justice through the courts is, as we have seen, a key function of the tribal leaders at the local level.[7] The second variable is the extent to which bribery is in evidence in the individual's location. In many places, bribery is an implicit part of the social norms (World Bank 2015, 60–61). But in Sudan, it is less likely to be part of the tribal, as opposed to the social, norms that dictate how decisions should be made. Indeed, bribery may be an attempt to circumvent those tribal norms. In many locations, given the powers of the tribal leadership, the ability to ask for bribes will ultimately stem from the tribal leader. Hence, we include a variable reflecting the average level of bribes requested from people in the individual's location, with the expectation that higher levels of requested bribes will signal reduced support for the tribal leaders and their decisions. This is consistent with much of the literature we have already reviewed.

The literature also suggests that overall evaluations of leaders will in part depend on the perceived fairness of their decisions (Tyler 1986). If we equate such overall evaluations with trust, as in Korsgaard, Schweiger, and Sapienza (1995), then perceptions of fairness will also influence trust. But trust may differ from perceived fairness, as the literature also suggests (Tyler 1986). For example, if the tribal leadership is perceived to be unfair, but in a way that benefits the individual, trust may not be eroded and may even be enhanced. Moreover, the literature suggests that leaders are evaluated on outcomes as well as on procedures (Tyler and Caine 1981). Hence, we would expect those who prosper under the tribal leadership to be more trusting. If the tribal leadership, despite being unfair, protects the tribe from outside influences and delivers other benefits, it still may be trusted. This is a hypothesis we will be testing. The hypothesis will be supported if, in a regression of leadership trust on perceived fairness, other socioeconomic variables linked to individual success are significant.

On the basis of both this analysis and the literature review, we formulate the following hypotheses. First, perceptions of fairness reflect the individual's position. Those who are doing well will tend to perceive the tribal leaders' decisions more favorably than those who are not. Second, increased education, both the individual's own and that of other inhabitants where they live, will tend to open individuals to nontribal norms and customs and potentially lead them to be more critical of the tribal leader's decisions. Third, a changing environment is likely to reduce the perceived fairness of decisions, if tribal norms tend to be slow to respond to changing circumstances. Finally, we anticipate that the larger the family unit, the more perceptions of fairness will decline, because the family unit presents an alternative to the tribe. We discussed this distinction at the beginning of the chapter, where we suggested that the two harmoniously coexist. Nonetheless, the family provides an alternative framework of support for the individual, and the larger the family, the greater potential importance of the alternative framework. Thus, in terms of the effect of perceived fairness on trust for the tribal leader, we anticipate, in line with the literature, that this will be a substantial factor but not the only one. The benefits—individual and collective—that the leadership brings to the individual will be relevant also.

The Data and Methodology

The dependent variables relate to the links with the tribal leader.[8] The first variable focuses on the extent to which the tribal leader's decisions are fair. If people perceive such decisions to be unfair, the response is coded 1; otherwise 0. We chose this specification because it then links in with the other variables in which an increase defines less fairness or trust. The second variable relates to whether respondents perceive men to be treated more fairly than women in decisions by the tribal leader. This is coded 1 if the respondent feels men are treated better and 0 otherwise. The alternative includes both those who thought everyone was treated fairly and those who thought tribal decisions were not fair but did not discriminate positively in favor of men. Both these variables are binomial, and we shall estimate the equations using binomial probit. The third dependent variable is not binomial. It relates to trust, or rather mistrust, in the tribal leader and is coded 1 for "trust a lot" up to 4 for "not at all." We shall therefore estimate the equations using ordered probit. Those who did not answer or who answered "did not know" were excluded from the analysis. The independent variables include marital status, age, gender, family size, and information on socioeconomic position, including employment status and education. In addition to variables that are individual specific, we also include the average values of individuals surveyed in the respondent's location with respect to certain variables. Those include education, income, and bribery and also perceptions on the overall level of the services they received.[9] For perceived service quality, the individual responses ranged from "at a very low level" (coded 1) to "excellent" (coded 5). The services we examined included electricity, hospitals, schools, water, sanitation, the police, and the courts. They represent a range of services that affect the individual, with some such as electricity directly facilitating economic, as well as social, development. All variables are defined in table 5.1. The expected effect of most of these variables has been made clear in the discussion, but will be further discussed in the results that follow.

Table 5.1 Data Definitions

Variable	Definition
Tribal trust	Trust local tribal leader coded 1 (a lot) to 4 (not at all)
Fair	Binary variable, coded 1 if decisions handed down by local tribal leader are perceived as not fair to everyone
Fairer to men	Binary variable, coded 1 if decisions handed down by local tribal leader are perceived as fairer to men than women
Bribe	Whether respondent has been asked for a bribe; responses coded 1–4 if asked in the past month, past six months, past year, and never
Age	Age in years
Education	Coded from 1 (illiterate) to 9 (PhD) as an increasing measure of education
Income	Household income, coded 1 (SDG 100–SDG 500), 2 (SDG 500–SDG 1,000), 3 (more than SDG 1,000), monthly income
Relative (to needs) income	Coded 1 if the household income is not enough to cover the household bills, 2 if it is enough to cover the household bills, 3 if it is enough to cover necessary expenses with nothing left over, and 4 if it is sufficient to allow saving
Marital variables	Binary variables taking a value of 1 if the person is single, married, divorced, or widowed
Male	Coded 1 if the individual is a male
Urban	Coded 1 if the individual lives in an urban area
Works	Coded 1 if the individual is in employment
Works for government/private firm	Coded 1 if the individual works for the government/private company
Locality variables (average of responses in individual's locality)	
Service	Individual response coded 1 if the services the individual received were at a very low level to 5 if they were excellent; services include electricity, water, sanitation, school, hospital, the police, the courts, and water

Figure 5.1 shows the histogram of trust in the tribal leader across the different states. It seems to be lowest—that is, the highest bars are on the left of the distribution—for South Kurdufan, North Kurdufan, and Northern. A number of states have a large number of "don't know" and "no response" answers. We have tended simply to exclude those responses from the analysis, as is common practice, but relatively high levels of abstentions might indicate a fear factor as mentioned by Crowther et al. (2014). For that reason, such nonresponses may well be worth analyzing in their own right, in a future analysis. (See also chapter 1 of this volume for a discussion on missing responses.)

Table 5.2 presents summary data relating to the three tribal leader variables and the way these vary across characteristics and between states. Column (2.1) shows summary figures for those who believed the tribal leader's decisions to be fair. Of those who responded, less than half thought they were fair in 2013 and slightly more than half in the 2014 data, thus reflecting only a limited amount of faith in the tribal leadership to deliver fair decisions.[10] Differences based on age, income, gender, urban or rural location, and whether the individual worked for the government are relatively small. But there were more substantial differences for other variables, such as perceptions of fairness were greater for less educated

Figure 5.1 Trust in Tribal Leader

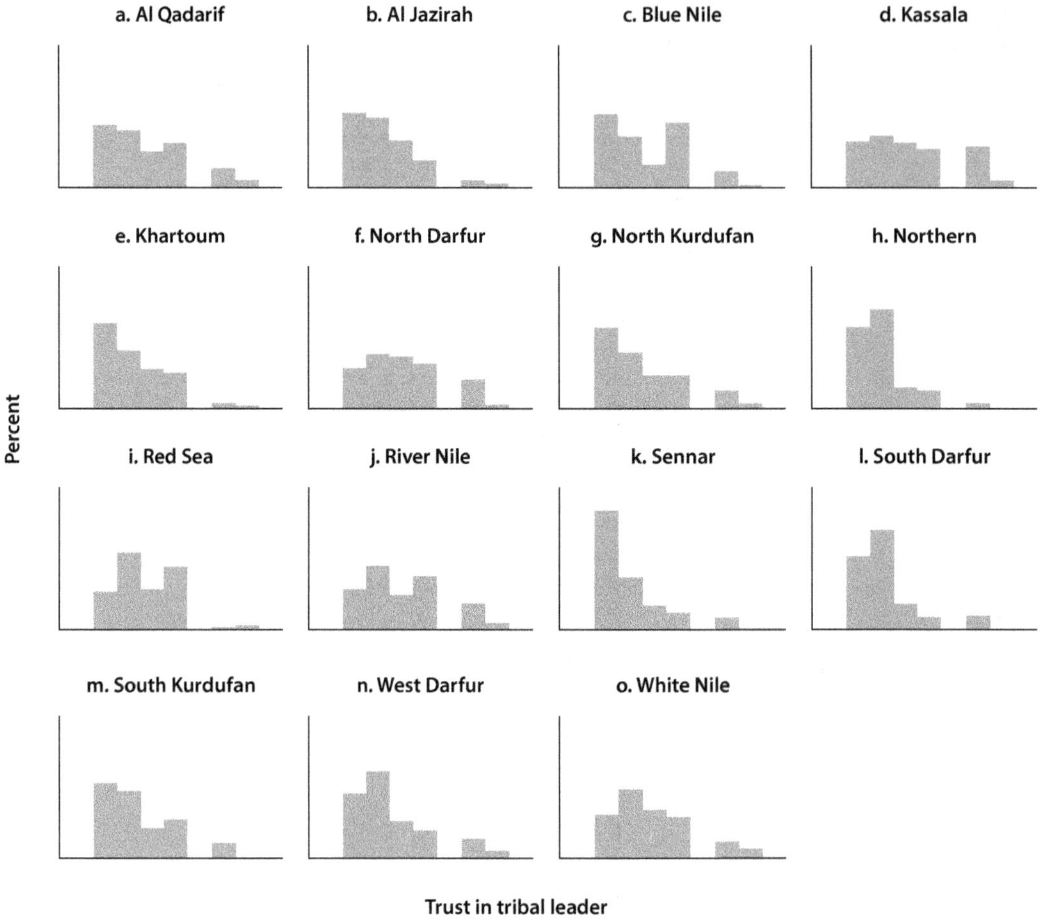

Source: World Bank staff.
Note: Each histogram shows the proportion of trust for the tribal leader by state. Levels of trust increase from left to right with bars indicating the lowest trust on the left. The last two bars on the right of each histogram indicate "don't know" and "no response."

people and for those who worked for the government. Perceptions of fairness were lower for widowed or divorced women, those who had been asked for a bribe, those who worked for a private company, and those whose income was supplemented from abroad.[11] Many of the differences are in line with a priori expectations. For example, working for a private company gives the individual a degree of independence from the tribe.

Column (2.2) relates to the proportion of respondents who think tribal decisions tend to favor women less than men; a bias seems to exist in favor of the latter. Slightly more than 20 percent of those who responded thought this to be the case in 2013. Again, there are some differences across different socioeconomic characteristics that may help explain the identity of those who think this way. The proportion who thought decisions favored men over women was

Table 5.2 Summary Data on Identification in 2013 and 2014 DFID Sudan Household Surveys

	2013			2014		
	Decisions	Fairer to trust		Decisions	Fairer to trust	
	Fair	Men		Fair	Men	
Variable	(2.1)	(2.2)	(2.3)	(2.4)	(2.5)	(2.6)
All	0.430	0.208	2.181	0.545[a]	0.159[a]	2.24
Individual characteristics						
Age < 34 years	0.428	0.215	2.193	0.526[a]	0.163[a]	2.265
Low education (< 5th grade)	0.498	0.191	2.034	0.623[a]	0.144	1.980
Low income (=1)	0.432	0.194	2.162	0.542[a]	0.165	2.180
Insufficient relative income (=1)	0.360	0.230	2.204	0.538[a]	0.149[a]	2.248
Bribe<4	0.274	0.277	2.387	0.450[a]	0.117[a]	2.382
Married	0.443	0.210	2.124	0.570[a]	0.152[a]	2.215
Single	0.405	0.210	2.283	0.506[a]	0.154[a]	2.294[a]
Male	0.435	0.186	2.195	0.539[a]	0.134[a]	2.238
Urban	0.426	0.209	2.141	0.564[a]	0.153[a]	2.187
Work	0.427	0.203	2.154	0.515[a]	0.166	2.264
Works for government	0.460	0.211	2.157	0.514	0.156	2.381[a]
Works for private company	0.344	0.243	2.337	0.508[a]	0.153	2.458
Divorced or widowed women	0.398	0.221	2.111	0.505	0.275	2.038
Divorced or widowed men	0.634	0.098	2.000	0.531	0.219	2.103
States						
Al Jazirah	0.356	0.227	2.431	0.552[a]	0.160	2.407[a]
Khartoum	0.300	0.354	2.244	0.333	0.217[a]	2.699[a]
Al Qadarif	0.203	0.220	1.938	0.446[a]	0.240	2.338
Northern	0.689	0.109	1.993	0.902[a]	0.000[a]	1.780
Red Sea	0.481	0.083	2.078	0.538	0.197	2.169
Blue Nile	0.554	0.231	1.993	0.731[a]	0.067[a]	2.258
Kassala	0.500	0.146	2.336	0.412	0.137	2.752[a]
River Nile	0.385	0.248	2.327	0.418	0.114	2.405
North Darfur	0.337	0.304	2.587	0.458	0.217	2.581
North Kurdufan	0.496	0.298	1.643	0.601	0.291	1.778
Sennar	0.388	0.216	2.392	0.839[a]	0.021	1.885[a]
South Darfur	0.550	0.159	2.264	0.417	0.161	2.367
South Kurdufan	0.341	0.159	1.902	0.483	0.217	1.875
West Darfur	0.392	0.192	2.436	0.442	0.225	2.437
White Nile	0.424	0.187	2.333	0.602[a]	0.080	1.846[a]

Source: Based on data from the 2013 and 2014 U.K. Department for International Development Sudan household surveys.
Note: The data represent the average percentage of respondents who perceived that decisions were fair (in contrast to the regressions where the variable is coded 1 if they are unfair) and that there was a bias from men toward women. The trust variable is the average response from the range of values indicated in table 5.1. A value of 2.24 lies between some trust (coded 2) and little trust (coded 3). DFID = U.K. Department for International Development.
a. Denotes that the 2014 estimate is significantly different from the 2013 estimate at the 1 percent significance level.

greater among those who had been asked for a bribe, who worked for a private company, and who were divorced or widowed women and less for relatively less educated people and men.

Column (2.3) relates to trust in the tribal leader. *This variable is defined to increase with levels of mistrust.* Hence, a higher value signals less trust and more mistrust. The average response for the full 2013 sample was 2.181. This lies between "some trust" (coded 2) and "little trust" (coded 3), being closer to the first. Trust is less—that is, the average for the variable is higher—for those who had been asked for a bribe and also those who worked for a private company. It is greater for those with relatively low levels of education. Different states also showed substantial differences. For example, those in Northern tended to have a favorable view of the tribal leader and particularly high levels of perceived fairness of the tribal leader's decisions. They also did not tend to think men were treated more favorably than women and had a particularly high level of trust in the tribal leader. Those in North Darfur, in contrast, tended to be more critical and have lower levels of perceived trust, higher perceived favoritism of men in tribal decisions, and lower levels of tribal trust. Such differences may well reflect local conditions and the behavior of local tribal leaders.

Columns (2.4), (2.5), and (2.6) relate to 2014. A shift appears to have occurred toward a more favorable view of the tribal leader. Thus, there seem to be higher levels of perceived fairness, lower levels of discrimination in favor of men, and slightly higher trust. Some of these figures are significantly different from the 2013 measures at the 1 percent level of significance, as table 5.2 shows. These changes since 2013 could reflect (a) genuine shifts in perceptions that are not linked to changing socioeconomic conditions, which may not be impossible given the large changes that continue to occur in the country; (b) a change in the characteristics of the people being interviewed, possibly linked to political changes in the country;[12] or (c) normal sampling variations. We return to this later once we have presented the results of the regression analysis. For now, we note that the relative ordering among different groups of people is relatively stable. Thus, in both years, the better educated, those who had been asked for a bribe, and those who worked for a private company tended to perceive tribal decisions as being more unfair than others perceived them to be. But, in addition, in 2014, so did young people and anybody who worked.

Figure 5.2 plots location-based tribal trust against location-based education. There is a clear upward slope. Given the many factors that can affect tribal trust, this is a very clear illustration that increasing levels of education in a given location will tend to undermine tribal trust there. We emphasize that there is no such clear relationship when we look at the effect of location-based income, both income relative to needs and absolute income, and, for example, location-based police services. This is, of course, not to say that in a multiple regression analysis these variables would not be significant—and indeed some do turn out to be significant—but it does make the clear link with education all the more remarkable (see figure 5.2). Figure 5.3 shows the relationship between location-based tribal trust and location-based perceived fairness. Both are defined so that higher

Using Survey Data from Sudan for Policy Making 93

Figure 5.2 Location-Based Tribal Trust and Location-Based Education

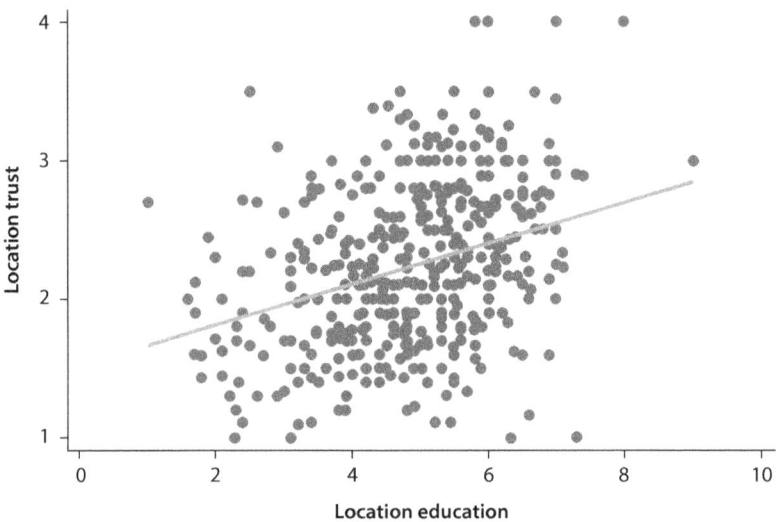

Source: World Bank staff.

Figure 5.3 Location-Based Tribal Trust and Location-Based Fairness

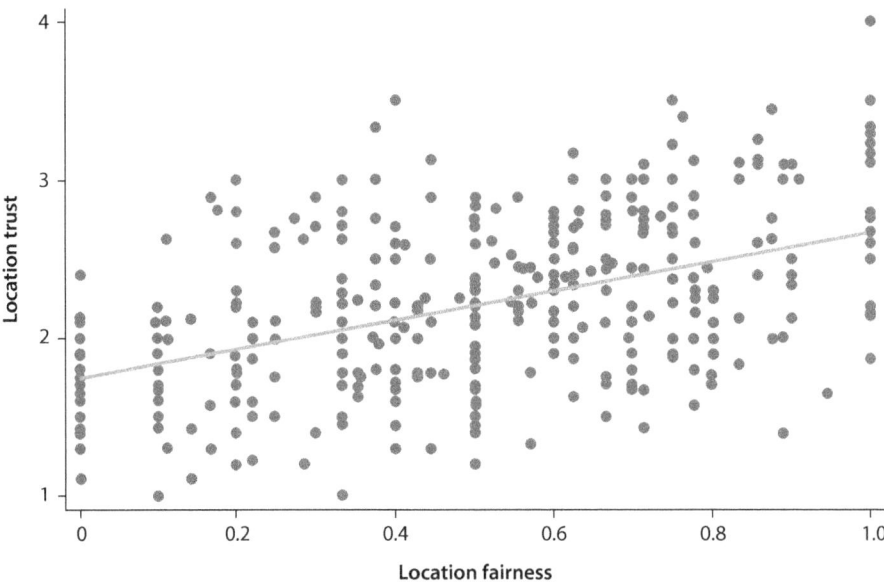

Source: World Bank staff.

values indicate less trust and fairness. As the latter increases, there is an increase in mistrust. But we can also see that the correlation is far from perfect, indicating a potential role for other variables in affecting trust.

Regression Results

The regression results presented in table 5.3 are pooled results obtained by combining the 2013 and 2014 survey data. Column (3.1) includes only the individual-based variables and relates to the perceived fairness of tribal decisions. *The dependent variable is coded 1 if perceived as unfair and 0 if fair; hence, a significantly positive coefficient indicates that as that variable increases, perceived fairness declines.* The results show that perceived fairness is higher for married people and divorced

Table 5.3 Regression Results

Variable	Fair (3.1)	Fair (3.2)	Fairer to men (3.3)	Fairer to men (3.4)	Trust (3.5)	Trust (3.6)	Trust (3.7)	Trust (3.8)
Married	−0.1113* (1.91)		−0.0262 (0.39)		−0.064 (1.33)			
Age	0.0205* (1.92)	0.0141 (1.42)	0.003 (0.25)		0.0191** (1.98)	0.01 (1.25)	0.0173* (1.88)	
Age² (× 100)	−0.024* (1.93)	−0.0210* (1.78)	−0.00045 (0.33)		−0.0023** (2.02)	−0.0016 (1.58)	−0.0023** (2.09)	
Gender	−0.0121 (0.10)		−0.2367* (1.65)	−0.1549*** (3.07)	−0.1028 (0.97)			
Education	0.0575*** (3.32)	0.0255* (1.74)	0.0247 (1.24)		0.0665*** (4.59)	0.035*** (3.16)	0.0491*** (4.02)	0.0293*** (2.71)
Absolute income	−0.0041 (0.16)	−0.0586* (1.93)	0.0392 (1.30)		−0.0085 (0.40)			
Urban location	−0.0217 (0.46)		0.0032 (0.06)		−0.048 (1.27)			
Relative (to needs) income	−0.0573*** (3.45)	−0.0456*** (2.69)	−0.0285 (1.49)		−0.0268* (1.94)	−0.0402*** (2.77)	−0.033** (2.05)	
Divorced or widowed and a woman	0.0572 (0.49)	0.1725* (1.69)	0.122 (0.96)	0.1827* (1.73)	−0.1649* (1.73)			
Divorced or widowed and a man	−0.4933*** (2.89)		−0.1002 (0.48)		−0.2938* (1.95)			
Divorced or widowed								−0.200*** (2.69)
Log of family size	0.0947** (2.38)	0.1446*** (3.56)	0.0826* (1.78)	0.1032** (2.24)	−0.0202 (0.60)			−0.0672* (1.93)
Works	0.0901 (1.39)	0.0928* (1.74)	0.0713 (0.97)		−0.0511 (0.93)		−0.0938** (2.17)	−0.0685* (1.77)
Works for government	−0.1056 (1.51)	−0.1237* (1.92)	−0.0223 (0.28)		0.0059 (0.10)			

table continues next page

Table 5.3 Regression Results *(continued)*

Variable	Fair (3.1)	Fair (3.2)	Fairer to men (3.3)	Fairer to men (3.4)	Trust (3.5)	Trust (3.6)	Trust (3.7)	Trust (3.8)
Works for private company	0.0184 (0.20)		−0.0089 (0.09)		0.1214 (1.64)	0.1091* (1.72)	0.1695** (2.31)	0.112* (1.67)
Women's education	0.002 (0.09)		−0.0055 (0.22)		−0.0224 (1.21)			
2013 Dummy variable	0.2913*** (6.02)	0.2316*** (4.70)	0.2242*** (4.16)	0.2018*** (3.76)	−0.0797** (2.03)	−0.0512 (1.31)	−0.0716* (1.71)	−0.2226*** (5.04)
Village-based variables								
Bribe		−0.3823*** (5.18)		−0.3445*** (4.72)		−0.0966* (1.72)		
Education		0.1182*** (4.12)		0.090*** (3.47)		0.0877*** (3.90)	0.0462** (1.99)	
Absolute income		0.1076* (1.69)		0.152** (2.39)		−0.0991** (2.19)	−0.113** (2.22)	
Relative (to needs) income						0.0876** (2.39)	0.1251*** (3.12)	0.1196*** (3.32)
Electricity		0.1679*** (3.38)				0.1002** (2.26)		
Sanitation		−0.1173** (2.36)		−0.1046** (2.19)		−0.1498*** (3.35)		−0.1214*** (2.74)
Courts		−0.338*** (5.87)				−0.2225*** (4.92)		
Hospital		0.0013 (0.03)		−0.1619** (2.04)		0.1026** (2.44)	0.1412*** (3.59)	
School				0.2344*** (3.23)				
Water						0.1204** (2.29)		0.1584*** (3.38)
Police							−0.100*** (2.61)	
Decisions—fair							0.5187*** (12.83)	
Predicted decision—fair							2.823***	(4.26)
Predicted decision Fair²							−1.397**	(2.34)
Constant	−0.8411*** (3.46)	0.7677* (1.75)	−1.446*** (5.30)	−0.7898* (1.86)				
Observations	3,594	3,529	3,594	3,742	3,742	3,932	3,344	3,677
Log likelihood	−2,315	−2,216	−1,648	−1,689	−4,888	−5,107	−4,238	−4,772
χ^2	324.5	392.3	158.3	220.6	274.2	348	456.9	321.4

Source: Based on data from the 2013 and 2014 U.K. Department for International Development Sudan household surveys.
Note: Columns (3.1)–(3.4) are estimated by binomial probit and columns (3.5)–(3.8) by ordered probit; *t* statistics are in parentheses. Significance level: * = 10 percent, ** = 5 percent, *** = 1 percent. Standard errors have been corrected for heteroskedasticity. Variables are defined in table 5.1, χ^2 represents the likelihood ratio test statistic. Regional variables are included in all regressions, for regions shown in figure 5.1.

or widowed men and increases with the extent to which income satisfies the individual's needs.[13] However, such trust tends to decline as the level of education and family size increase. Age also can be seen to have a significant U-shaped effect on perceived unfairness. That is, as people age, perceived unfairness at first increases but then apparently starts to decline. The turning point, however, is 86 years, which is longer than most people live. Thus, in effect, trust declines with age, flattening out for very old people, with no effective turning point.

In column (3.2), which includes mainly significant variables, we add further variables defined at the level of the respondent's location to the individual-based variables. These emerge as very significant. In particular, the tribal leader's decisions are more likely to be perceived as being unfair the higher the average level of education in the location. Perceived fairness declines as requests for a bribe in the location increase and as people's access to the courts declines. Poor access to sanitation also decreases perceived fairness, whereas better electricity services have the opposite effect. Once more, we will delay further discussion on these effects until we have done further regressions. The inclusion of these additional locational variables has changed the significance of some of the individual-based variables, increasing it for some, decreasing it for others. Furthermore, the two age variables, which are less significant, now indicate a turning point at 37 years for decreasing trust. This method therefore indicates a genuine turning point with age, with perceived fairness at first decreasing and then increasing.

Columns (3.3) and (3.4) relate to perceptions of whether men are treated more fairly than women. The first of these two regressions is again limited to individual-based variables, with very few being significant. Such perceptions increase with family size and are significantly less for men than for women, although neither is significant at the 10 percent level. However, both increase substantially in significance when we add the location-based variables in column (3.4). In addition in this regression, divorced or widowed women are now more likely to perceive the decisions as being biased toward men. With respect to the location-based variables, perceptions that men are treated more fairly than women increase with the average level of village income, education, and requests for a bribe. They decline with better access to sanitation and hospitals but increase with better access to schools. We will discuss these effects further in the concluding section.

The final set of regressions relates to tribal trust, with the regression in column (3.5) once more excluding location-centered variables, being based only on the full set of individual-based variables. *We again emphasize that higher values of the dependent variable reflect less trust—that is, greater mistrust.* The two age variables are again significant and suggest that trust first decreases with age and then starts to increase with age at 40.7 years. Trust also declines with the individual's education and is lower for those who worked for a private company. The latter is insignificant here, but it becomes significant in subsequent regressions. Trust is higher for divorced or widowed people, both men and women. In column (3.6), we again add the location-centered variables. Trust declines with increases in the average level of education and relative income in the individual's location.

Trust is, however, greater the higher the local absolute income, access to the courts, and sanitation. But it declines with better access to water, electricity, hospitals, and requests for bribes. This differential effect of better services, sometimes increasing trust and sometimes decreasing it, is something we discuss further in the conclusion.

In the next regression, column (3.7), we add perceptions of the tribal leader's fairness as an explanatory variable. This is very significant. The individual-based variables remain significant along with location-based ones. The results suggest that perceived fairness is an important factor in determining overall trust for the tribal leader, but it is far from being the only factor that influences this trust. One possible problem here is endogeneity, that individuals who do not trust the leader find reasons to perceive a lack of fairness, as well as the reverse relationship. That is, the causality may go from trust to perceived fairness, as well as in the reverse direction. Thus, in the final regression, we replace individual perceptions of fairness with average perceived fairness in the locality. This is again very significant. The other variables remain largely significant, once more indicating that perceived fairness is an important determinant of overall trust but not the only such factor.

In all of these regressions, dummy variables relating to the different states were included, and it is to these that we now turn. In general, the dummy variables were very significant and signify substantial differences in attitudes among states that do not disappear, or even decline substantially, when we include the location-based variables. This finding therefore indicates that the differences do not simply relate to different stages of development but also reflect something more fundamental, such as relating to the institution of the tribal leader. Given the substantial differences in tribes, tribal structures, and governance noted earlier, this is not surprising. The coefficients on these state dummy variables are shown in figure 5.4. They are based on the regressions in columns (3.2), (3.4), and (3.6) in table 5.3. They tend to move together, so that people in South Darfur, for example, perceive most fairness both overall and with respect to women, and they also have relatively low levels of mistrust. People from Red Sea State, in contrast, tend to be the opposite on all three dimensions. However, Al Qadarif State is more heterogeneous with very low levels of mistrust, slightly higher perceptions of unfairness to women relative to other states, and substantially higher perceptions of unfairness per se.

Finally, in most cases, the dummy variable that distinguishes between the two samples is significant, although less so in most of the trust equations. We cannot say whether this reflects genuine changes caused by an overall change in culture or whether it reflects sampling variations. However, because the socioeconomic variables were included in this regression, it cannot be due to differences in the socioeconomic characteristics of the two samples. Further insights into this will need to wait until more surveys are available.

We have one more set of regressions to discuss. These relate to locational variables alone, with no individual or state variables. They were estimated using the Tobit methodology. The Tobit model was proposed by James Tobin and is a limited dependent variable technique. The term *Tobit* was derived by combining

Figure 5.4 Regression Coefficients on State Variables

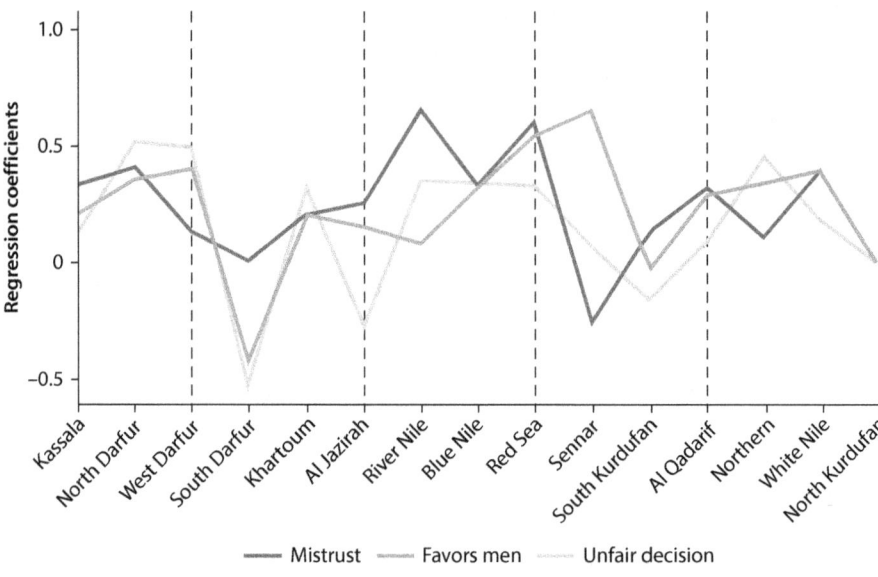

Source: Based on regressions from columns (3.2), (3.4), and (3.6) in table 5.3.

Table 5.4 Regressions Based on Location Variables Only

Variable	Fairness (4.1)	Fairness to women (4.2)	Trust (4.3)	Fairness (4.4)	Fairness to women (4.5)	Trust (4.6)
Bribes	−0.1825***	−0.1797***	−0.0851	−0.1727***	−0.1787***	−0.0746
	(4.06)	(4.87)	(1.08)	(4.95)	(4.23)	(1.02)
Education	0.0701***	0.0281**	0.1491***	0.0388***	0.0698***	0.1394***
	(5.13)	(2.45)	(6.32)	(3.52)	(5.64)	(6.58)
Relative (to needs) income	−0.007	0.0164	0.0686*			
	(0.30)	(0.85)	(1.69)			
Absolute income	−0.0363	0.009	−0.0543			
	(1.41)	(0.43)	(1.22)			
Services						
Electricity	0.086***	0.0184	0.1879***	0.0116	0.0513	0.1926***
	(2.88)	(0.74)	(3.59)	(0.46)	(1.80)	(3.96)
Schools	−0.042	0.0742**	−0.1777**	0.0673	−0.0381	−0.1823**
	(1.01)	(2.16)	(2.46)	(1.89)	(0.97)	(2.45)
Police	−0.0062	−0.0116	−0.1633*			
	(0.13)	(0.29)	(1.95)			
Sanitation	−0.0811**	−0.0647**	−0.044	−0.0887***	−0.0707**	−0.0454
	(2.36)	(2.28)	(0.73)	(3.64)	(2.45)	(0.87)
Courts	−0.0839	0.0044	−0.1255	0.0026	−0.0949**	−0.2437***
	(1.62)	(0.10)	(1.39)	(0.08)	(2.51)	(3.86)
Hospitals	0.0126	−0.0468	0.208***	−0.0608	−0.0133	0.1695**
	(0.28)	(1.24)	(2.61)	(1.60)	(0.30)	(2.10)

table continues next page

Table 5.4 Regressions Based on Location Variables Only (continued)

Variable	Fairness (4.1)	Fairness to women (4.2)	Trust (4.3)	Fairness (4.4)	Fairness to women (4.5)	Trust (4.6)
Water	(0.0319) (0.96)	−0.0192 (0.71)	0.012 (0.21)			
Constant	1.268*** (6.64)	0.6907*** (4.45)	2.065*** (6.18)	0.727*** (5.12)	1.238*** (7.54)	2.123*** (7.75)
Observations	379	379	381	368	368	382
Log likelihood	−105.1	−76.67	−268.3	−67.43	−77.35	−272.9

Source: Based on data from the 2013 and 2014 U.K. Department for International Development Sudan household surveys.
Note: Regressions are estimated by Tobit with both upper and lower limits imposed. Regional variables are not included. For further notes, see table 5.3.

Tobin with probit. The model can be used when the variable is bounded from above, from below, or both. The results are shown in table 5.4, and there are, of course, substantially fewer observations than before. The first three regressions, in columns (4.1), (4.2), and (4.3), include the majority of possible locational variables, and the final three, in columns (4.4), (4.5), and (4.6), focus on the significant variables. We note the significance of education across the board, bribery for the two fairness regressions, and the differential impact of services. For example, better sanitation increases both dimensions of perceived fairness. Better access to the courts increases both perceived overall fairness and trust and better access to electricity reduces trust. Thus these results largely confirm the individual-based regressions.

Conclusions and Implications

The survey data collected in Sudan over recent years present a valuable resource that helps monitor the effect of current conflict and in the future will enable us to monitor Sudan as the situation evolves. Moreover, it helps illuminate everyday life in Sudan. In this chapter, we show how these data can be used to present a snapshot of circumstances on the ground as they relate to objective variables; subjective attitudinal variables, such as trust; and other variables, such as perceptions of services. Our analysis also shows how these data can then be used to understand the determinants of a specific set of attitudes, in this case, those related to tribal leadership. In this analysis, we use both individual responses and locational variables that have been derived from those individual responses. The results show that, although attitudes to leadership are determined in part by factors unique to Sudan, they are also determined by factors similar to those in other countries around the world, even much more developed ones. In particular, our results support the view that leadership trust is based on both procedures and outcomes, as Tyler and Caine (1981) suggested would be the case when they evaluated political and other leadership in the United States.

In illustrating how the data set can be used, we focus on attitudes toward tribal leaders. People's attitudes toward tribal leaders and leadership in Sudan are linked to individual characteristics, the characteristics of others in the same locality, and the characteristics of that locality itself. The locality variables in particular may reflect the behavior of tribal leaders themselves. Education is a critical individual characteristic. The more educated the people surveyed, the less likely they were to view decisions as being fair and tribal leaders as being trustworthy, and, to an extent, the more likely they were to perceive leadership decisions as being biased toward men. These findings were tempered by the finding that those who worked tended to have a more favorable view of tribal leaders and their decisions, although that case was less common for those who worked for a private company. The effect of individual education was reinforced by the level of education of those who lived in the same location. Thus, a multiplier effect occurs with a person's education affecting the views of other individuals. The coefficients on age suggest that as people get older, they first become less and then become more favorable toward the leadership. This finding may reflect genuine life-cycle effects because as people age, they may come to depend more on the tribe and become perhaps less rebellious. Another possibility is that increasing age combines life-cycle and generational effects. With respect to the former, people gain more knowledge and experience about the leadership as they age, along with more information on alternatives to the tribal norms. Because of this, older people should be more skeptical than younger ones. But that view might be countered if there is a generational gap and, for whatever reason, older generations are more respectful than younger ones.

We notice how similar these results are to Hudson's (2006) when he analyzed trust in the EU, particularly with respect to income, divorce, work status, and age. This similarity is remarkable, given the substantial differences between the societies, and it suggests that similar dynamics are driving perceptions of fairness and leadership trust in vastly different circumstances. But, of course, there are also differences. One substantial difference relates to the differential effect of education. Given the different backgrounds of people in the EU and Sudan, that is not surprising. People in the EU often have little direct knowledge about institutions of governance, with ignorance breeding skepticism, a skepticism reduced by education. Many people in Sudan, however, understand the tribal norms very well but do not know other viewpoints, and education may then drive a wedge between the individual and the tribal norms and hence the tribal leadership.

The results with respect to whether decisions favor men are of particular interest. First, we note that the effect of individual characteristics was relatively weak, although there was evidence that men perceived this bias less than women did and that divorced or widowed women tended to perceive this bias even more than other women did. Divorce and widowhood are often linked to the transfer of property, and in Sudan, that process often brings an individual into direct contact with the tribal leadership. Women often experienced particular problems in this respect. The results in relation to the incidence of requests for bribery in the individual's location were particularly important, and its significance in this equation suggests that attempts to extract bribes often targeted women. But it was the effect of the service variables that was perhaps most interesting. Good local access to sanitation and hospitals increased perceptions of equal treatment for men and women. Women have specific sanitation needs, yet many areas lack adequate toilet facilities. Meeting these needs in public can be humiliating and also dangerous, especially at night when assault is a genuine risk (Fisher 2008). Hence, the provision of sanitation facilities particularly benefits women, without being a catalyst for further societal change. Access to modern health care is particularly important in pregnancy, childbirth, and family planning (Puentes-Markides 1992). Without access to hospitals, people resort to traditional medicine. However, in many societies, traditional medical practices see illness in women as somehow attributable to a woman's inappropriate behavior (Okojie 1994). More surprising perhaps is that better provision of schools increases perceptions of unequal treatment between men and women. However, because the raising of children is the traditional and most important role of women in many societies, their importance within society may be reduced when schools take away some of the responsibility for this role from mothers. If that is the case, it can be an example of how policy can have unintended consequences.[14]

More generally, better access to sanitation tends to lead to an individual having a more favorable view of the tribal leader and the tribe on all dimensions. The same is also largely true for access to the courts. However, better access to other services tends to worsen people's perceptions of fairness and trust in the tribe. Better access to water and electricity can be catalysts for indirect effects such as opening up new opportunities to individuals in agriculture,[15] over and above the direct effects of better access to the service itself for an individual's personal benefit. In addition, in opening the way for societal change, better access to water and electricity also may lead indirectly to a reduction in support for traditional behavior, including respect for tribal institutions.

At best, we can say that support for the tribal leaders, in terms of trust in them and perceptions of their fairness, is lukewarm, and in some states and among some villages and people of certain characteristics, it is positively hostile. Given the volatile nature of Sudan, and the way the tribal system has been used and misused over the decades by central governments, this finding may not be too surprising. But the attitude matters in the sense that tribal leaders exercise authority, authority that is linked to that of the state itself. If support for tribal leaders were to decline still further, the leaders' ability to exercise this authority might be compromised. In addition, if individuals themselves are moving further from the group norm and becoming more heterogeneous in their attitudes, Sudanese society overall might become more difficult to govern and the state might need to respond by becoming more flexible and less dogmatic. In contrast, the change could all be part of the normal evolution from a tribal society to a more modern one, potentially at least, based more on democratic government.

Annex 5A: Generating Locational Variables in Stata

Generating Locational Variables

The objective is to generate a variable ("educloc") that equals the average level of education of all the people in each individual's location. Obviously for all the people in the same location, this variable will take the same value. Education is stored as "educ14." There are 229 locations. The variable "location14" is coded 1 if the individual lives in the first location, 2 in the second, and so on up to 229. First, we generate a variable called "educloc" (setting it equal to 0), which will eventually represent the average level of education of everyone in the same location as the individual. The following command, *quietly summ educ14 if location14==k1 & educ14<70*, summarizes the level of education of everyone in location k1 (the first time through the loop k1=1, second time =2, and so on). The summarized data also are restricted to those who gave valid responses (*educ14<70*). The next command, *replace educloc=r(mean) if location14n==k1*, places a value equal to the mean of the previously summarized data for all the people living in location k1 in the variable educloc. If we had wished, we could have captured the median rather than the mean, or indeed a particular percentile. We also could have captured the heterogeneity of the location by using the standard deviation of the distribution. The *quietly* commands instruct the computer not to echo, because with many locations and locational variables to generate, the output on the screen would otherwise be considerable.

```
generate educloc =0
scalar k1=0
forvalues i1=1(1)229{
scalar k1=k1+1
quietly summ educ14 if location14==k1 & educ14<70
quietly replace educloc=r(mean) if location14==k1
}
```

Showing Summary Data by Locational Variables

The following is a short routine to summarize the data on two variables, "tribedecfair14" and "tribedecfairw14," for all valid responses by (a) those of ages less than 34 years, (b) those with a level of education coded less than 5, and (c) those with the "income14" variable coded 1. This approach facilitates the calculation of summary data as in table 5.2.

```
foreach var1 of varlist tribedecfair14 tribedecfairw14 {
summ `var1' if `var1' !=. & tribedec14 <5
summ `var1' if age14<34 & `var1' !=. & tribedec14 <5
summ `var1' if educ14<5 & `var1' !=. & tribedec14 <5
summ `var1' if income14==1 & `var1' !=. & tribedec14 <5
}
```

Notes

1. An earlier pilot exercise was carried out in 2012, but it will not be analyzed here.
2. We emphasize once again that this and the following sections are an expansion of the work in Hamilton and Hudson (2014b).
3. To an extent, the current tribal structure is an artificial construction, built by the British for reasons of effective control over the country. This is certainly the case in Darfur, even down to the construction of the tribal dars (Bassil 2014).
4. Of course, there can be more complex splits than simply urban and rural areas. Some rural areas may be close to large cities, and hence the inhabitants may be closer to city people than rural people in their attitudes. In addition, differences between cities may exist. The largest city in Sudan is Khartoum, and the state dummy variables may pick up some of these differences. Nonetheless, a single dummy variable, capturing the rural–urban split, still might be expected to capture any general differences. In anticipation of the results, this variable is not significant, but there are very substantial differences among states.
5. As far back as several millennium BCE in ancient Egypt, Ptahhotep emphasized the importance of leaders to both (a) be generous and (b) listen to someone's plea in full, because the very act of making that plea can bring comfort. He therefore stressed both outcome and procedure or process.
6. Bassil (2014) notes that in parts of Darfur there are clear signs that urbanization, education, nationalism, and economic development together are undermining the solidarity of the tribal unit.
7. Of course, access to the courts does not guarantee an outcome that the individual perceives to be fair. But the literature suggests that such perceptions are linked with judicial procedures, and the possibility of attending a court for a decision may in itself promote perceived fairness (Tyler 1986).
8. As noted earlier, the concept of the tribe and hence the tribal leader is likely to vary from place to place. Our question allows individuals to interpret this in their own way. Any differences may then be reflected in the various locally defined variables and the state dummy variables that affect the dependent variables.
9. We do not include locational fairness and trust because we seek to understand the determinants of individual perceived fairness and trust, and saying they depend on locational trust and fairness is not very illuminating.
10. As already indicated, different people were estimated in the two years.
11. In the regression analysis, this was not significant and has been omitted from the variables included in that analysis.
12. Over such a short period of time, though, this is perhaps unlikely.
13. This variable relates to the ability to cover household bills. Obviously, different households will have different aspirations and hence different expenses. Nonetheless, those who have the ability to cover their bills perceive decisions to be fairer than those who cannot cover their household bills.
14. Schools provide knowledge, and the knowledge may filter through to the mother and thus change perceptions. But the insignificance of either individual or locational levels of education in the regression suggests that increased knowledge is not an important factor.
15. These cannot, however, include greater access to television or the Internet in providing people with information. We have data on individual access to these media, and there is no evidence that such access tended to reduce tribal links.

Bibliography

Assal, M. 2009. "The Question of Identity in the Sudan: New Dimensions for an Old Problem." *Maghreb Review* 34: 181–94.

Barr, A. 2003. "Trust and Expected Trustworthiness: Experimental Evidence from Zimbabwean Villages." *Economic Journal* 113: 614–30.

Bassil, N. R. 2014. "Beyond 'Culture' and 'Tradition' in Sudan. The Role of the State in Reinventing Darfur's Tribal Politics." In *Informal Power in the Greater Middle East: Hidden Geographies*, edited by L. Anceschi, G. Gervasio, and A. Teti, 103–16. New York: Routledge.

Brewer, P., K. Gross, S. Aday, and D. Willnat. 2004. "International Trust and Public Opinion about World Affairs." *American Journal of Political Science* 48 (1): 93–109.

CIA (U.S. Central Intelligence Agency). 2012. *World Factbook*. https://www.cia.gov/library/publications/the-world-factbook.

Collier, P., and A. Hoeffler. 2004. "Greed and Grievance in Civil War." *Oxford Economic Papers* 56: 563–95.

Crowther, N., K. Okamura, C. Raja, D. Rinnert, and E. Spencer. 2014. "Inequalities in Public Services in the Sudan—Using a Perceptions-Informed View to Drive Policy in Education, Health and Water Provision." LSE Master of Public Administration (MPA) Capstone Report, London School of Economics and Political Science, London. http://r4d.dfid.gov.uk/Output/195649/Default.aspx.

Deng, F. 2009. *Customary Law in the Modern World: The Crossfire of Sudan's War of Identities*. New York: Routledge.

De Waal, A. 2005. "Who Are the Darfurians? Arab and African Identities, Violence and External Engagement." *African Affairs* 104: 181–205.

Fisher, J. 2008. "Women in Water Supply, Sanitation and Hygiene Programmes." *Proceedings of the Institute of Civil Engineers—Municipal Engineer* 161: 223–29.

Fjeldstad, O. H. 2004. "What's Trust Got to Do with It? Non-payment of Service Charges in Local Authorities in South Africa." *Journal of Modern African Studies* 42: 539–62.

Fried, M. H. 1975. *The Notion of Tribe*. Vol. 342. Menlo Park, CA: Cummings Publishing Company.

Gaviria, A., and S. Raphael. 2001. "School-Based Peer Effects and Juvenile Behavior." *Review of Economics and Statistics* 83: 257–68.

Glaeser, E. L., D. Laibson, J. A. Scheinkman, and C. L. Soutter. 2000. "Measuring Trust." *Quarterly Journal of Economics* 65: 811–46.

Hall, S. 2002. "Political Belonging in a World of Multiple Identities." In *Conceiving Cosmopolitanism: Theory, Context and Practice*, edited by S. Vertovec and R. Cohen. Oxford, U.K.: Oxford University Press.

Hamilton, A. 2013a. "Small Is Beautiful, at Least in High-Income Democracies: The Distribution of Policy-Making Responsibility, Electoral Accountability, and Incentives for Rent Extraction." Policy Research Working Paper WPS 6305, World Bank, Washington, DC.

———. 2013b. *MPA PIP Talk*. London School of Economics and Political Science, London. November 7.

Hamilton, A., and J. Hudson. 2014a. "Bribery and Identification: Evidence from Sudan." University of Bath Working Paper 30/14, Bath, U.K.

———. 2014b. "The Tribes that Bind: Attitudes to the Tribe and Tribal Leader in Sudan." University of Bath Working Paper 31/14, Bath, U.K.

Hardin, R. 1993. "The Street Level Epistemology of Trust." *Politics and Society* 21: 505–29.

———. 2002. *Trust and Trustworthiness*. New York: Russell Sage Foundation.

Hetherington, M. J. 1998. "The Political Relevance of Political Trust." *American Political Science Review* 92: 791–808.

Hollander, E. P., and J. W. Julian. 1970. "Studies in Leader Legitimacy, Influence, and Innovation." *Advances in Experimental Social Psychology* 5: 33–69.

Hudson, J. 2006. "Institutional Trust and Subjective Well-Being across the EU." *Kyklos* 59: 43–62.

Inglehart, R. 1997. *Modernization and Postmodernization, Cultural, Economic and Political Change in 41 Societies*. Princeton, NJ: Princeton University Press.

Johnson, D. H. 2003. *The Root Causes of Sudan's Civil Wars*. Vol. 5. Bloomington, IN: Indiana University Press.

Korsgaard, M. A., D. M. Schweiger, and H. J. Sapienza. 1995. "Building Commitment, Attachment, and Trust in Strategic Decision-Making Teams: The Role of Procedural Justice." *Academy of Management Journal* 38: 60–84.

Leventhal, G. S., J. Karuza Jr., and W. R. Fry. 1980. "Beyond Fairness: A Theory of Allocation Preferences." In *Justice and Social Interaction*, edited by G. Mikula, 167–218. New York: Springer-Verlag.

Lind, E. A., R. Kanfer, and P. C. Earley. 1990. "Voice, Control, and Procedural Justice: Instrumental and Noninstrumental Concerns in Fairness Judgments." *Journal of Personality and Social Psychology* 59: 952–59.

Lind, E. A., and T. R. Tyler. 1988. *The Social Psychology of Procedural Justice*. New York: Plenum.

Madibbo, A. I. 2012. "Conflict and the Conceptions of Identities in the Sudan." *Current Sociology* 60: 302–19.

Miguel, E. 2004. "Tribe or Nation? Nation Building and Public Goods in Kenya versus Tanzania." *World Politics* 56: 327–62.

Mishler, W., and R. Rose. 2001. "What Are the Origins of Political Trust? Testing Institutional and Cultural Theories in Post Communist Societies." *Comparative Political Studies* 34: 30–62.

North, D. C. 1990. *Institutions, Institutional Change and Economic Performance*. New York: Cambridge University Press.

Nugent, J. B., and N. Sanchez. 1999. "The Local Variability of Rainfall and Tribal Institutions: The Case of Sudan." *Journal of Economic Behavior and Organization* 39: 263–91.

Okojie, C. E. 1994. "Gender Inequalities of Health in the Third World." *Social Science and Medicine* 39: 1237–47.

Puentes-Markides, C. 1992. "Women and Access to Health Care." *Social Science and Medicine* 35: 619–26.

Putnam, R. D. 2000. *Bowling Alone: The Collapse and Revival of American Community*. New York: Touchstone.

Rawls, J. 1971. *A Theory of Justice*. Cambridge, MA: Harvard University Press.

Schweer, M. K. W. 1997. "Trust in Central Social Institutions—Results of an Empirical Study of Young Adults." *Gruppendynamik-Zeitschrift Fur Angewandte Sozialpsychologies* 28: 201–10.

Seligson, M. A. 2002. "The Impact of Corruption on Regime Legitimacy: A Comparative Study of Four Latin American Countries." *Journal of Politics* 64: 408–33.

———. 2006. "The Measurement and Impact of Corrupt Victimization: Survey Evidence from Latin America." *World Development* 34: 381–404.

Sun, W. K., and X. H. Wang. 2012. "Do Governments Affect Social Trust? Cross City Evidence in China." *Social Science Journal* 49: 447–57.

Tyler, T. R. 1986. "The Psychology of Leadership Evaluation." In *Justice in Social Relations*, edited by H. W. Bierhoff, R. L. Cohen and J. Greenberg, 299–316. New York: Plenum Press.

Tyler, T. R., and A. Caine. 1981. "The Influence of Outcomes and Procedures on Satisfaction with Formal Leaders." *Journal of Personality and Social Psychology* 41: 642–55.

Uslaner, E. M. 2002. *The Moral Foundations of Trust*. New York: Cambridge University Press.

Wallerstein, I. 1960. "Ethnicity and National Integration in West Africa." *Cahiers d'études Africaines* 1: 129–39.

World Bank. 2015. *World Development Report 2015: Mind, Society, and Behavior.* Washington, DC: World Bank.

Zain, M. E. 1996. "Tribe and Religion in the Sudan." *Review of African Political Economy* 23: 523–29.

CHAPTER 6

The Vicious Circle of Poverty, Poor Public Service Provision, and State Legitimacy in Sudan

Alexander Hamilton and Jakob Svensson

Introduction

Well-functioning public services can lift people out of poverty by improving their health, their education, and ultimately their earning opportunities. Conversely, if public services are missing and dysfunctional—as is the case in many developing countries—people remain in or may fall into poverty. Even worse, poverty and the lack of basic services may be linked: when public services are bad, they are often worse for the poor.

Public services are of course not bad by accident. Instead, policy makers decide whether investing in such services is worth their while. Important variables that determine that decision are the strength of common interest and the structure of political institutions (Acemoglu and Robinson 2012; Besley and Persson 2011; Collier 2009). In particular, when institutions are noninclusive, they tend to generate both poverty and negative feedback loops that help ensure the persistence of bad equilibria. This factor may lead to a vicious circle: exclusion from public services leads to poverty and distrust in state institutions and a questioning of state legitimacy, which in turn creates political apathy. As a result, people are unlikely to hold policy makers accountable, making investment in public services even less likely. Ultimately, if the state loses its legitimacy, responding with force and repression in the short term may be easier than taking on the arduous and long-winded task of building trust in state institutions and providing quality public services.

Authors' Note: This chapter is a nontechnical summary of our 2014 paper, "The Vicious Circle of Poverty, Poor Public Service Provision, and State Legitimacy: A View from the Ground in Sudan." The copyrights of this paper remain with the U.K. Department for International Development, which gave permission for use of the above-noted material.

This chapter summarizes and elaborates on the findings from our recent research paper (Hamilton and Svensson 2014) that attempts to quantify the mechanisms above using the unique U.K. Department for International Development (DFID) Sudan household survey data set from rural and urban areas of Sudan. We show that poverty and poor public service delivery go hand in hand in Sudan. Being poor makes one twice as likely to suffer from poor access to low-quality public services. Moreover, we show that this relationship is not attributable to just a rural–urban divide (where both the poor and the low-quality public services are concentrated in rural areas). Even within states and within urban and rural areas, the poor are always less likely to have access to well-functioning public services.

Does poor access to public services affect the trust and legitimacy in state institutions? We suggest the answer is yes. We find that households with poor access are significantly less likely to report that they trust various central and local state institutions. However, although the data show that households are significantly more likely to distrust central and government institutions in charge of public service provision, they are not more distrustful in general: they have no less trust in actors like the local imam or the tribal chief, who presumably have little influence over service provision.

We identify two channels through which poor service delivery influences households' views on the legitimacy and trustworthiness of public institutions. First, we show that households experiencing poor public service outcomes are more likely to distrust the formal public institutions. Second, we show that households in states with widespread inequalities are more likely to distrust the formal public institutions. That is, there is both a direct link and a link that appears to work through aversion against inequality in public service access.

Is political apathy caused by distrust in state institutions and a questioning of state legitimacy? We again suggest an affirmative answer. According to the data, households with poor public service access are less likely to be politically active. Importantly, we show that poverty in itself does not have these effects. On the contrary, the poor are slightly more inclined to associate themselves with political parties rather than with their tribe, and in states with widespread poverty, households are more inclined to express their views through elections.

This chapter briefly discusses the context and general literature regarding trust and public service provision, outlines the data used in Hamilton and Svensson (2014), presents the key findings, and summarizes the key insights.

Background: Sudan

Sudan is a federal entity with 18 states. Despite a number of decentralization reforms, the central authority—particularly the president—has retained dominance over all major sources of power. An authoritarian country considered to be one of the most fragile in the world, Sudan has a long and complex history of instability with a succession of civil wars, war in the Darfur region, and, more recently, conflict in South Kurdufan and Blue Nile. The secession of South Sudan in 2011 and the conflict there have further exacerbated much of that instability, particularly in the border areas. The World Bank (2012) classifies Sudan as a lower-middle-income country, but the classification masks the large inequality within Sudan—from the relative prosperity of Khartoum to most rural areas that remain desperately poor.

On human development and political freedoms, Sudan ranks very low, at 171 of 186 countries in the 2013 Human Development Index (UNDP 2014). The Brookings Institution's *Index of State Weakness in the Developing World* (Rice and Patrick 2008) is derived from aggregating eight indicators that capture the effectiveness and legitimacy of the state in the security, political, economic, and social spheres; Sudan is ranked sixth of 141 countries, with only Somalia, Afghanistan, the Democratic Republic of Congo, Iraq, and Burundi ranked higher (the higher the score, the weaker the state).

The 2013 DFID Sudan Household Survey Data

We use data from a household survey conducted by DFID Sudan in July 2013. As described in detail in chapter 4 of this book, information was collected from 2,365 households using a stratified random sample design. Unlike other sources of data in Sudan, the DFID Sudan household survey data set contains information on the quality of public service delivery experienced by households, information on householders' views of the state, their willingness to participate in political activities, and basic socioeconomic information.

From the data, our paper defines the following eight key variables:

- *Headcount ratio* is calculated on the basis of self-reported data about monthly household income and self-reported income supplemented by earnings of family members living abroad. Total income is then defined per capita, and the headcount ratio measures the share of households below the poverty line.

- *No access to public services* is a binary variable taking the value 1 if the household has no access to education, health, electricity, water, or sanitation services. The variable is created as follows: for each service, the respondent was asked to assess, using a four-grade scale ("completely inaccessible," "infrequent access possible," "frequent access possible," "completely accessible"), whether that service was accessible. A household is deemed to have no access to a service if the respondent answered "completely inaccessible" or "infrequent access possible" for that service. Households with *no access* therefore reported "completely inaccessible" or "infrequent access possible" for all five services.

- *No access, quality adjusted* combines the data used to define *no access* with (self-reported) data on the quality of the service. The quality score, for each service, is reported on a five-grade scale: "extremely poor quality," "poor quality," "adequate quality," "good quality," and "excellent quality." For each service, a household is labeled as having *no access, quality adjusted* if the respondent assessed the service as not accessible (that is, "completely inaccessible" or "infrequent access possible") or if the respondent assessed the service as accessible but the quality was viewed as poor or extremely poor. Households with *no access, quality adjusted* thus reported no access, quality adjusted for all five services.

- *Trust central state institutions* is based on the questions relating to whether the respondent trusted the parliament, the judiciary, the armed forces, and the federal government. The respondent was asked to assess each institution on a four-grade scale ("a lot of trust," "some trust," "little trust," or "no trust"). A respondent is viewed as having trust (value 1) in a particular central state institution if the answer given was "a lot of trust" or "some trust" for that institution, and 0 otherwise. The variable *trust central state institutions* is the sum of the five binary indicators for having trust in central state institutions, normalized by dividing the sum by the number of indicators (5) used in its construction.

- *Trust local state institutions* is based on questions relating to whether the respondent trusted the local government, the local public hospital, or the local public school. Similar to the derivation of the *trust central state institutions*, the respondent was asked to assess each institution on a four-grade scale ("a lot of trust," "some trust," "little trust," or "no trust"). A respondent is viewed as having trust (value 1) in a particular local state institution if the answer given was "a lot of trust" or "some trust" for that institution, and 0 otherwise. The variable *trust local state institutions* is the sum of the three binary indicators for having trust in local state institutions, normalized by dividing the sum by the number of indicators (3) used in its construction.

- *Trust nonstate institutions* is based on questions relating to whether the respondent had trust in the local imam and in the tribal chief. Again, similar to the derivation of the *trust state institutions*, the respondent was asked to assess each institution on a four-grade scale ("a lot of trust," "some trust," "little trust," or "no trust"). A respondent is viewed as having trust (value 1) in a nonstate institution if the answer given was "a lot of trust" or "some trust" for that institution, and 0 otherwise. The variable *trust nonstate institutions* is the sum of the two binary indicators for having trust in nonstate institutions, normalized by dividing the sum by the number of indicators (2) used in its construction.

- *Voting* is a binary variable taking the value 1 if the respondent answered yes to the question as to whether—were a general election held tomorrow—he or she would vote, and 0 otherwise.

- *Party vs. tribe* is a binary variable taking the value 1 if the respondent identified more closely with a political party rather than with the tribe, and 0 otherwise.

The Vicious Circle of Poverty, Poor Public Service Provision, and State Legitimacy

Table 6.1 reports summary statistics for the eight variables. For the poverty measure, *no access* and *no access, quality adjusted*, both individual means and state means are reported. Table 6.1 clearly shows that, on average, every third household surveyed was estimated to live on an income below the official poverty line of US$1.07 per day. The average score, however, masks great variation across states in estimated poverty, with the *headcount ratio* at the state level varying from 2 percent to 75 percent.

Of the households surveyed, 13 percent reported no access to any of the five basic public services, and 33 percent reported no access to decent quality services (*no access, quality adjusted*). The variation across states is again large: only 1 percent of the respondents reported no quality-adjusted access in the best-performing state, and 80 percent of the respondents reported no quality-adjusted access in the worst-performing state.

On average, 60 percent of the respondents reported having trust in central state institutions, and 59 percent reported having trust in local state institutions. Trust in nonstate institutions is more widespread, with 75 percent reported having trust in the local imam and the tribal chief.

Table 6.1 Summary Statistics

Variable	Obs.	Mean	Std. dev.	Minimum	Maximum
Income					
Poor	2,376	0.327	0.469	0.000	1.000
Headcount ratio (by state)	2,376	0.327	0.197	0.020	0.747
Public service provision					
No access	2,245	0.127	0.333	0.000	1.000
No access, quality adjusted	2,102	0.333	0.472	0.000	1.000
No access (state)	2,376	0.129	0.105	0.000	0.347
No access, quality adjusted (by state)	2,376	0.335	0.233	0.007	0.796
Public trust					
Trust central state institutions	1,912	0.601	0.362	0.000	1.000
Trust local state institutions	2,139	0.585	0.376	0.000	1.000
Trust nonstate institutions	1,957	0.749	0.325	0.000	1.000
Voting	2,286	0.701	0.458	0.000	1.000
Party vs. tribe	2,376	0.678	0.467	0.000	1.000

Source: Hamilton and Svensson 2014.
Note: Mean outcomes are by subgroup. Obs. = observations; Std. dev. = standard deviation.

Table 6.2 Summary Statistics: Urban vs. Rural and Poor vs. Nonpoor

Variable	Urban	Rural	Poor	Nonpoor
Poor	0.254	0.390	–	–
No access	0.097	0.153	0.204	0.091
No quality-adjusted access	0.285	0.377	0.405	0.301

Source: Hamilton and Svensson 2014.
Note: — = not available. Mean outcomes are by category.

Seventy percent of the respondents reported that they would vote in a general election if the election were held tomorrow.[1] A clear majority of the respondents, 68 percent, reported that they identified more closely with a political party than a tribe.

Table 6.2 breaks down the findings into rural and urban areas and whether the household is below (poor) or above (relatively less poor) the estimated poverty line. The headcount ratio is 14 percentage points higher in rural areas relative to urban areas. Households in rural areas are 58 percent (or 5.6 percentage points) more likely to suffer from complete lack of services (*no access*) and 32 percent (or 9.2 percentage points) more likely to suffer from complete lack of service adjusted for quality (*no access, quality adjusted*).

The poor are more than twice as likely to report no access to any public services, and a striking 40 percent of the poor report complete lack of services, quality adjusted. We show that these differences between poor and relatively less poor continue to hold when controlling for other differences, such as education, family size, or age. We further show that the strong significant relationship between poverty and poor access also holds when considering only households residing in urban areas or when considering only households residing in rural areas. Thus, although both the extent of poverty and the extent of service provision are lower in rural areas, the strong correlation between poverty and no access is not driven by an urban–rural divide.

We turn next to the question of whether poor access to public services affects the trust and legitimacy in state institutions, as suggested in recent political economy literature on state capacity and development. Table 6.3 splits the sample into three subgroups: (a) households with no access to public services, (b) households with some access, and (c) households with good access. Panel A reports results for *no access*. Panel B reports results for *no access, quality adjusted*. Panel C splits the sample between state means in the inequality of access by comparing states with an above-median (in the full sample) share of households lacking access (states with relatively higher inequality) and states with a below-median (in the full sample) share of households lacking access (states with relatively lower inequality).

For households with good access to public services (panel A), trust in institutions is uniformly high at an average of 70 percent across all three types of institutions (central state, local state, and nonstate). As for the total sample (see table 6.1), trust is most widespread for nonstate institutions (70 percent trust central and local state institutions versus 79 percent who trust nonstate institutions).

Table 6.3 State Legitimacy: Summary Statistics

Variable	Trust central state institutions	Trust local state institutions	Trust nonstate institutions
Panel A			
No access	0.507	0.463	0.667
Some access	0.617	0.603	0.764
Good access	0.703	0.699	0.788
Panel B			
No quality-adjusted access	0.521	0.523	0.729
Some quality-adjusted access	0.651	0.627	0.764
Good quality-adjusted access	0.835	0.833	0.852
Panel C			
Above-median share lacking access (state)	0.551	0.552	0.718
Below-median share lacking access (state)	0.665	0.625	0.790

Source: Hamilton and Svensson 2014.
Note: Mean outcomes are by category.

The pattern is strikingly different for those without access to public services. Two results stand out. First, trust in institutions is generally lower for these households, with only about half of the households with no access trusting the central and local state institutions and two-thirds trusting nonstate institutions. Second, the difference in trust between state and nonstate institutions is much more pronounced: households completely lacking access are 32 percent (or nearly 20 percentage points) more likely to trust nonstate institutions than state institutions.

Panel B assesses differences in trust as a function of quality-adjusted access. As is evident, the difference in trust in formal state institutions between those who have good access and those who have none becomes even more striking: more than 80 percent of those who reported good quality-adjusted access have trust in all three types of institutions, and trust is uniformly high for all categories of institutions. Those with no quality-adjusted access are 30 percentage points more likely to distrust state institutions. For nonstate institutions, however, the difference in access to quality service does not seem to play an important role. Trust in these institutions is only 13 percentage points lower for people with no quality-adjusted access to public services.

If households care about their own access yet have an aversion to inequality, as the recent literature in behavioral economics suggests, poor access in the state—even holding own access constant—may translate into lower trust in state institutions.[2] Panel C provides summary statistics that support this hypothesis.

In states with a relatively higher share of households with no access to public services, the trust in government institutions is on average 23 percent, or 17 percentage points, lower than trust in nonstate institutions. In states with a relatively lower share of households with no access to public services, this difference in trust is significantly smaller.

The results in panel C, table 6.3, are unconditional: one cannot separate out the direct effects of having no access from the indirect effect from aversion against inequality in access. To address this problem, we estimate an empirical model where trust in institutions is regressed on own and state-level average access to public services and show that the conditional results broadly confirm the unconditional findings.

The results so far suggest that poor access to public services is generally associated with lower trust in institutions and those who are involved in service delivery and those who are not differentiate between those institutions. When service delivery is poor, mistrust is particularly high for the former, but not the latter. We turn next to the question of whether poor public service provision—and as a result, a questioning of state legitimacy—also creates political apathy.

Table 6.4 presents summary statistics for the relationship between access to services and the two measures of political participation described above (*voting, party vs. tribe*). As evident, those without access to public services and without access to public services of adequate quality are less likely to intend to vote and less likely to affiliate with a party rather than their tribe. The effects are again large in magnitude, with the households completely lacking quality-adjusted services being 15 percent less likely to report that they would vote and 25 percent less likely to affiliate themselves with a party rather than a tribe.

The bottom two rows in table 6.4 show that the relationship is also apparent at the state level: households in states with lower-than-average access to public services are less likely to vote and are more likely to identify with tribes than households in states with higher-than-average access to public services.

We further investigate the channel from poor public service provision to reduced political participation. In an empirical model, linking no access and no access at the state level to trust (in central state institutions), we then use only that variation in trust that is predicted by access to public services to explain political participation.

Table 6.4 Political Participation: Summary Statistics

Variable	Voting	Party vs. tribe
No access	0.658	0.614
Some access	0.711	0.686
Good access	0.703	0.731
No quality-adjusted access	0.661	0.595
Some quality-adjusted access	0.728	0.713
Good quality-adjusted access	0.776	0.792
Above-median share lacking access (state)	0.665	0.636
Below-median share lacking access (state)	0.747	0.732

Source: Hamilton and Svensson 2014.
Note: Mean outcomes are by category. See main text for definitions of the variables.

Figure 6.1 Political Participation and State Legitimacy

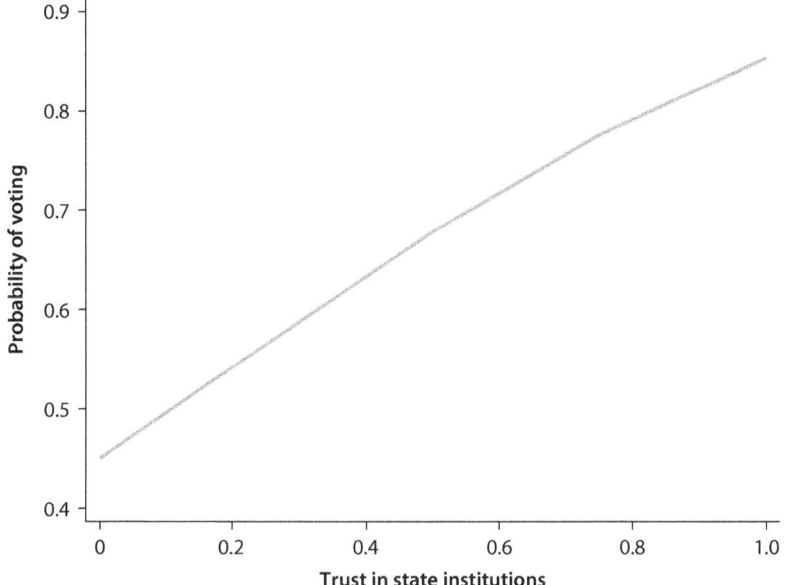

Source: Hamilton and Svensson 2014.
Note: The figure illustrates the two-stage least squares result discussed in Hamilton and Svensson 2014. Trust in state institutions is predicted on poor public service access.

Figure 6.1 illustrates the findings. That component of trust in central state institutions, which is predicted by access to public services, has a quantitatively large effect on both measures of political participation. Going from trust in all government institutions to no trust implies a 40 percentage point reduction in the likelihood of voting and an 70 percentage point reduction in the likelihood of affiliating with political parties rather than with tribes.

The findings so far suggest that mistrust of government institutions and lack of political participation are related to poor access to public services. An alternative explanation for the results is that poor access is a proxy for income poverty; that is, poverty, not lack of access to services, drives both lower trust in state institutions and a lower likelihood of political participation.

Combining data on poverty and poor access, we examine this hypothesis and reject it. Being poor is not associated with lower trust in any of the three types of institutions or with lower political participation. In fact, higher poverty at the state level is associated with a stronger intention to vote. However, poor access to public services is significantly and negatively correlated with both trust in central and local state institutions and political participation, even when controlling for own poverty and state-level headcount ratio.

Taken together, the findings suggest that the poor have significantly worse access to public services, and those with worse access distrust government institutions more. Poverty in itself does not make people distrust government. Rather, lack of trust in government is a direct effect of poor service delivery—at any income level. This factor is important because it suggests that the vicious circle of poor service delivery as it relates to lack of state legitimacy and political participation—leading to even lower incentives to invest in service delivery to the poor—could be turned into a virtuous circle if the government made a concerted effort to improve public services.

Discussion

This chapter discusses and summarizes the findings in Hamilton and Svensson (2014). Using microdata on access to and quality of public services collected at the household level in Sudan, we investigate the link between poor access to public services and state legitimacy and political participation. The results are broadly consistent with recent macroeconomic models of the occurrence of a vicious circle connecting poverty and state legitimacy to low investment in public services.

Unlike the recent macro-models (such as Besley and Persson 2011), in which common interest, state legitimacy, or both are exogenous variables, we show that people's views about the state are a function of how the state treats them: when the state does not provide basic public services, trust in government is eroded. Importantly, evidence exists that the link from lack of access to services to lack of political participation works through trust, which is endogenous in our model. The results also show that even though poverty and lack of public services are highly correlated, poverty per se does not lead to a lack of trust in government and political apathy. Those who are poor are more likely to be disadvantaged with regard to service delivery, and that in turn leads them to mistrust government and abstain from political activity.

Although the findings paint a bleak picture of the vicious circle of poverty, poor public service provision, and state legitimacy, there is also a potential upside. The results provide suggestive evidence of ways in which the government can turn the vicious circle into a virtuous circle. Specifically, it can strengthen its legitimacy by improving basic services to the poor, which might lead to more political participation, in turn giving more incentives for good service delivery. Importantly, improving basic services to the poor may in principle be a simpler problem to solve than addressing poverty itself, which is potentially much more entrenched.

Notes

1. These numbers are interesting in themselves. To our knowledge, no reliable official data on voting exist in Sudan. The formally reported partition rate in elections is very high, but also highly suspect.
2. See, for example, Camerer, Loewenstein, and Rabin (2011).

References

Acemoglu, D., and J. A. Robinson. 2012. *Why Nations Fail: The Origins of Power, Prosperity, and Poverty*. New York: Crown.

Besley, T., and T. Persson. 2011. *Pillars of Prosperity*. Princeton, NJ: Princeton University Press.

Camerer, C. F., G. Loewenstein, and M. Rabin. 2011. *Advances in Behavioral Economics*. Princeton, NJ: Princeton University Press.

Collier, P. 2009. *Wars, Guns and Votes: Democracy in Dangerous Places*. New York: HarperCollins.

Hamilton, A., and J. Svensson. 2014. "The Vicious Circle of Poverty, Poor Public Service Provision, and State Legitimacy: A View from the Ground in Sudan." Seminar Paper 772, Institute for International Economic Studies, Stockholm University, Stockholm.

Rice, S. E., and S. Patrick. 2008. *Index of State Weakness in the Developing World*. Washington, DC: Brookings Institution.

UNDP (United Nations Development Programme). 2014. *The Human Development Report 2014*. New York: UNDP.

World Bank. 2012. *The World Development Report 2012: Gender Equality and Development*. Washington, DC: World Bank.

CHAPTER 7

Geography and Correlates of Attitudes toward Female Genital Mutilation in Sudan: What Can We Learn from Successive Sudan Opinion Poll Data?

Alexander Hamilton and Ngianga-Bakwin Kandala

Background

Female genital mutilation (FGM), or cutting, is considered to be a violation of human rights and has life-long implications for women, including ongoing infection, infertility, psychological trauma, and complications during childbirth. In recent years, an estimated 125 million women and girls are thought to have undergone FGM in 29 countries in Africa and the Middle East. The United Nations Children's Fund (UNICEF) reports that nearly 9 out of 10 Sudanese women age 15–49 years have undergone some form of cutting with various degrees of severity (DFID 2013; *Sudan Tribune* 2014; UNICEF 2013). The procedure, also known as infibulation or pharaonic circumcision, is usually performed on girls by traditional practitioners who have no medical training. However, a comparison of the 2006 and 2010 Sudanese government household surveys shows a notable decrease in the practice of cutting. This is likely a result of an ongoing changing attitude toward FGM because more Sudanese women believe the practice should be discontinued amid growing awareness about its health dangers.

Authors' Note: This chapter is a nontechnical summary of our 2016 article, "Geography and Correlates of Attitude toward Female Genital Mutilation (FGM) in Sudan: What Can We Learn from Successive Sudan Opinion Poll Data?" *Spatial and Spatio-temporal Epidemiology* 16: 59–76. Copyrights of this paper remain with the *Spatial and Spatio-temporal Epidemiology* periodical, which gave permission for use of the above-noted material.

The FGM procedure is irreversible, and no modern medical procedures can fully repair its long-term psychological and physical complications, such as urinary and genital tract infections; pain and hemorrhage; complications in childbirth; social, psychological, and sexual complications for mother or daughter; mortality; and ongoing morbidity concerns (Kandala 2014; Kandala and Komba 2014; Kandala, Nwakeze, and Kandala 2009; Karmaker et al. 2011). In other countries in the region, there have been some efforts by multilateral agencies, such as the World Health Organization (WHO) and United Nations Children's Fund (UNICEF), and nongovernmental organizations (NGOs) advocating attitude change and the abandonment of FGM. In Ethiopia, some successful public health programs have been documented by NGOs such as Kembatti Mentti Gezzimma-Tope (KMG)[1] and TOSTAN in The Gambia, Guinea, Guinea-Bissau, Mali, Mauritania, and Senegal.[2]

However, a comparison of the 2006 and 2010 Sudanese government household surveys shows a notable decrease in the practice of cutting among, for instance, girls age 5–9 years: 34.5 percent had been cut in 2010, compared to 41.0 percent in 2006 with a further decrease expected in the next household survey (DFID 2013; *Sudan Tribune* 2014; UNICEF 2013). Eastern Sudan's Kassala state is most affected; 78.9 percent of girls and women are reported to have undergone the procedure—the third-highest prevalence in the country, according to the 2010 Sudan Household Health Survey (DFID 2013; *Sudan Tribune* 2014; UNICEF 2013). The origin of the practice is steeped in traditional (especially in the north of the country) and societal ideals of beauty and cleanliness, as well as religion and morality. In addition, it is used as a method of stifling female libido (DFID 2013; *Sudan Tribune* 2014; UNICEF 2013).

The Sudanese government has introduced stiff penalties for those who continue to perform the procedure, but the practice, which is still not criminalized by law in Sudan, remains widespread, particularly in rural communities (DFID 2013; *Sudan Tribune* 2014; UNICEF 2013). The eradication of FGM is complicated further by cultural and societal pressures, as well as religious sensitivities surrounding the issue. UNICEF is providing support for a national strategy to abolish FGM known as the Saleema Initiative. Conceived in 2008, the campaign is supervised by the National Council for Child Welfare (UNICEF 2013). However, despite the extensive media campaign by the Sudanese government, the strategy of changing attitudes and tribal habits is not easy or swift within the diverse population of Sudan (*Sudan Tribune* 2014). Very few studies have investigated attitudes toward FGM in high-FGM-prevalence countries such as Sudan. The study by UNICEF (2013) is the most comprehensive to date on attitudes toward FGM. However, it was limited in scope and performed only an exploratory analysis using descriptive data without examining many of the control variables that can confound attitudes toward FGM (UNICEF 2013).

This chapter is an extension of our work published elsewhere (Hamilton and Kandala 2016). Here we are able to expand on many issues discussed in our previous work by giving more detailed explanations of our key findings using figures and maps. In this chapter, we examine the geographical variation of an attitude toward the abandonment of FGM, as well as a wide range of potential correlates toward the continuation of FGM (pro-FGM). We analyze the 2012/13 and 2014 U.K. Department for International Development (DFID) Sudan Household Health Survey data sets consisting of responses from 4,741 individuals. We use Bayesian geo-additive mixed models to identify the factors that are more likely to result in individual respondents supporting the continuation of FGM. This chapter investigates the geographic variation of attitude shifts toward the eradication of FGM, as well as a wide range of potential correlates toward the continuation of FGM, using the 2014 DFID Sudan Household Health Survey data set, while accounting for a number of potential risk factors and sociodemographic correlates. This kind of data is valuable in informing public health policy that educates younger generations in the prevention of avertable health conditions associated with FGM in Sudan and other settings (DFID 2013).

Methods

Study Population

The 2014 DFID Sudan Household Health Surveys, which employed similar methodologies, were carried out across the country in government-controlled areas (thus excluding some rebel-controlled and high-conflict areas) using a random stratified sampling methodology. Respondents were asked about a range of subjects covering governance, service delivery, and humanitarian and social development areas. The Institutional Review Board at the Sudan Polling Statistics Center validated the survey procedures and instruments, and the DFID Sudan statistics adviser assured their quality (DFID 2013). The response rates for the two surveys were 100 percent.

The overall methods, objectives, organization, sample design, and questionnaires used in the DFID Sudan Household Health Surveys have been described in detail in the preceding chapters. But for FGM specifically, responses collected from participants included whether they would like the practice to be stopped or to be continued (and, if so, why); their individual attitudes and beliefs about FGM; and their political, cultural, and economic profiles.

Outcome Variable

We studied attitude shifts surrounding FGM as the main outcome in terms of "whether a participant, when asked, would like FGM practice to continue or to stop." This question was converted into a binary variable, with two categories defined as 1 if participants wanted the practice to continue and 0 if they wanted it to stop as the two possible outcomes, after exclusion of participants who did not respond to the question or were undecided.

Control Variables

The main control variable in the analysis was the "state of residence," defined by the Sudanese 2008 Census and numbering 16, including the capital city,

Khartoum, as shown in map 7.1 later in this chapter. Other control variables included sociodemographic and environmental factors associated with FGM attitudes (DFID 2013). Other cultural, political, and geographic factors that might have influenced the outcome—sex; age; education level; income; marital status; family size; place of residence; trust in tribal leader, imam, police, and local and federal government; identity; decision-making power (autonomy); and willingness to vote in general election—also were included as confounders. Age was recorded in the data set as a continuous variable and was recoded into a categorical variable of four categories in the preliminary analysis, with a truncated first category for 18–24 year olds. Education level was categorized as "No education," "Primary/interim," "Secondary/diploma," "BSc" and "Higher (higher diploma, MSc, PhD)." Income was precalculated in the data set, categorized as "<100 SDG," "100–500 SDG," "501–1,000 SDG," "1,001–2,000 SDG," and "2,001–3,000 SDG." The variable for family size was recoded into three categories of "small (1–4 children)," "middle (5–7 children)," and "large (8+ children)." Trust in tribal leader, imam, federal government, local government, police, and judiciary and degree of choice about their future were predefined from "a lot" to "not at all." Identity was recorded as "Sudanese," "my state," "Arab," "African," "my tribe," and "my religious affiliation." The 16 Sudanese states were also recoded into 15 states according to administrative divisions set up with the aforementioned states in the 2008 census (DFID 2013). The category "Sudanese" in the identity variable and the category "Northern State" in the state variable were used as references, because both categories contained the fewest pro-FGM participants.

Statistical Analysis

The 2012/13 and 2014 DFID Sudan Household Health Survey data sets include geographical information that might identify spatial patterns in FGM attitude toward the continuation of FGM. This information in turn can help policy makers target at-risk locations for FGM abandonment programs. This new information about the geographic location can be incorporated when those data are analyzed.

In the analysis of survey data, the commonly adopted models are logistic or probit and the standard measure of effect is the odds ratio (Kandala 2014; Kandala and Komba 2014; Kandala, Nwakeze, and Kandala 2009; Karmaker et al. 2011). In our study, however, because the DFID Sudan Household Health Survey data sets contain geographical or spatial information (for example, state of residence) and nonlinear effects for some covariates (for example, age of the respondent), strictly linear predictors cannot be assumed. Analyzing and modeling geographical patterns for attitude shifts surrounding the eradication of FGM, in addition to the effect of the cultural and political environment of a respondent, is of obvious interest.

In this chapter, we use a well-grounded advanced statistical methodology to explore various dynamics influencing pro-FGM attitude. In the context of Sudan, the spatial patterns of pro-FGM attitudes, sociocultural factors, state factors, and the possibly nonlinear effects of other factors are explored within a simultaneous, coherent regression framework, using a geo-additive, semiparametric mixed model that simultaneously controls spatial dependence and possibly nonlinear or time effects of covariates in the complex sampling design. The methodologies can identify key drivers of pro-FGM factors associated with high-risk groups that can be targeted for rapid intervention at state level to assess the potential effect of abandonment programs and the enforcement of laws banning FGM (Kandala 2014; Kandala and Komba 2014; Kandala, Nwakeze, and Kandala 2009; Karmaker et al. 2011).

The Bayesian model used here is a special class of generalized linear mixed model (Belitz et al. 2012; Fahrmeir and Lang 2001). Fahrmeir and Lang (2001) extended classical geostatistical methods such as kriging to allow, among other features, formal incorporation of (a) sampling error in the observed data, (b) relationships with covariates (and the uncertainty in the form of these relationships), and (c) uncertainty in the spatial autocorrelation structure of the outcome variable.

In brief, the strictly linear predictor:

$$\eta_i = x'\beta + w_i'\gamma + \varepsilon_i \qquad (7.01)$$

is replaced with a logit link function with dynamic and spatial effects, $\Pr(y_i = 1|h_i) = e^{h_i}/(1 + e^{h_i})$, and a geo-additive semiparametric predictor $\mu_i = h(h_i)$:

$$h_i = f_1(x_{i1}) + \ldots + f_p(x_{ip}) + f_{spat}(s_i) + w'_i g + \varepsilon_i, \qquad (7.02)$$

where h is a known response function with a logit link function, $f_1, \ldots, f_p$ are nonlinear smoothed effects of the metrical covariates (respondent's age), and $f_{spat}(s_i)$ is the effect of the spatial covariate $s_i \in \{1,\ldots,S\}$ labeling the state in Sudan. Covariates in w'_i are categorical variables such as education and urban–rural residence. Regression models with predictors such as those in equation (7.02) are sometimes referred to as geo-additive models (Belitz et al. 2012; Fahrmeir and Lang 2001). In a further step, we may split up the spatial effect f_{spat} into a spatially correlated (structured) and an uncorrelated (unstructured) effect: $f_{spat}(s_i) = f_{str}(s_i) + f_{unstr}(s_i)$. The rationale is that a spatial effect is usually a surrogate of many unobserved influences, some of them obeying a strong spatial structure and others presenting only locally.

To estimate smooth effect functions and model parameters, we used a fully Bayesian approach, as developed in Fahrmeir and Lang (2001). For all parameters and functions, we have to assign appropriate priors. The nonlinear effects in equation (7.02) of $f_1, \ldots, f_p$ are modeled by cubic penalized splines (P-splines) with second-order random walk penalty. For the structured spatial effect $f_{spat}(s_i)$, we experimented with different prior assumptions (two-dimensional P-splines or Gaussian random field, priors based on radial basis functions, or Markov random field priors common in spatial statistics). In the final model, P-spline priors were assigned to the functions $f_1,...,f_p$, while a Markov random field prior was used for f_{spat} (s_i) because it outperformed the other priors (Belitz et al. 2012; Fahrmeir and Lang 2001; Kandala, Nwakeze, and Kandala 2009). The standard measure of effect was the posterior odds ratios (PORs) and 95 percent credible region (CR). Although the estimation process with this model is complex, the estimated PORs that were produced could be interpreted as similar to those of ordinary logistic models.

The analysis was carried out using version 2.0.1 of the BayesX software package (Belitz et al. 2012), which permits Bayesian inference based on Markov chain Monte Carlo simulation techniques. The statistical significances of associations between potential risk factors and pro-FGM attitude were explored in chi-square and Mann-Whitney U-tests, as appropriate.

We used multivariate Bayesian geo-additive regression models to evaluate the significance of the POR, determined for the fixed effects and spatial effects between pro-FGM attitudes in Sudan. Each factor was viewed separately in unadjusted models using conventional logistic regression models. We then performed fully adjusted multivariate Bayesian geo-additive regression analyses to look again for a statistically significant correlation between these variables, but further controlling for any influence from individual (age), cultural (identity), political (trust in government and so on), and state factors (see table 7.1). A p-value of < 0.05 was considered indicative of a statistically significant difference.

Table 7.1 Baseline Characteristics of the Study Population[a]

Variable	2012/13 (N = 2,364)	2014 (N = 2,376)
Mean age[b] (SD) for respondent	34.8(12.5)	35.8(12.9)
FGM should stop (%)		
Yes	72.5	81.7
No	27.5	18.3
Why FGM should continue (%)		
Required for good marriage	51.6	28.7
Important for tradition	34.4	30.8
Part of culture	11.9	20.2
Part of Islamic instruction	2.1	20.2
Age (%)		
<25 years	17.4	23.2
25–30 years	19.9	35.7
36–50 years	15.5	25.5
>50 years	47.2	15.6
Gender (%)		
Female	49.9	47.6
Male	50.1	52.4

table continues next page

Table 7.1 Baseline Characteristics of the Study Population *(continued)*

Variable	2012/13 (N = 2,364)	2014 (N = 2,376)
Married (%)		
Yes	58.0	63.7
No	42.0	36.3
Education (%)		
No education	14.1	7.2
Primary interim education	21.5	13.9
Secondary education/diploma	37.2	23.8
BSc	22.0	42.0
Higher education (higher diploma, MSc, PhD)	5.2	13.1
Household income (%)		
<100 SDG	46.0	33.9
100–500 SDG	31.8	37.1
501–1,000 SDG	22.2	19.1
1,001–2,000 SDG		6.0
2,001–3,000 SDG		3.9
Family size (%)		
Small (1–4 children)	61.9	52.9
Middle (5–7 children)	28.5	31.9
Large (8+ children)	9.6	15.2
Place of residence (%)		
Urban	35.7	35.4
Rural	64.3	64.6
Trust in the tribal leader (%)		
A lot	43.0	31.6
Some	36.2	31.4
A little	20.8	18.3
Not at all		18.6
Trust in imam (%)		
A lot	60.5	69.3
Some	21.0	16.6
A little	10.0	6.8
Not at all	8.5	7.3
Trust in the federal government (%)		
A lot	15.8	23.5
Some	30.6	29.1
A little	27.6	22.9
Not at all	26.0	24.5
Trust in the local government (%)		
A lot	12.8	22.0
Some	30.8	26.1
A little	29.5	26.0
Not at all	27.0	25.9

table continues next page

Table 7.1 Baseline Characteristics of the Study Population *(continued)*

Variable	2012/13 (N = 2,364)	2014 (N = 2,376)
Trust in the police (%)		
A lot	23.9	33.3
Some	34.4	31.4
A little	23.9	19.4
Not at all	17.8	15.9
Trust in the judiciary system (%)		
A lot	25.0	35.0
Some	38.1	31.3
A little	21.7	20.5
Not at all	15.2	13.2
Islamic law (%)		
Should be at the heart of the constitution	55.2	82.4
Should be part of the constitution	11.8	17.6
Have a choice about my future		
A lot	39.7	42.8
Some	25.8	23.7
A little	20.3	19.6
Not at all	14.2	13.9
Identity		
Sudanese	81.2	78.3
My state	2.6	1.9
Arab	1.3	1.8
African	2.0	1.4
My tribe	4.6	4.3
My religious affiliation	8.3	12.2
Able to hold decision makers to account		
A lot	20.5	22.3
Some	21.7	21.2
A little	19.9	17.6
Not at all	37.9	38.9
If election held would vote		
Yes	80.8	70.1
No	19.2	29.9
State of residence (%)		
Al Qadarif	6.3	6.3
Al Jazirah	7.3	7.6
Blue Nile	6.3	5.9
Kassala	5.9	6.3
Khartoum	10.9	10.9
North Darfur	4.3	3.8
North Kurdufan	6.3	6.3
Northern	6.3	6.3

table continues next page

Table 7.1 Baseline Characteristics of the Study Population *(continued)*

Variable	2012/13 (N = 2,364)	2014 (N = 2,376)
Red Sea	6.3	6.3
River Nile	6.3	6.3
Sennar	6.3	6.3
South Darfur	8.4	8.7
South Kurdufan	6.1	6.3
West Darfur	6.4	6.3
White Nile	6.3	6.3

Source: Based on data from the 2012/13 and 2014 U.K. Department for International Development Sudan Household Health Surveys.
Note: BSc = bachelor of science; FGM = female genital mutilation; MSc = master of science; N = number; PhD = doctor of philosophy; SD = standard deviation; SDG = Sudanese pound.
a. Data are expressed as mean (standard deviation) or as percentages.
b. Age ranges from 18 to 97 years of age.

Results

Descriptive Results

Baseline sociodemographic and state characteristics are shown in table 7.1, and response results for intent to stop or continue FGM practice are presented in table 7.2. The overall proportion of pro-FGM attitudes was different between the two surveys (27.5 percent in 2012/13 and 18.3 percent in 2014). However, the two survey populations are comparable for the selected variables in terms of a higher proportion of pro-FGM among rural residents, and similar proportions in both female and male respondents.

The mean age for men was slightly higher than that for women in both the 2012/13 survey (36.2 versus 32.7 years) and the 2014 survey (38.0 versus 33.5 years) as expected from the sample strategy. Overall, the mean age of the two samples was comparable (age range: 18–75 years in 2012/13 and 18–97 years for 2014). For 2012/13, the mean age was 34.8 years, with a standard deviation of ±12.5 years. For 2014, the mean age of the sample was 35.8 years, with a standard deviation of ±12.9 years, and most of the population sampled lived in rural settings (64.6 percent), and 63.7 percent were married.

In the 2014 survey population, 24 percent of individuals had a secondary education and only 7.2 percent had no education compared to 37.2 percent having secondary education and 14.1 percent having no education in 2012/13 (see figure 7.1). When asked why FGM should continue, in 2012/13, 51.6 percent of participants cited the requirement for a good marriage, 34.4 percent cited the importance of tradition, and 2.1 percent cited it as being part of Islamic instruction. In 2014, 28.7 percent of participants cited the requirement for a good marriage, 30.8 percent cited the importance of tradition, and 20.2 percent cited it as being part of Islamic instruction (see figure 7.2).

In the 2012/13 survey versus the 2014 survey, respondents in favor of FGM were mostly married (29.7 percent versus 19.3 percent), had no education or primary education (68.8 percent versus 50.0 percent), had a low income (32.1 percent versus 28.1 percent), had a large family (26.4 percent

Table 7.2 Baseline Characteristics of the Study Population, by Intent to Continue FGM[a]

Variable	2012/13			2014		
	Stop FGM (N–1,616)	Continue FGM (N–612)	P-value[b]	Stop FGM (N–1,800)	Continue FGM (N–404)	P-value[b]
Age			$p = 0.37$			$p = 0.67$
<25 years	478(74.9)	160(25.1)		406(81.0)	95(19.0)	
25–30 years	511(70.7)	212(29.3)		648(82.0)	142(18.0)	
36–50 years	407(72.6)	154(27.4)		474(82.9)	98(17.1)	
>50 years	220(71.9)	86(28.1)		272(79.8)	69(20.2)	
Gender			$p\,0.06$			$p\,0.74$
Female	817(74.3)	282(25.7)		881(81.9)	194(18.1)	
Male	799(70.8)	330(29.2)		919(81.4)	210(18.6)	
Married			$p = 0.005$			$p = 0.07$
Yes	906(70.3)	383(29.7)		1,125(80.7)	269(19.3)	
No	709(75.7)	228(24.3)		652(83.8)	126(16.2)	
Education (%)			$p < 0.001$			$p < 0.001$
No education	201(62.4)	121(37.6)		121(79.6)	31(20.4)	
Primary/Interim education	332(68.9)	150(31.1)		207(70.4)	87(29.6)	
Secondary education/ Diploma	624(76.1)	196(23.9)		420(79.8)	106(20.2)	
BSc	370(75.7)	119(24.3)		804(85.8)	133(14.2)	
Higher educ. (higher diploma, MSc, PhD)	89(77.4)	26(22.6)		250(83.9)	44(16.1)	
Household income			$p < 0.001$			$p < 0.001$
<100 SDG	621(67.9)	293(32.1)		520(71.9)	203(28.1)	
100–500 SDG	486(77.3)	143(22.7)		722(86.7)	111(13.3)	
501–1000 SDG	312(74.3)	108(25.7)		377(87.7)	53(12.3)	
1001–2000 SDG				107(82.9)	22(17.1)	
2001–3000 SDG				74(83.1)	15(16.9)	
Family size			$p = 0.03$			$p < 0.001$
Small (1–4 children)	960(70.6)	399(29.4)		986(84.6)	180(15.4)	
Middle (5–7 children)	494(76.1)	155(23.9)		570(81.0)	134(19.0)	
Large (8+ children)	162(73.6)	58(26.4)		244(73.0)	90(27.0)	
Place of residence (%)			$p < 0.001$			$p\,0.003$
Urban	603(77.3)	177(22.7)		663(85.0)	117(15.0)	
Rural	1,013(70.0)	435(30.0)		1,137(79.8)	287(20.2)	
Trust in the tribal leader			$p = 0.66$			$p < 0.001$
A lot	555(70.5)	232(29.5)		457(76.9)	137(23.1)	
Some	465(71.5)	185(28.5)		518(86.9)	78(13.1)	
A little	264(73.1)	97(26.9)		265(78.6)	72(21.4)	
Not at all				286(83.6)	56(16.4)	
Trust in Imam			$p = 0.001$			$p < 0.001$
A lot	883(83.5)	384(30.3)		1,243(83.5)	245(16.5)	
Some	336(75.0)	112(25.0)		268(81.5)	61(18.5)	

table continues next page

Table 7.2 Baseline Characteristics of the Study Population, by Intent to Continue FGM[a] *(continued)*

	2012/13			2014		
Variable	Stop FGM (N–1,616)	Continue FGM (N–612)	P-value[b]	Stop FGM (N–1,800)	Continue FGM (N–404)	P-value[b]
A little	153(72.9)	57(27.1)		99(72.3)	38(27.7)	
Not at all	147(83.1)	30(16.9)		107(71.3)	43(28.7)	
Trust in federal government			p – 0.005			p – 0.02
A lot	211(65.1)	113(34.9)		383(81.0)	90(19.0)	
Some	424(71.3)	171(28.7)		501(85.8)	83(14.2)	
A little	399(74.2)	139(25.8)		355(78.9)	95(21.1)	
Not at all	400(75.9)	127(24.1)		402(83.6)	79(16.4)	
Trust in local government			p = 0.003			p = 0.03
A lot	181(65.8)	94(34.2)		376(80.7)	90(19.3)	
Some	451(70.7)	187(29.3)		455(84.3)	85(15.7)	
A little	426(72.0)	166(28.0)		412(78.3)	114(21.7)	
Not at all	433(77.3)	127(22.7)		445(84.4)	82(15.6)	
Trust in the police			p < 0.001			p = 0.099
A lot	331(64.4)	183(35.6)		592(82.3)	127(17.7)	
Some	540(76.4)	167(23.6)		563(84.8)	101(15.2)	
A little	380(73.6)	136(26.4)		313(78.8)	84(21.2)	
Not at all	284(75.1)	94(24.9)		258(81.4)	59(18.6)	
Trust in the judiciary			p = 0.15			p = 0.06
A lot	376(70.4)	158(29.6)		622(84.4)	115(15.6)	
Some	570(73.4)	206(26.6)		519(79.4)	135(20.6)	
A little	328(72.4]	125(27.9)		338(83.1)	69(16.9)	
Not at all	251(77.5)	73(22.5)		208(79.4)	54(20.6)	
Islamic law			p = 0.003			p = 0.23
Should be at the heart of the constitution	788(69.9)	339(30.1)		1,421(82.4)	303(17.6)	
Should be part of the constitution	705(75.7)	226(24.3)		296(79.8)	75(20.2)	
Choice about my future			p < 0.001			P – 0.90
A lot	561(66.7)	280(33.3)		757(81.6)	171(18.4)	
Some	394(77.0)	118(23.0)		425(82.9)	88(17.1)	
A little	336(79.1)	89(20.9)		331(81.5)	75(18.5)	
Not at all	229(75.8)	73(24.2)		240(80.8)	57(19.2)	
Identity			p < 0.001			P < 0.001
Sudanese	1,331(74.5)	456(25.5)		1,440(83.8)	279(16.2)	
My state	27(56.3)	21(43.7)		22(68.8)	10(31.2)	
Arab	17(60.7)	11(39.3)		24(64.9)	13(35.1)	
African	28(62.2)	17(37.8)		23(76.7)	7(23.3)	
My tribe	60(59.4)	41(40.6)		50(55.6)	40(44.4)	
My religious affiliation	125(72.7)	47(27.3)		223(81.4)	51(18.6)	

table continues next page

Table 7.2 Baseline Characteristics of the Study Population, by Intent to Continue FGM[a] *(continued)*

	2012/13			2014		
Variable	Stop FGM (N–1,616)	Continue FGM (N–612)	P-value[b]	Stop FGM (N–1,800)	Continue FGM (N–404)	P-value[b]
Hold decision makers to account			p < 0.001			p = 0.03
A lot	255(63.4)	147(36.6)		364(80.9)	86(19.1)	
Some	283(68.4)	131(31.6)		335(80.1)	83(19.9)	
A little	277(77.2)	82(22.8)		272(78.2)	76(21.8)	
Not at all	585(79.7)	149(20.3)		656(85.0)	116(15.0)	
If election held would vote			p – 0.002			p – 0.09
Yes	1,283(74.3)	444(25.7)		1,247(82.8)	260(17.2)	
No	279(66.9)	138(33.1)		497(79.7)	127(20.3)	
State of residence (%)			p < 0.001			p < 0.001
Al Qadarif	105(70.5)	44(29.5)		141(96.6)	5(3.4)	
Al Jazirah	142(83.5)	28(16.5)		153(92.7)	12(7.3)	
Blue Nile	90(60.0)	60(40.0)		89(81.6)	20(18.4)	
Kassala	125(90.6)	13(9.4)		119(90.8)	12(9.2)	
Khartoum	187(89.0)	23(11.0)		206(84.4)	38(15.6)	
North Darfur	51(59.3)	35(40.7)		64(79.0)	17(21.0)	
North Kurdufan	113(80.1)	28(19.9)		109(72.7)	41(27.3)	
Northern	130(87.2)	19(12.8)		148(98.7)	2(1.3)	
Red Sea	81(54.0)	69(46.0)		122(81.9)	27(18.1)	
River Nile	101(69.2)	45(30.8)		131(89.1)	16(10.9)	
Sennar	79(54.1)	67(45.9)		135(90.6)	14(9.4)	
South Darfur	151(79.9)	38(20.1)		80(44.7)	99(55.3)	
South Kurdufan	84(68.3)	39(31.7)		118(80.3)	29(19.7)	
West Darfur	103(76.3)	32(23.7)		86(76.8)	26(23.2)	
White Nile	74(50.7)	72(49.3)		99(68.3)	46(31.7)	

Source: Based on data from the 2012/13 and 2014 U.K. Department for International Development Sudan Household Health Surveys.
Note: BSc = bachelor of science; FGM = female genital mutilation; MSc = master of science; N = number; PhD = doctor of philosophy; SDG = Sudanese pound.
a. Data are expressed as mean (standard deviation) or as percentages.
b. P-values for comparison between pro-FGM and ant-FGM subjects.

versus 27.0 percent), and lived in rural areas (30.0 percent versus 20.2 percent). Pro-FGM respondents had a lot of trust in tribal leaders (29.5 percent versus 23.1 percent), had a lot of trust in the imam (30.3 percent versus 16.5 percent), had a lot of trust in federal government (34.9 percent versus 19.0 percent), and had some trust in local government (29.3 percent versus 15.7 percent). They identified mostly with the state rather than their tribe (43.7 percent versus 31.2 percent) (see figure 7.3), held decision makers to account a lot (36.6 percent versus 19.1 percent), and lived in White Nile (49.3 percent versus 31.7 percent) or South Darfur (20.1 percent versus 55.3 percent) (table 7.2 and maps 7.1a and 7.1b).

Figure 7.1 Share of Study Participants, by Educational Attainments

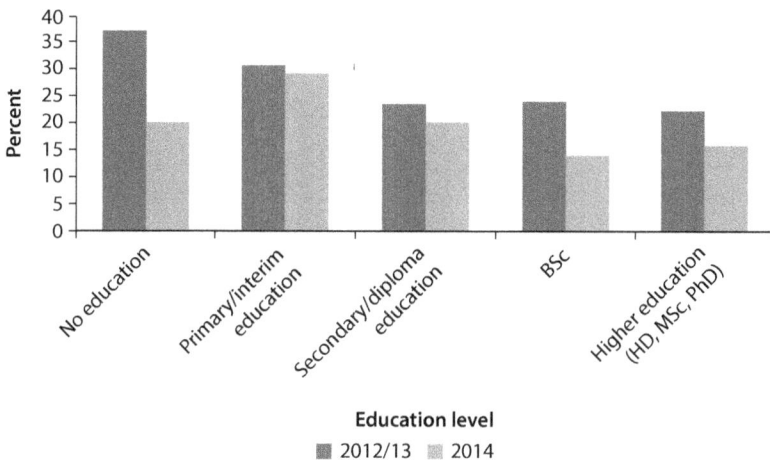

Source: Based on data from the 2012/13 and 2014 U.K. Department for International Development Sudan Household Health Surveys.
Note: BSc = bachelor of science; HD = higher diploma; MSc = master of science; PhD = doctor of philosophy.

Figure 7.2 Share of Study Participants, by Reasons That FGM Should Continue

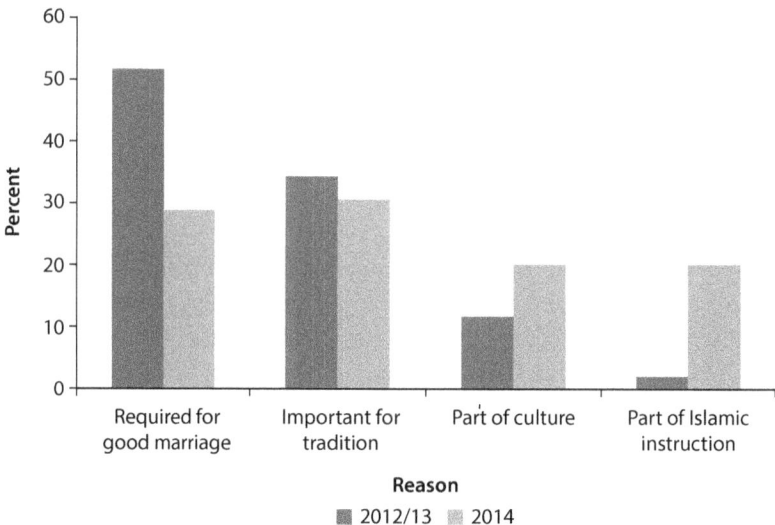

Source: Based on data from the 2012/13 and 2014 U.K. Department for International Development Sudan Household Health Surveys.

What is interesting about the distribution of support across the states is that the areas historically associated with FGM (in the North) are now less likely to support the practice. Although speculation on the underlying reasons for this shift is beyond the scope of this paper, given the better socioeconomic and political environment observed in these areas,

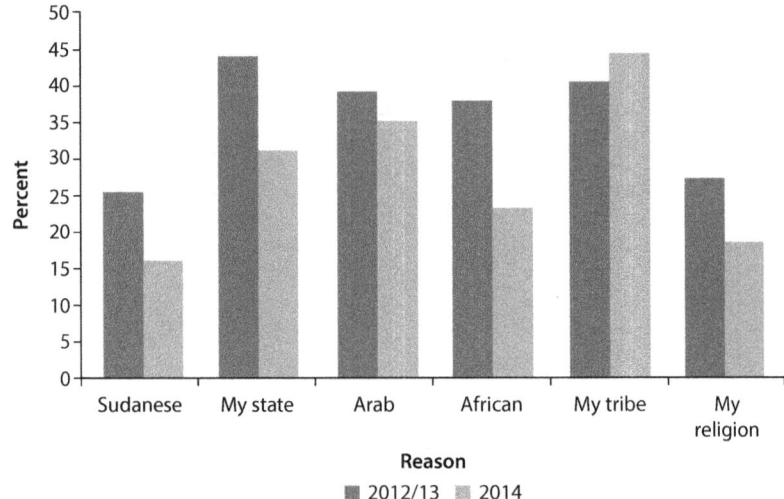

Figure 7.3 Proportion of Study Participants, by Self-Perceived Identity

Source: Based on data from the 2012/13 and 2014 U.K. Department for International Development Sudan Household Health Surveys.

the shift possibly may be associated with the fact that these areas are powerful politically and therefore enjoy higher socioeconomic development (factors associated with a decreasing rate of FGM support). Indeed, the statistically significant factors associated with pro-FGM were people having trust in local government compared to the federal government.

Regression Analysis Results

Unadjusted and fully adjusted marginal odds ratios (ORs) are presented in table 7.3. Factors that helped explain (unadjusted analysis) a positive attitude for the continuation of FGM (pro-FGM) in the 2012/13 survey were being married (OR = 1.31, 95 percent confidence interval [CI] = 1.09–1.59); having no education (OR = 2.06, 95 percent CI = 1.26–3.37) compared to people with higher education (master of science [MSc] and doctor of philosophy [PhD]); having a household income of < SDG 100 (OR = 1.60, 95 percent CI = 1.27–2.02) compared to people with a household income of SDG 501–SDG 1,000; having a small-size family of 1–4 children (OR = 1.32, 95 percent CI = 1.07–1.64) compared to a large-size family of 8+ children versus middle-size families of 5–7 children; having a place of residence in a rural area versus an urban area (OR = 1.46, 95 percent CI = 1.20–1.79); having trust in the imam, having trust in federal government, being able to make a choice about their own future, having trust in local government, having trust in the judiciary system, and being able to hold decision makers to account, as well as self-identity and state of residence.

After adjusting for all other factors (adjusted model), we found that the likelihood of people with only primary or interim education being pro-FGM became

Table 7.3 Unadjusted and Fully Adjusted Odds Ratios of Intent to Continue FGM across Selected Covariates

Variable	2012/13		2014	
	Unadjusted OR & 95%CI[a]	Fully adjusted OR & 95% CI[b]	Unadjusted OR & 95% CI[a]	Fully adjusted OR & 95% CI[b]
Age				
<25 years	1.00	1.00	1.13(0.83, 1.55)	1.49(0.87, 2.55)
25–30 years	1.24(0.97, 1.58)	1.50(0.99, 2.25)	1.06(0.80, 1.41)	1.41(0.92, 2.18)
36–50 years	1.13(0.87, 1.46)	1.27(0.78, 2.06)	1.00	1.00
>50 years	1.17(0.86, 1.59)	0.90(0.50, 1.62)	1.23(0.87, 1.73)	1.11(0.65, 1.89)
Gender				
Female	1.20(0.99, 1.44)	0.97(0.71, 1.32)	0.96(0.78, 1.20)	1.03(0.73, 1.44)
Male	1.00	1.00	1.00	1.00
Marriage				
Yes	1.31(1.09, 1.59)	1.15(0.80, 1.66)	1.24(0.98, 1.56)	1.44(0.94, 2.21)
No	1.00	1.00	1.00	1.00
Education (%)				
No education	2.06(1.26, 3.37)	1.97(0.86, 4.50)	1.55(1.00, 2.39)	0.70(0.30, 1.63)
Primary/interim education	1.55(0.96, 2.49)	1.65(0.78, 3.49)	2.54(1.86, 3.47)	1.95(1.18, 3.22)
Secondary education/diploma	1.08(0.68, 1.71)	1.12(0.55, 2.27)	1.53(1.15, 2.02)	1.31(0.87, 1.98)
BSc	1.10(0.68, 1.79)	1.24(0.60, 2.54)	1.00	1.00
Higher educ. (higher diploma, MSc, PhD)	1.00	1.00	1.16(0.80, 1.68)	0.74(0.42, 1.32)
Household income				
<100 SDG	1.60(1.27, 2.02)	1.30(0.88, 1.91)	2.78(2.00, 3.86)	1.41(0.87, 2.28)
100–500 SDG	1.00	1.00	1.09(0.77, 1.55)	1.12(0.69, 1.81)
501–1000 SDG	1.18(0.88, 1.57)	1.33(0.86, 2.06)	1.00	1.00
1001–2000 SDG			1.46(0.85, 2.51)	1.34(0.64, 2.82)
2001–3000 SDG			1.44(0.77, 2.69)	0.83(0.25, 2.72)
Family size				
Small (1–4 children)	1.32(1.07, 1.64)	0.99(0.69, 1.41)	1.00	1.00
Middle (5–7 children)	1.00	1.00	1.29(1.01, 1.65)	0.94(0.63, 1.39)
Large (8+ children)	1.14(0.80, 1.62)	1.02(0.57, 1.84)	2.02(1.51, 2.70)	1.61(1.00, 2.61)
Place of residence (%)				
Urban	1.00	1.00	1.00	1.00
Rural	1.46(1.20, 1.79)	1.04(0.73, 1.48)	1.43(1.13, 1.81)	1.12(0.77, 1.63)
Trust in the tribal leader				
A lot	1.14(0.86, 1.50)	1.00(0.66, 1.52)	1.99(1.47, 2.70)	1.52(0.96, 2.42)
Some	1.08(0.81, 1.44)	1.02(0.66, 1.58)	1.00	1.00
A little	1.00	1.00	1.80(1.27, 2.57)	1.62(0.96, 2.71)
Not at all			1.30(0.90, 1.89)	1.25(0.71, 2.21)
Trust in Imam				
A lot	2.13(1.41, 3.21)	1.45(0.69, 3.07)	1.00	1.00
Some	1.63(1.01, 2.55)	1.28(0.58, 2.86)	1.15(0.85, 1.57)	0.68(0.41, 1.15)
A little	1.83(1.11, 3.00)	1.86(0.78, 4.47)	1.95(1.31, 2.90)	1.04(0.52, 2.06)
Not at all	1.00	1.00	2.04(1.40, 2.98)	1.00(0.47, 2.12)

table continues next page

Table 7.3 Unadjusted and Fully Adjusted Odds Ratios of Intent to Continue FGM across Selected Covariates (continued)

	2012/13		2014	
Variable	Unadjusted OR & 95%CI[a]	Fully adjusted OR & 95% CI[b]	Unadjusted OR & 95% CI[a]	Fully adjusted OR & 95% CI[b]
Trust in the federal government				
A lot	1.69(1.25, 2.28)	0.94(0.54, 1.63)	1.42(1.02, 1.97)	1.54(0.90, 2.63)
Some	1.27(0.97, 1.66)	1.32(0.82, 2.12)	1.00	1.00
A little	1.10(0.83, 1.45)	0.97(0.60, 1.57)	1.62(1.17, 2.23)	1.12(0.68, 1.85)
Not at all	1.00	1.00	1.19(0.85, 1.66)	1.22(0.67, 2.22)
Trust in the local government				
A lot	1.77(1.29, 2.43)	1.55(0.90, 2.66)	1.30(0.93, 1.81)	1.91(0.99, 3.68)
Some	1.41(1.09, 1.84)	1.64(1.05, 2.57)	1.01(0.73, 1.41)	2.00(1.09, 3.67)
A little	1.33(1.02, 1.74)	1 51(0.96, 2.39)	1.50(1.10, 2.06)	2.07(1.17, 3.65)
Not at all	1.00	1.00	1.00	1.00
Trust in the police				
A lot	1.79(1.39, 2.30)	1.70(1.12, 2.57)	1.00	1.00
Some	1.00	1.00	0.84(0.63, 1.11)	1.16(0.72, 1.87)
A little	1.16(0.89, 1.50)	1.25(0.82, 1.93)	1.25(0.92, 1.70)	1.02(0.58, 1.79)
Not at all	1.07(0.80, 1.43)	1.64(0.97, 2.77)	1.07(0.76, 1.50)	0.96(0.51, 1.81)
Trust in the judiciary system				
A lot	1.44(1.05, 1.99)	1.14(0 64, 2.05)	1.00	1.00
Some	1.24(0.92, 1.69)	1.35(0.78, 2.32)	1.41(1.07, 1.85)	0.92(0.57, 1.48)
A little	1.31(0.94, 1.83)	1.28(0.73, 2.27)	1.10(0.80, 1.53)	0.64(0.37, 1.10)
Not at all	1.00	1.00	1.40(0.98, 2.01)	1.51(0.81, 2.84)
Islamic law				
Should be at the heart of the constitution	1.34(1.10, 1.63)	0.90(0.66, 1.25)	0.84(0.63, 1.12)	0.75(0.50, 1.13)
Should be part of the constitution	1.00	1.00	1.00	1.00
Choice about my future				
A lot	1.88(1.43, 2.48)	0.86(0.53, 1.38)	1.09(0.82, 1.45)	1.05(0.69, 1.61)
Some	1.13(0.83, 1.54)	0.74(0.44, 1.23)	1.00	1.00
A little	1.00	1.00	1.09(0.78, 1.54)	0.68(0.40, 1.17)
Not at all	1.20(0.85, 1.71)	0.88(0.48, 1.62)	1.15(0.79, 1.66)	1.53(0.81, 2.88)
Identity				
Sudanese	1.00	1.00	1.00	1.00
My state	2.27(1.27, 4.06)	2.20(0.84, 5.77)	2.35(1.10, 5.01)	1.83(0.56, 5.93)
Arab	1.89(0.88, 4.06)	1.26(0.29, 5.41)	2.79(1.41, 5.56)	2.57(0.69, 9.56)
African	1.77(0.96, 3.27)	2.91(1.17, 7.26)	1.57(0.67, 3.70)	0.78(0.20, 3.02)
My tribe	1.99(1.32, 3.01)	1.39(0.68, 2.81)	4.13(2.67, 6.38)	3.10(1.57, 6.14)
My religious affiliation	1.10(0.77, 1.56)	0.89(0.52, 1.53)	1.18(0.85, 1.64)	1.35(0.81, 2.26)
Hold decision makers to account				
A lot	2.26(1.73, 2.97)	1.49(0.94, 2 35)	1.34(0.98, 1.82)	1.06(0.65, 1.74)
Some	1.82(1.38, 2.39)	1.41(0.90, 2.20)	1.40(1.03, 1.91)	1.40(0.87, 2.26)

table continues next page

Table 7.3 Unadjusted and Fully Adjusted Odds Ratios of Intent to Continue FGM across Selected Covariates *(continued)*

	2012/13		2014	
Variable	Unadjusted OR & 95%CI[a]	Fully adjusted OR & 95% CI[b]	Unadjusted OR & 95% CI[a]	Fully adjusted OR & 95% CI[b]
A little	1.16(0.86, 1.58)	1.26(0.80, 2.01)	1.58(1.14, 2.18)	1.42(0.88, 2.29)
Not at all	1.00	1.00	1.00	1.00
If election held would vote				
Yes	0.70(0.56, 0.88)	0.67(0.45, 1.01)	0.82(0.64, 1.03)	0.76(0.51, 1.13)
No	1.00	1.00	1.00	1.00
State of residence (%)				
Al Qadarif	4.03(2.06, 7.88)	1.68(0.62, 4.56)	0.35(0.12, 1.03)	0.11(0.02, 0.57)
Al Jazirah	1.89(0.94, 3.82)	1.64(0.64, 4.21)	0.78(0.34, 1.79)	0.57(0.17, 1.86)
Blue Nile	6.41(3.32, 12.4)	2.00(0.77, 5.22)	2.23(1.04, 4.80)	0.99(0.35, 2.76)
Kassala	1.00	1.00	1.00	1.00
Khartoum	1.18(0.58, 2.42)	1.18(0.42, 3.34)	1.83(0.92, 3.64)	0.88(0.33, 2.38)
North Darfur	6.60(3.23, 13.5)	3.53(1.15, 10.8)	2.63(1.18, 5.86)	1.35(0.47, 3.93)
North Kurdufan	2.38(1.18, 4.82)	1.64(0.51, 5.32)	3.73(1.86, 7.47)	1.08(0.39, 2.95)
Northern	1.41(0.67, 2.97)	1.11(0.31, 3.97)	0.13(0.03, 0.61)	0.05(0.01, 0.28)
Red Sea	8.19(4.25, 15.8)	6.00(2.05, 17.6)	2.19(1.06, 4.53)	0.98(0.38, 2.51)
River Nile	4.28(2.19, 8.38)	3.19(1.09, 9.38)	1.21(0.55, 2.66)	0.47(0.16, 1.37)
Sennar	8.15(4.23, 15.7)	6.00(2.56, 14.1)	1.03(0.46, 2.31)	0 24(0.07, 0.81)
South Darfur	2.42(1.23, 4.74)	2.30(0.92, 5.74)	12.3(6.33, 23.8)	7.93(2.98, 21.1)
South Kurdufan	4.46(2.25, 8.86)	4.36(1.57, 12.2)	2.44(1.19, 5.00)	1.00(0.36, 2.79)
West Darfur	2.99(1.49, 5.99)	1.58(0.58,4.32)	3.00(1.43, 6.27)	1.71(0.61, 4.84)
White Nile	9.36(4.85, 18.0)	7.14(3.04, 16.8)	4.61(2.31, 9.18)	1.56(0.54, 4.45)

Source: Based on data from the 2012/13 and 2014 U.K. Department for International Development Sudan Household Health Surveys.
Note: BSc = bachelor of science; CI = confidence interval; FGM = female genital mutilation; MSc = master of science; N = number; OR = odds ratio; PhD = doctor of philosophy; SDG = Sudanese pound.
a. Unadjusted marginal odds ratio (OR) from standard logistic regression models.
b. Adjusted marginal odds ratio (OR) from standard logistic regression models.

statistically insignificant. The effect disappeared also for those in a large family; the statistically significant effect remained only for people with some trust in local government. They were 1.64 times more likely to be pro-FGM than people with no trust at all (95 percent CI = 1.05–2.57); people with a lot of trust in the police were 1.70 times more likely to be pro-FGM (95 percent CI = 1.12–2.57) than people with some trust in the police; and people who identified as African were 2.91 times more likely to be associated with pro-FGM than people who identified as Sudanese (95 percent CI = 1.17–7.26).

In the 2012/13 survey, pro-FGM respondents were least likely to be living in Northern state and most likely to be living in White Nile (OR = 7.14, 95 percent CI = 3.04–16.8), in Sennar (OR = 6.00, 95 percent CI = 2.56–14.1), and in Red Sea (OR = 6.00, 95 percent CI = 2.05–17.6).

In the 2014 survey, factors associated with pro-FGM attitude in the unadjusted analysis were having no education (OR = 1.55, 95 percent

CI = 1.00–2.39), having primary or interim education (OR = 2.54, 95 percent CI = 1.86–3.47), and having secondary education/diploma versus people with MSc and PhD (OR = 1.53, 95 percent CI = 1.15–2.02); having a household income of < SDG 100 (OR = 2.78, 95 percent CI = 2.00–3.86) versus a household income of SDG 501–SDG 1,000; having a middle-size family of 5–7 children (OR = 1.29, 95 percent CI = 1.01–1.65) and having a large-size family of 8+ children versus having a small-size family of 1–4 children (OR = 2.02, 95 percent CI = 1.51–2.70); having a place of residence in a rural area versus an urban area (OR = 1.43, 95 percent CI = 1.13–1.81); having trust in the tribal leader; having trust in the imam; having trust in federal government; having trust in local government; having trust in the judiciary system; and being able to hold decision makers to account, as well as self-identity and respondent's state of residence.

After adjusting for all other factors, we found the likelihood of being pro-FGM in people with only primary or interim education was almost twice that of people with a bachelor of science (OR = 1.95, 95 percent CI = 1.18–3.22). People from large families (8 children or more) were 1.61 times more likely to be pro-FGM than people from small families (1–4 children) (OR = 1.61, 95 percent CI = 1.00–2.61). People with little trust in local government were 2.07 times more likely to be pro-FGM than people with no trust at all (95 percent CI = 1.17–3.65). People who identified with their tribe were 3.10 times more likely to be associated with pro-FGM than people who identified as Sudanese (95 percent CI = 1.57–6.14). Pro-FGM people were least likely to live in Northern state and most likely to live in West Darfur (OR = 1.71, 95 percent CI = 0.61–4.84), White Nile (OR = 1.56, 95 percent CI = 0.54–4.45), or North Darfur (OR = 1.35, 95 percent CI = 0.47–3.93).

Results of a Shift in Pro-FGM Attitude at State Level during the Three-Year Period

Monitoring pro-FGM respondents using national proportions can mask within-country variability and thereby lead to the design and implementation of generic policies and interventions that may have limited effect at the local level. The national pro-FGM percentage shown in the DFID Sudan Household Health Surveys data sets conceals important spatial variation at the state level from 2012/13 to 2014. For example, in the 2014 data set, the national percentage of pro-FGM respondents was 18.3 percent but ranged from 1.3 percent (Northern state) to 55.3 percent (South Darfur). Between 2012/13 and 2014, although the national percentage of pro-FGM respondents decreased dramatically, South Darfur state moved from being a lower-prevalence area in 2012/13 (20.1 percent) to a higher-prevalence area in 2014 (55.3 percent). The state of Sennar went from the highest-prevalence area in 2012/13 (45.9 percent) to a lower-prevalence area in 2014 (9.4 percent). The proportion of pro-FGM respondents remains stable at a lower level during the same period in states such as Kassala and Khartoum.

Unadjusted marginal odds ratios indicate that in 2012/13, the highest pro-FGM attitude was in White Nile (OR = 9.36, 95 percent CI =

4.85–18.0), Red Sea (OR = 8.19, 95 percent CI = 4.25–15.8), and Sennar (OR = 8.15, 95 percent CI = 4.23–15.7), followed by North Darfur, Blue Nile, South Kurdufan, River Nile, Al Qadarif, West Darfur, South Darfur, and North Kurdufan, with the lowest percentages in Kassala, Khartoum, and Al Jazirah. In 2014, the highest percentages were in South Darfur (OR = 12.3, 95 percent CI = 6.33–23.8) and White Nile (OR = 4.61, 95 percent CI = 2.31–9.18), followed by North Kurdufan, West Darfur, North Darfur, South Kurdufan, Blue Nile, and Red Sea, and the lowest percentage was again in Al Qadarif, Al Jazirah, and Kassala. Khartoum state, a highly urbanized area, was among the lowest-percentage states in both 2012/13 and 2014. The underlying reasons of this shift in pro-FGM attitude are unclear. However, in recent decades, South Darfur has received increased attention owing to the conflict, and there has been an influx of NGOs in this area working with the local population on various aspects of improving their well-being.

The pattern of shifts in pro-FGM attitude by state differed markedly between the two surveys, though there was a consistently higher proportion of pro-FGM attitude in South Darfur and a lower proportion in Khartoum state (maps 7.1a, 7.1b, 7.2, and 7.3). The observed proportion of pro-FGM attitude at the state level shown in table 7.2 (see also map 7.1a, 7.1b) indicates that the states in which the proportion of pro-FGM attitude is lowest and below the national average in both surveys are Kassala, Northern state, and Khartoum. In 2012/13, states in which the proportion of pro-FGM attitude are higher than the national average are Al Qadarif, Blue Nile, North Darfur, Red Sea, River Nile, Sennar, South Kurdufan, and White Nile. In 2014, the states with a higher proportion of pro-FGM attitude than the national average are North Darfur, South Darfur, North Kurdufan, South Kurdufan, West Darfur, and White Nile. White Nile and Sennar are no longer among the states with the highest marginal odds ratios, which in 2014 is only South Darfur.

Bayesian Spatial Regression Analysis Results

Maps 7.2–7.5 show the adjusted residual spatial effects of pro-FGM attitude, that is, the spatial effects that have not been explained by the survey's characteristics and that have not been explained by fixed effect variables such as income and education level after multiple adjustments of individual, household, and community and state factors. The total residual spatial effects in maps 7.2 and 7.4 were allocated to structured neighboring and global effects and unstructured localized spatial effects. Overall, socioeconomic and cultural factors are able to explain a fair amount of the spatial variation of pro-FGM attitude in the two data sets. We also calculated that the average residual spatial effects in maps 7.2a and 7.4a are about 20–30 percent lower than the original observed spatial effects plotted in map 7.1, showing that the socioeconomic effects explain some but not all of the spatial variation.

However, the total spatial residuals of maps 7.2 and 7.4 show that much of the variation in pro-FGM attitude is as yet unexplained. These spatial effects are then allocated by the model into structured effects (maps 7.3a and 7.5a) and unstructured residual effects (maps 7.3b and 7.5b).

Several important findings emerge. First, many of these total residual spatial effects are significant as indicated by the probability map (maps 7.3a and 7.5a). Map 7.2b shows the posterior probability maps of pro-FGM attitude at a 95 percent confidence interval. The states in black indicate a significant positive spatial effect (higher pro-FGM attitude), while the states in white imply a significant negative spatial effect associated with lower pro-FGM attitude. The rest of the states (in gray) have no significant effect on pro-FGM attitude. Thus we clearly see a pattern of higher pro-FGM attitude in the eastern states of Sudan in 2012/13 and the southern state of South Darfur and the southeastern state of White Nile in 2014.

Second, and conversely, pro-FGM attitude was significantly less in Kassala state in 2012/13 and Northern, River Nile, and Kassala states in 2014. Second, although these structured effects suggest higher pro-FGM attitude in 2012/13 in

Map 7.1 The Observed Proportion of People with Positive Attitudes Surrounding FGM Continuation (Pro-FGM), by State

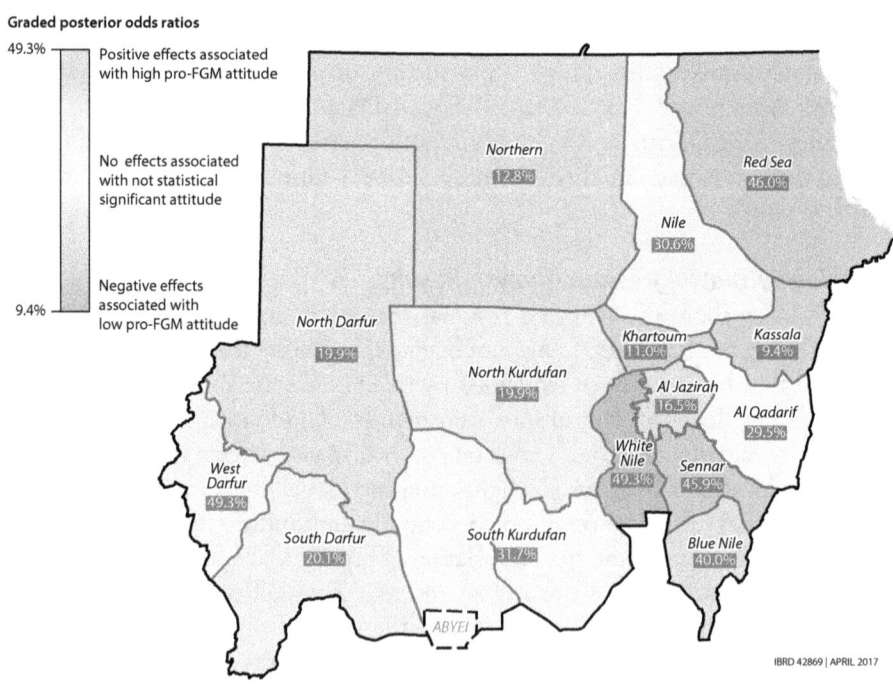

map continues next page

Map 7.1 The Observed Proportion of People with Positive Attitudes Surrounding FGM Continuation (Pro-FGM), by State *(continued)*

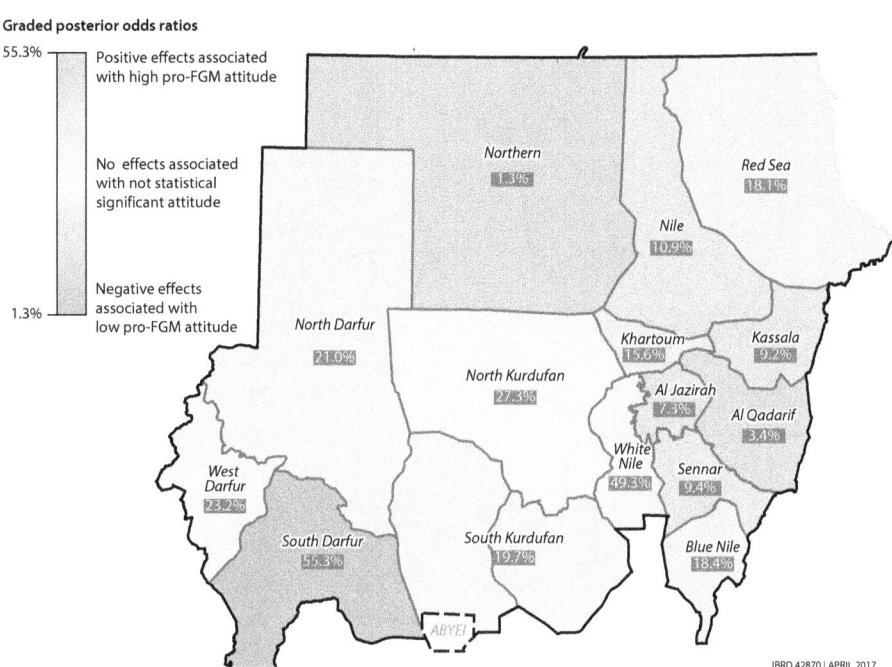

b. DFID Sudan Household Survey Data, 2014

Source: Based on data from the 2012/13 and 2014 U.K. Department for International Development Sudan Household Health Surveys.
Note: DFID = U.K. Department for International Development; FGM = female genital mutilation.

a belt ranging from northeastern (Red Sea) to southeastern states, the districts in northern Sudan are not significant components in that belt. Thus, whereas some spatial residuals do spill significantly across borders, between South and West Kurdufan states for example, some borders do seem to matter in the sense that spatial residuals remain noticeably distinct in the analysis of the two sides of the border.

Third, the unstructured spatial effects shown in maps 7.3b and 7.5b, while being much smaller and not significant, also display an interesting pattern. Although in 2012/13, South Darfur had significantly lower pro-FGM attitude, this was not the case in 2014, which showed a significant increase. This increase may be related to the effect of the decline in government control of this part of the country owing to the ongoing unrest and the effect of the conflict on social norms by increasing circumstances of extreme resource inequality (Macro International 1997).

Map 7.2 Adjusted Total Residual Spatial Effects of Positive Attitudes Surrounding FGM Continuation (Pro-FGM), State Level, 2012/13

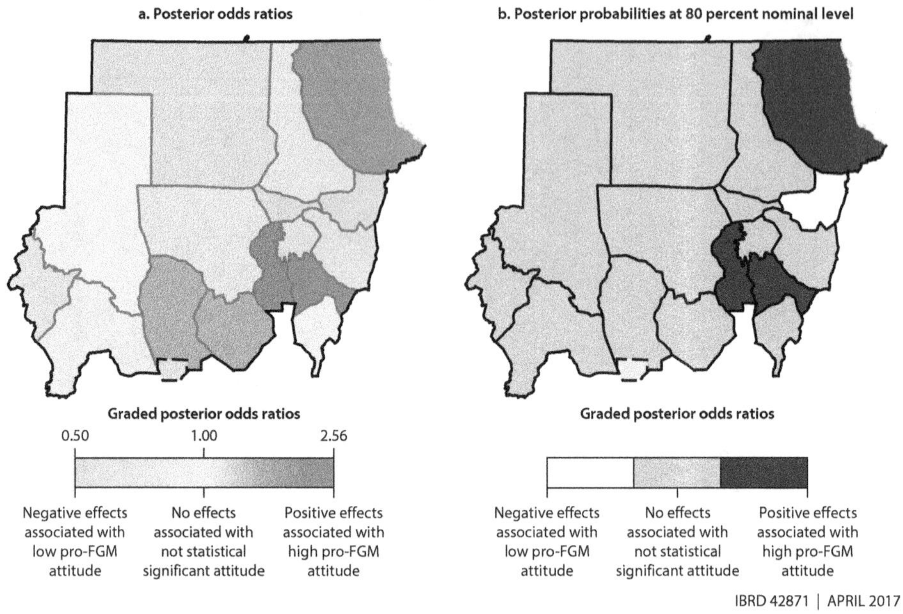

a. Posterior odds ratios

b. Posterior probabilities at 80 percent nominal level

Graded posterior odds ratios

0.50   1.00   2.56

Negative effects associated with low pro-FGM attitude | No effects associated with not statistical significant attitude | Positive effects associated with high pro-FGM attitude

Graded posterior odds ratios

Negative effects associated with low pro-FGM attitude | No effects associated with not statistical significant attitude | Positive effects associated with high pro-FGM attitude

IBRD 42871 | APRIL 2017

Source: Based on data from the 2012/13 U.K. Department for International Development Sudan Household Health Surveys.
Note: FGM = female genital mutilation.

Map 7.3 Spatial Residual Effects of Positive Attitudes Surrounding FGM Continuation (Pro-FGM), State Level, 2012/13

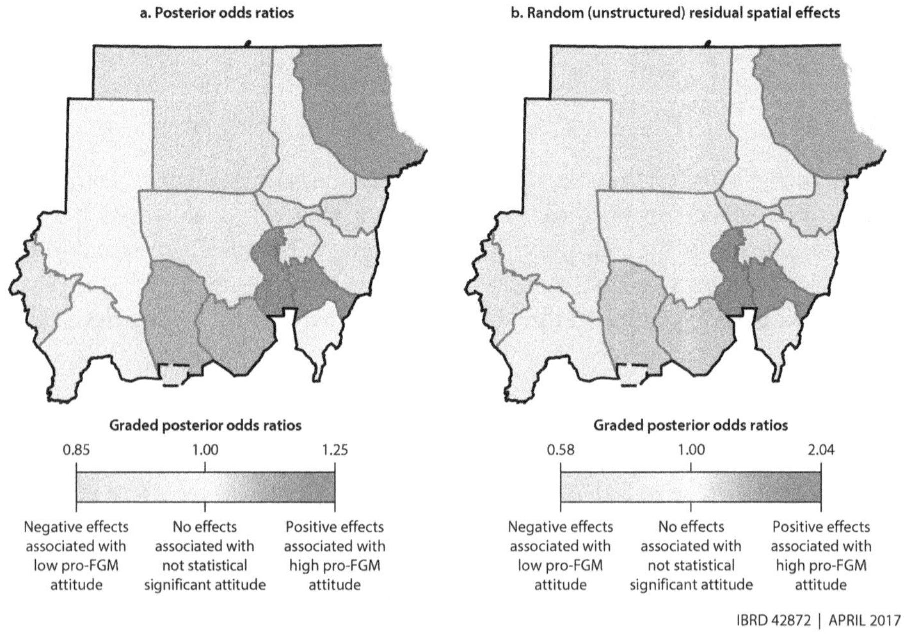

a. Posterior odds ratios

b. Random (unstructured) residual spatial effects

Graded posterior odds ratios

0.85   1.00   1.25

Negative effects associated with low pro-FGM attitude | No effects associated with not statistical significant attitude | Positive effects associated with high pro-FGM attitude

Graded posterior odds ratios

0.58   1.00   2.04

Negative effects associated with low pro-FGM attitude | No effects associated with not statistical significant attitude | Positive effects associated with high pro-FGM attitude

IBRD 42872 | APRIL 2017

Source: Based on data from the 2012/13 U.K. Department for International Development Sudan Household Health Surveys.
Note: FGM = female genital mutilation.

Geography and Correlates of Attitudes toward Female Genital Mutilation in Sudan   141

Map 7.4 Adjusted Total Residual Spatial Effects of Positive Attitudes Surrounding FGM Continuation (Pro-FGM), State Level, 2014

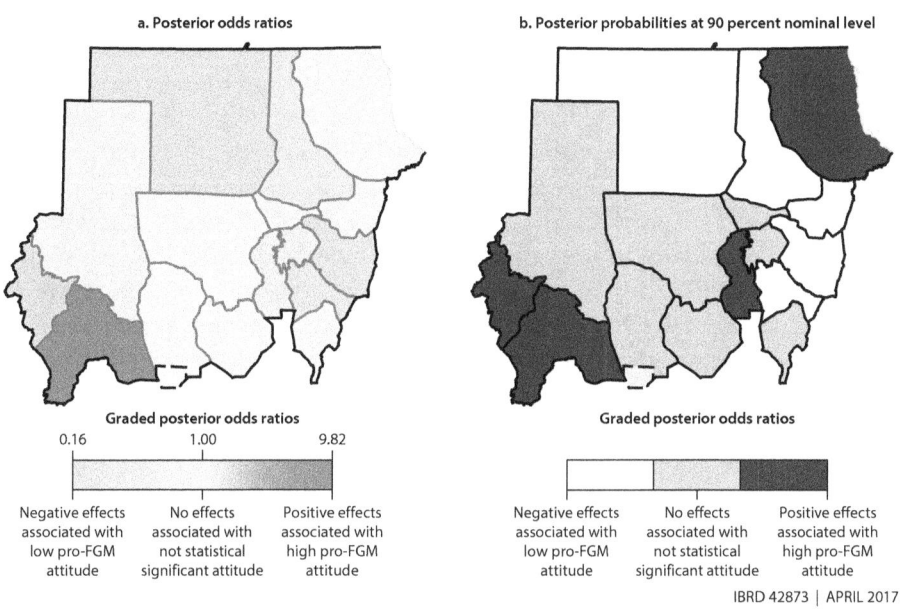

Source: Based on data from the 2014 U.K. Department for International Development Sudan Household Health Surveys.
Note: FGM = female genital mutilation.

Map 7.5 Spatial Residual Effects of Positive Attitudes Surrounding FGM Continuation (Pro-FGM), State Level, 2014

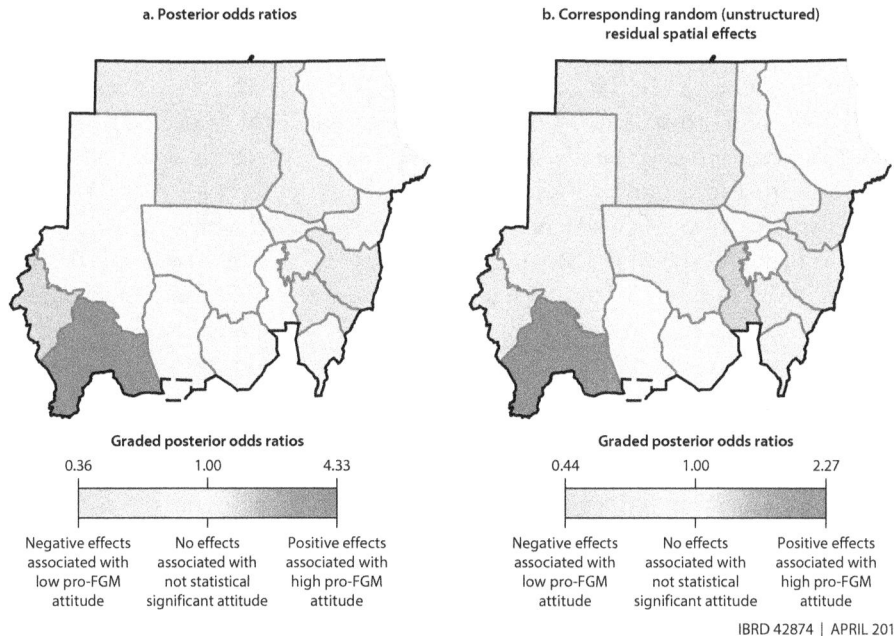

Source: Based on data from the 2014 U.K. Department for International Development Sudan Household Health Surveys.
Note: FGM = female genital mutilation.

Data-Driven Decision Making in Fragile Contexts: Evidence from Sudan
http://dx.doi.org/10.1596/978-1-4648-1064-0

The clear structured pattern demands an explanation. None of the socioeconomic and cultural variables we tried in addition to the ones mentioned were able to reduce these pronounced spatial effects. One common factor to most of the states that have lower pro-FGM attitude is the higher prevalence of FGM. This distinction is most noticeable and clear in the state of Kassala, but it is also noticeable elsewhere. The difference could well be due to differences in educational and abandonment programs and other religious and cultural factors that have a spatial structure and were not measured in the two surveys. In an exploratory analysis, we compared the spatial pattern of FGM prevalence with the structured spatial pattern of the pro-FGM attitudes and found that the spatial distribution of FGM (results not shown here) has a fairly close resemblance to the structured spatial effects, whereas the others did not appear to play a significant role. Future research should explore this link further.

In multivariable Bayesian geo-additive regression analyses, the fixed effects factors that were consistently associated with higher pro-FGM attitude in both samples are no education (POR = 2.15, 95 percent credible region (CR) = 1.03–3.80) in 2012/13 and primary or interim education (POR = 2.07, 95 percent CR = 1.29–3.18) in 2014 (figures 7.4 and 7.5); some trust in local government (POR = 1.59, 95 percent CR = 1.05–2.64) in 2014 or little trust in local government (POR = 1.47, 95 percent CR = 1.03–2.03) in 2012/13 and little trust in local government in 2014 (POR = 2.10, 95 percent CR = 1.03–4.04) (figures 7.6 and 7.7); African identity (POR = 3.16, 95 percent CR = 1.24–6.48) in 2012/13 and tribal identity (POR = 3.23, 95 percent CR = 1.75–6.34) in 2014 (figures 7.8 and 7.9); and state of residence of Sennar, Red Sea, and White Nile in 2012/13 and South Darfur, West Darfur, and White Nile in 2014.

Other factors associated with higher pro-FGM attitude in each sample were, in 2012/13, household income (SDG 501–SDG 1,000) (POR = 1.43, 95 percent CR = 1.03–2.36) and a lot of trust in police (POR = 1.71, 95 percent CR = 1.11–2.47) or no trust at all (POR = 1.67, 95 percent CR = 1.00–2.89). In 2014, those factors were large family size (POR = 1.72, 95 percent CR = 1.19–2.78) and little trust in the tribal leader (POR = 1.73, 95 percent CR = 1.05–2.80). People willing to vote in a general election were associated with a reduced likelihood of being pro-FGM (POR = 0.65, 95 percent CR = 0.46–0.89) in 2012/13.

Results of both multivariate standard logistic regression and multivariate Bayesian geo-additive analyses displayed in table 7.4 support the role of lack of education, family size, trust in the local government, self-identity, willingness to vote in a general election, and residence in certain states as associated risk factors for pro-FGM attitude in both data sets. The association between urban–rural residence and pro-FGM attitude risk was not statistically significant. Perhaps the effect of urban–rural residence has been attenuated by the geographic location and accounted for as spatial effects.

Age of the respondent at the time of interview (as a continuous variable using a flexible nonlinear curve in figure 7.10) and state of residence (as a spatial variable in maps 7.2–7.5) remained significant risk factors in both surveys. Overall, results of the 2012/13 DFID Sudan Household Health Survey (map 7.2)

Geography and Correlates of Attitudes toward Female Genital Mutilation in Sudan 143

Figure 7.4 Likelihood of Pro-FGM Attitude, by Educational Attainments, 2012/13

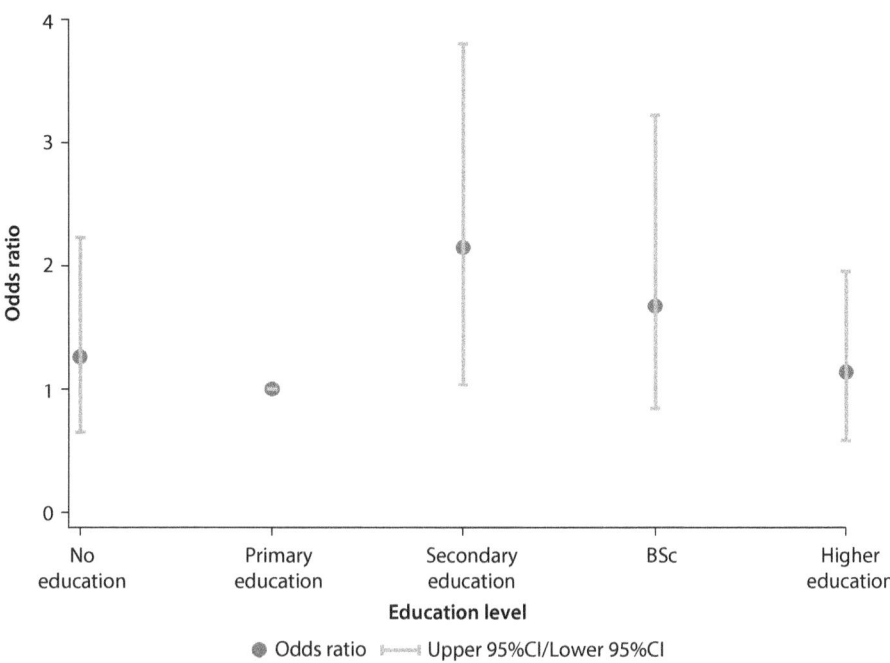

Source: Based on data from the 2012/13 U.K. Department for International Development Sudan Household Health Surveys.
Note: BSc = bachelor of science; CI = confidence interval.

Figure 7.5 Likelihood of Pro-FGM Attitude, by Educational Attainments, 2014

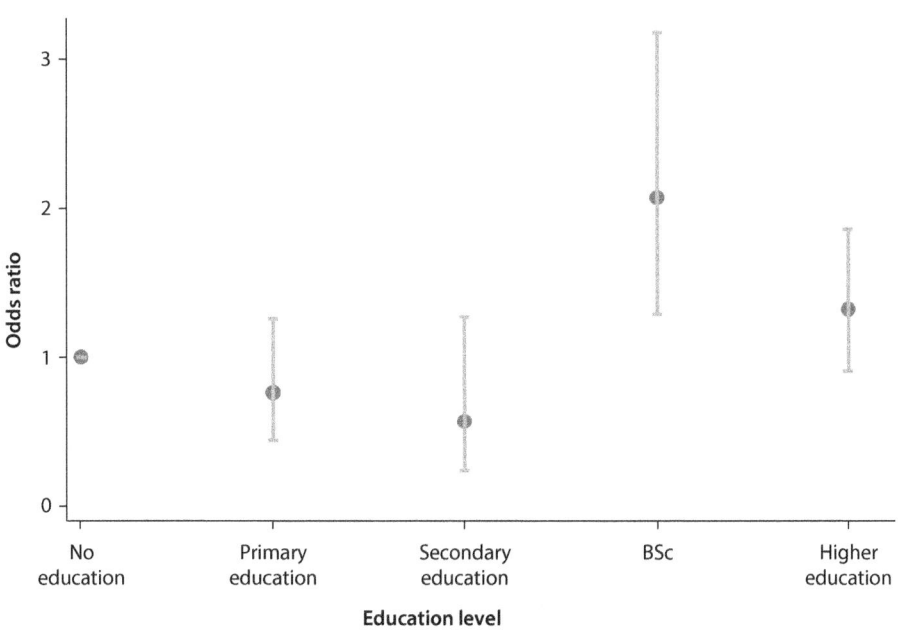

Source: Based on data from the 2014 U.K. Department for International Development Sudan Household Health Surveys.
Note: BSc = bachelor of science; CI = confidence interval.

Data Driven Decision Making in Fragile Contexts: Evidence from Sudan
http://dx.doi.org/10.1596/978-1-4648-1064-0

Figure 7.6 Likelihood of Pro-FGM Attitude, by Trust in Local Government, 2012/13

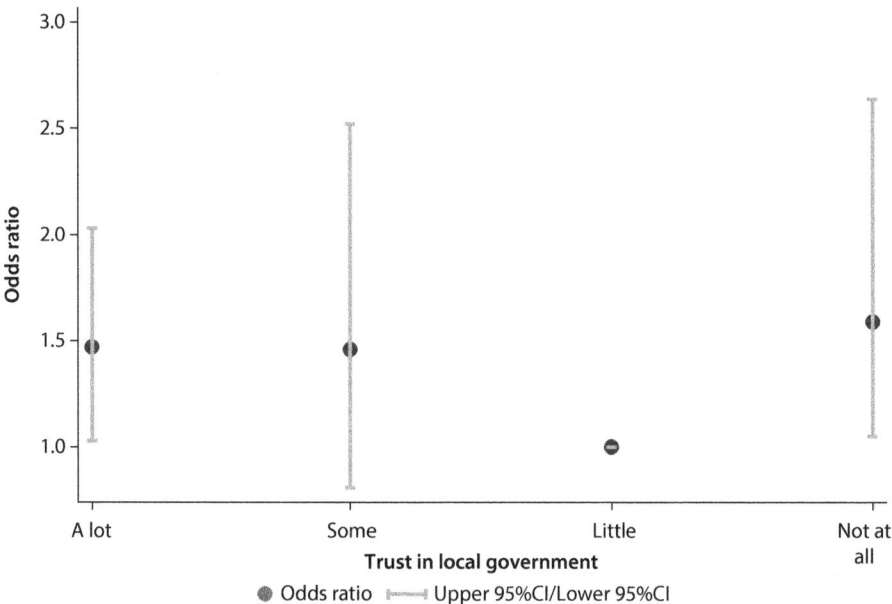

Source: Based on data from the 2012/13 U.K. Department for International Development Sudan Household Health Surveys.
Note: CI = confidence interval.

Figure 7.7 Likelihood of Pro-FGM Attitude, by Trust in Local Government, 2014

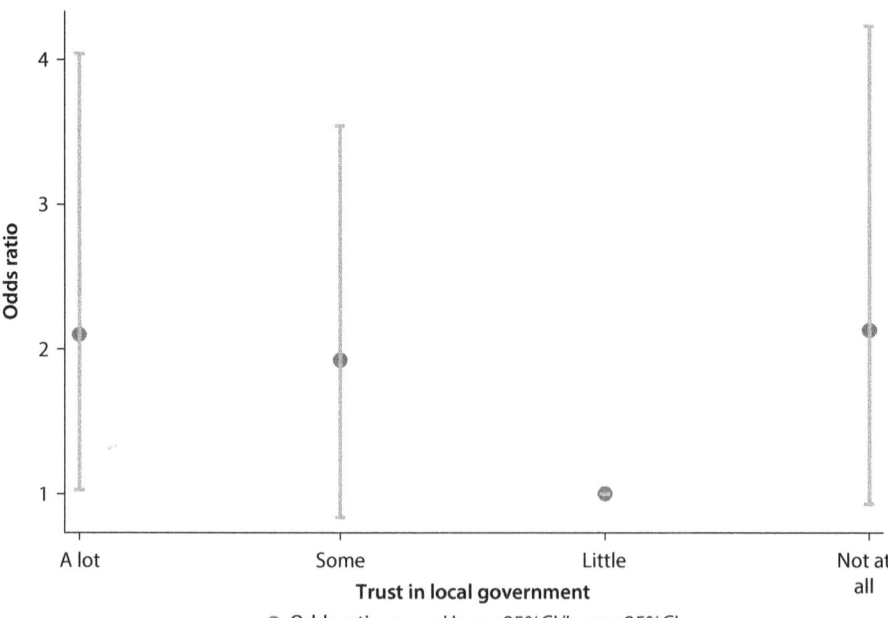

Source: Based on data from the 2014 U.K. Department for International Development Sudan Household Health Surveys.
Note: CI = confidence interval.

Figure 7.8 Likelihood of Pro-FGM Attitude, by Self-Perceived Identity, 2012/13

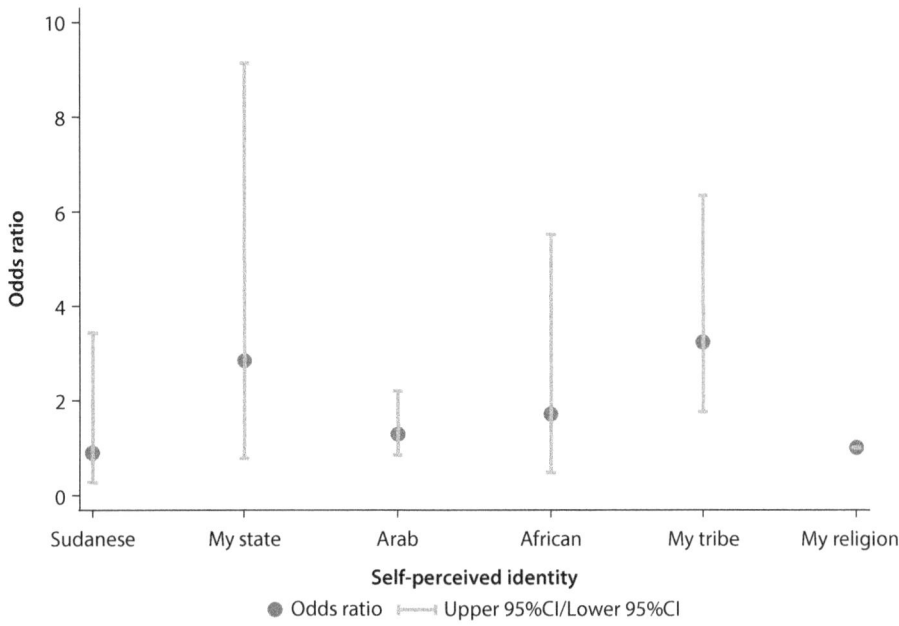

Source: Based on data from the 2012/13 U.K. Department for International Development Sudan Household Health Surveys.
Note: CI = confidence interval.

Figure 7.9 Likelihood of Pro-FGM Attitude, by Self-Perceived Identity, 2014

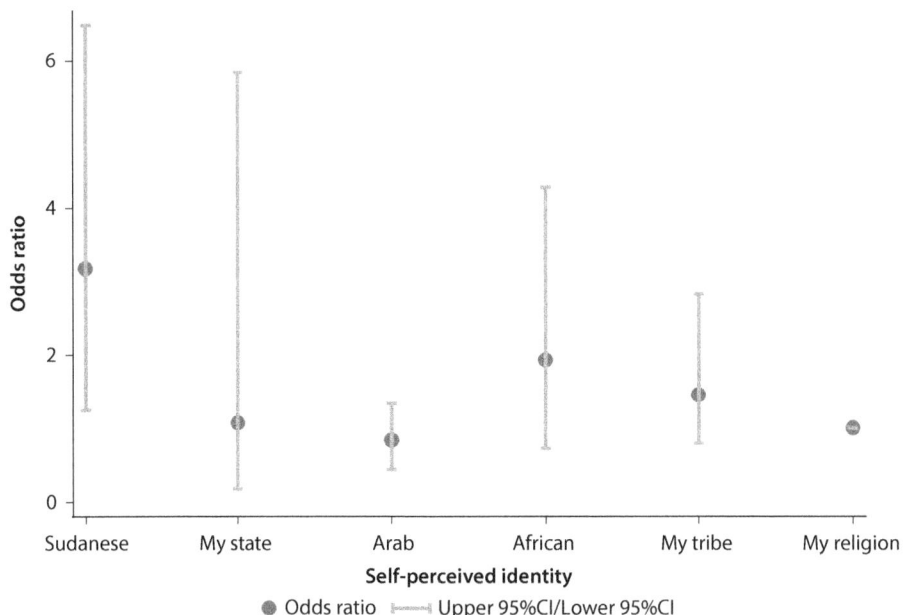

Source: Based on data from the 2014 U.K. Department for International Development Sudan Household Health Surveys.
Note: CI = confidence interval.

Table 7.4 Fully Adjusted and Bayesian Odds Ratios of Intent to Continue FGM across Selected Covariates

Variable	2012/13		2014	
	Fully adjusted OR & 95% CI[a]	Baycsian OR & 95% CI[b]	Fully adjusted OR & 95% CI[a]	Bayesian OR & 95% CI[b]
Age				
<25 years	1.00		1.49 (0.87, 2.55)	
25–30 years	1.50 (0.99, 2.25)		1.41 (0.92, 2.18)	
36–50 years	1.27 (0.78, 2.06)		1.00	
>50 years	0.90 (0.50, 1.62)		1.11 (0.65, 1.89)	
Gender				
Female	0.97 (0.71, 1.32)	0.94 (0.75, 1.27)	1.03 (0.73, 1.44)	1.00 (0.71, 1.33)
Male	1.00	1.00	1.00	1.00
Marriage				
Yes	1.15 (0 80, 1.66)	1.12 (0.85, 1.55)	1.44 (0.94, 2.21)	1.54 (0.95, 2.66)
No	1.00	1.00	1.00	1.00
Education (%)				
No education	1.97 (0.86, 4.50)	2.15 (1.03, 3.80)	0.70 (0.30, 1.63)	0.57 (0.24, 1.27)
Primary/interim education	1.65 (0.78, 3.49)	1.67 (0.84, 3.22)	1.95 (1.18, 3.22)	2.07 (1.29, 3.18)
Secondary education/diploma	1.12 (0 55, 2.27)	1.14 (0.58, 1.95)	1.31 (0.87, 1.98)	1.32 (0.91, 1.86)
BSc	1.24 (0.60, 2.54)	1.26 (0.65, 2.23)	1.00	1.00
Higher educ. (higher diploma, MSc, PhD)	1.00	1.00	0.74 (0.42, 1.32)	0.76 (0.44, 1.26)
Household income				
<100 SDG	1.30 (0.88, 1.91)	1.40 (0.97, 2.07)	1.41 (0.87, 2.28)	1.43 (0.90, 2.38)
100–500 SDG	1.00	1.00	1.12 (0.69, 1.81)	1.05 (0.59, 1.76)
501–1000 SDG	1.33 (0.86, 2.06)	1.43 (1.03, 2.36)	1.00	1.00
1001–2000 SDG			1.34 (0.64, 2.82)	1.22 (0.56, 2.61)
2001–3000 SDG			0.83 (0.25, 2.72)	0.73 (0.21, 1.87)
Family size				
Small (1–4 children)	0.99 (0.69, 1.41)	1.04 (0.71, 1.51)	1.00	1.00
Middle (5–7 children)	1.00	1.00	0.94 (0.63, 1.39)	1.01 (0.67, 1.46)
Large (8+ children)	1.02 (0.57, 1.84)	1.06 (0.65, 1.79)	1.61 (1.00, 2.61)	1.72 (1.19, 2.78)
Place of residence (%)				
Urban	1.00	1.00	1.00	1.00
Rural	1.04 (0.73, 1.48)	1.07 (0.74, 1.58)	1.12 (0.77, 1.63)	1.17 (0.84, 1.72)
Trust in the tribal leader				
A lot	1.00 (0.66, 1 52)	0.97 (0.66, 1.31)	1.52 (0.96, 2.42)	1.52 (0.85, 2.38)
Some	1.02 (0.66, 1.58)	1.03 (0.72, 1.44)	1.00	1.00
A little	1.00	1.00	1.62 (0.96, 2.74)	1.73 (1.05, 2.80)
Not at all			1.25 (0.71, 2.21)	1.25 (0.77, 2.11)
Trust in Imam				
A lot	1.45 (0.69, 3.07)	1.48 (0.81, 271)	1.00	1.00
Some	1.28 (0.58, 2.86)	1.27 (0.63, 254)	0.68 (0.41, 1.15)	0.72 (0.44, 1.12)
A little	1.86 (0.78, 447)	1.82 (0.81, 398)	1.04 (0.52, 2.06)	1.08 (0.57, 2.35)
Not at all	1.00	1.00	1.00 (0.47, 2.12)	1.07 (0.50, 1.89)

table continues next page

Table 7.4 Fully Adjusted and Bayesian Odds Ratios of Intent to Continue FGM across Selected Covariates *(continued)*

	2012/13		2014	
Variable	Fully adjusted OR & 95% CI[a]	Baycsian OR & 95% CI[b]	Fully adjusted OR & 95% CI[a]	Bayesian OR & 95% CI[b]
Trust in the federal government				
A lot	0.94 (0.54, 1.63)	0.91 (0.60, 1 78)	1.54 (0.90, 2.63)	1.63 (0.89, 2.75)
Some	1.32 (0.82, 2.12)	1.24 (0.86, 1.97)	1.00	1.00
A little	0.97 (0.60, 1.57)	0.93 (0.66, 1.54)	1.12 (0.68, 1.85)	1.15 (0.76, 1.90)
Not at all	1.00	1.00	1.22 (0.67, 2.22)	1.29 (0.68, 2.30)
Trust in the local government				
A lot	1.55 (0.90, 2.66)	1.46 (0.81, 2.52)	1.91 (0.99, 3.68)	1.92 (0.84, 3.54)
Some	1.64 (1.05, 2.57)	1.59 (1.05, 2.64)	2.00 (1.09, 3.67)	2.13 (0.93, 4.23)
A little	1.51 (0.96, 2.39)	1.47 (1.03, 2.03)	2.07 (1.17, 3.65)	2.10 (103, 4.04)
Not at all	1.00	1.00	1.00	1.00
Trust in the police				
A lot	1.70 (1.12, 2.57)	1.71 (1.11, 2.47)	1.00	1.00
Some	1.00	1.00	1.16 (0.72, 1.87)	1.15 (0.72, 1.89)
A little	1.25 (0.82, 1.93)	1.26 (0.84, 1.94)	1.02 (0.58, 1.79)	1.03 (0.59, 1.86)
Not at all	1.64 (0.97, 2.77)	1.67 (1.00, 2.89)	0.96 (0.51, 1.81)	0.94 (0.58, 1 74)
Trust the judiciary system				
A lot	1.14 (0.64, 2.05)	1.21 (0 69, 2.15)	1.00	1.00
Some	1.35 (078, 2.32)	1.47 (0.92, 2.54)	0.92 (0.57, 1.48)	0.95 (0.66, 1.35)
A little	1.28 (0.73, 2.27)	1.33 (0.82, 2.24)	0.64 (0.37, 1.10)	0.66 (0.38, 1.17)
Not at all	1.00	1.00	1.51 (0.81, 2.84)	1.51 (0.83, 2.79)
Islamic law				
Should be at the heart of the constitution	0.90 (0.66, 1.25)	0.89 (0.67, 1.23)	0.75 (0.50, 1.13)	0.81 (0.59, 1.21)
Should be part of the constitution	1.00	1.00	1.00	1.00
Choice about my future				
A lot	0.86 (0.53, 1.38)	0.95 (0.64, 1.54)	1.05 (0.69, 1.61)	1.04 (0.71, 1.68)
Some	0.74 (0.44, 1.23)	0.78 (0.50, 1.29)	1.00	1.00
A little	1.00	1.00	0.68 (0.40, 1.17)	0.72 (0.42, 1.15)
Not at all	0.88 (0.48, 1.62)	0.91 (0.52, 1.61)	1.53 (0.81, 2.88)	1.38 (0.77, 3.22)
Identity				
Sudanese	1.00	1.00	1.00	1.00
My state	2.20 (0.84, 5.77)	1.92 (0.72, 1.27)	1.83 (0.56, 5.93)	1.71 (0.47, 5.51)
Arab	1.26 (0.29, 5.41)	1.07 (0.17, 5.84)	2.57 (0.69, 9.56)	2.85 (0.77, 9.14)
African	2.91 (1.17, 7.26)	3.16 (1.24, 6.48)	0.78 (0.20, 3.02)	0.89 (0.27, 3.43)
My tribe	1.39 (0.68, 2.81)	1.44 (0.79, 2.82)	3.10 (1.57, 6.14)	3.23 (1.75, 6.34)
My religious affiliation	0.89 (0.52, 1.53)	0.83 (0.43, 1.33)	1.35 (0.81, 2.26)	1.28 (0.85, 2.20)
Hold decision makers to account				
A lot	1.49 (0.94, 2.35)	0.00 (0.00, 0.65)	1.06 (0.65, 1.74)	0.07 (0.00, 28.9)
Some	1.41 (0.90, 2.20)	0.00 (0.00, 0.57)	1.40 (0.87, 2.26)	0.10 (0.00, 22.3)

table continues next page

Table 7.4 Fully Adjusted and Bayesian Odds Ratios of Intent to Continue FGM across Selected Covariates *(continued)*

	2012/13		2014	
Variable	Fully adjusted OR & 95% CI[a]	Baycsian OR & 95% CI[b]	Fully adjusted OR & 95% CI[a]	Bayesian OR & 95% CI[b]
A little	1.26 (0.80, 2.01)	0.00 (0.00, 0.49)	1.42 (0.88, 2.29)	0.10 (0.00, 21.1)
Nod al all	1.00	0.00 (0.00, 0.42)	1.00	0.06 (0.00, 23.5)
If election held would vote				
Yes	0.67 (0.45, 1.01)	0.65 (0.46, 0.89)	0.76 (0.51, 1.13)	0.78 (0.56, 1.09)
No	1.00	1.00	1.00	1.00
State of residence (%)				
Al Qadarif	1.68 (0.62, 456)	0.80 (0.47, 1.46)	0.11 (0.02, 0.57)	0.23 (0.07, 0.67)
Al Jazirah	1.64 (0.64, 4.21)	0.69 (0.33, 1.22)	0.57 (0.17, 1.86)	0.71 (0.30, 1.81)
Blue Nile	2.00 (0.77, 5.22)	0.86 (0.47, 1.45)	0.99 (0.35, 2.76)	1.22 (0.62, 2.51)
Kassala	1.00	0.50 (0.24, 0.80)	1.00	1.19 (0.56, 2.73)
Khartoum	1.18 (0.42, 3.34)	0.57 (0.28, 1.04)	0.88 (0.33, 2.38)	1.05 (0.44, 2.19)
North Darfur	3.53 (1.15, 10.8)	1.26 (0.68, 2.80)	1.35 (0.47, 3.93)	1.63 (0.62, 2.89)
North Kurdufan	1.64 (0.51, 5.32)	0.79 (0.36, 1.84)	1.08 (0.39, 2.95)	1.44 (0.76, 3.41)
Northern	1.11 (0.31, 3.97)	0.61 (0.24, 1.33)	0.05 (0.01, 0.28)	0.16 (0.04, 0.48)
Red Sea	6.00 (2.05, 17.6)	1.88 (1.00, 3.74)	0.98 (0.38, 2.51)	1.28 (0.67, 2.34)
River Nile	3.19 (1.09, 9.38)	1.17 (0.63, 2.49)	0.47 (0.16, 1.37)	0.50 (0.21, 0.95)
Sennar	6.00 (2.56, 14.1)	2.24 (1.47, 4.08)	0.24 (0.07, 0.81)	0.36 (0.14, 0.90)
South Darfur	2.30 (0.92, 5.74)	0.88 (0.49, 1.50)	7.93 (2.98, 21.1)	9.82 (5.39, 21.4)
South Kurdufan	4.36 (1.57, 12.2)	1.62 (0.83, 3.21)	1.00 (0.36, 2.79)	1.41 (0.56, 2.65)
West Darfur	1.58 (0.58, 4.32)	0.69 (0.34, 1.39)	1.71 (0.61, 4.84)	2.44 (1.25, 4.25)
White Nile	7.14 (3.04, 16.8)	2.56 (1.64, 4.59)	1.56 (0.54, 4.45)	1.83 (1.04, 4.57)

Source: Based on data from the 2012/13 and 2014 U.K. Department for International Development Sudan household surveys.
Note: BSc = bachelor of science; CI = confidence interval; FGM = female genital mutilation; MSc = master of science; N = number; OR = odds ratio; PhD = doctor of philosophy; SDG = Sudanese pound.
a. Adjusted marginal odds ratio (OR) from standard logistic regression models.
b. Spatially adjusted posterior odds ratio (POR) from Bayesian geo-addictive regression models after controlling for nonlinear effect of age, categorical variables, and the state of residence (spatial effects).

show that after accounting for (a) sampling errors in the observed data, (b) relationships with covariates and the uncertainty in the form of these relationships, and (c) uncertainty in the spatial autocorrelation structure of the outcome variable, the states with the highest pro-FGM risk included White Nile, Sennar, and Red Sea, whereas South Kurdufan and North Darfur no longer ranked among states with the highest prevalence as suggested by the marginal OR (map 7.2 and table 7.2). A year later, in 2014 (map 7.4), the highest-risk states included South Darfur, West Darfur, and White Nile but not Sennar.

Figure 7.10 shows an inverse U-shape association and a bell-shaped nonlinear relationship between the probability of pro-FGM attitude and respondent's age at interview. The nonlinear association between age and the probability of pro-FGM at age 18 years does not differ in the two data sets starting at zero, the lowest probability of pro-FGM attitude with a gradual increase in both years.

Figure 7.10 Estimated Nonparametric Effect of Respondent's Age

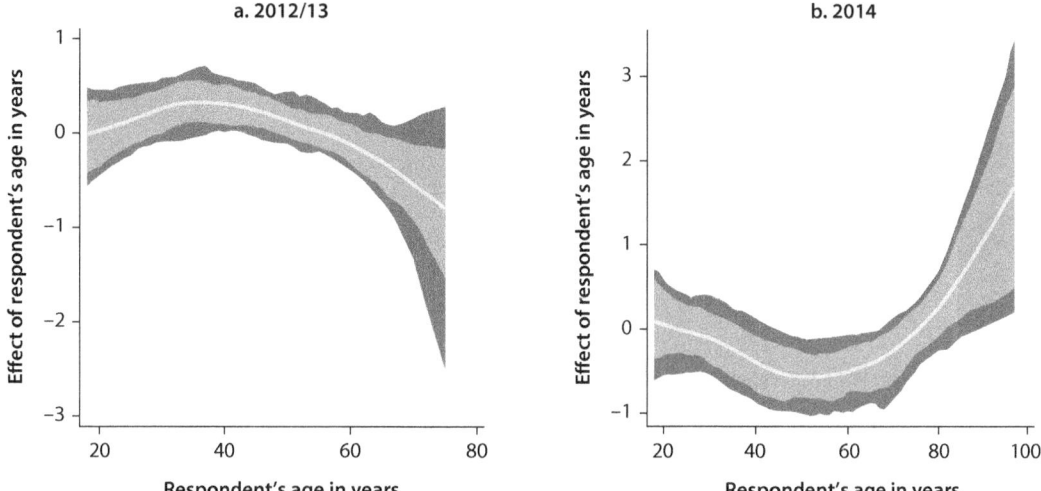

Source: Based on data from the 2014 U.K. Department for International Development Sudan Household Health Surveys.
Note: The posterior mean is shown within 80 percent credible regions.

At all other ages, the two data sets show agreement in the pattern of probability of pro-FGM attitude until the age of 60 years. A watershed is present between 30 and 35 years of age, when both samples have the highest observed probability of pro-FGM attitude. Before age 30 years, this probability rises quickly as age increases. Beyond age 34 years, there is a declining probability of pro-FGM attitude, although the variation in probability increases rapidly at the same time as age continues to increase. For age 60 years and above, there are wide confidence intervals, suggesting too few observations in both data sets that make it difficult to discern a consistent upward increase in pro-FGM attitude (instability of the estimates) in either data set. We note that at first glance, the figures seem to be different. However, a careful examination reveals that, in both figures, the age's effects start at an estimate of 0 with a gradual increase thereafter. Nevertheless, the two figures have a problem of scaling on the y axis. This is an estimation problem and a difficult one to resolve now.

With regard to pro-FGM attitude by states, in both data sets, the spatial analysis has captured the striking variation in pro-FGM risk across states observed in the marginal regression analyses. Maps 7.2–7.5 show results for covariate-adjusted state-level pro-FGM attitude spatial variation captured by the global total residual state effects (that is, the sum of the unstructured and structured spatial effects). A clear pattern emerged of states with a higher risk of pro-FGM attitude, mostly the southeastern states of Sennar and White Nile, including the eastern state of Red Sea in 2012/13 (map 7.2) and the southern state of South Darfur in 2014 (map 7.4), which were associated with a higher risk of pro-FGM attitude. States such as Kassala in 2012/13 and Northern, River Nile, Kassala, and Al Qadarif in 2014, however, were associated with lower pro-FGM attitude (maps 7.4 and 7.5). These spatial patterns confirm the observed marginal model findings shown in table 7.3.

Map 7.2a shows estimated posterior total residual state odds of pro-FGM attitude for each state in 2012/13, ranging from a lower POR of 0.50 (0.24–0.80) in Kassala to a higher POR of 2.56 (1.64–4.59) in White Nile. In 2014, the POR ranges as low as 0.16 (0.04–0.48) to a higher POR of 9.82 (5.39–21.4) in South Darfur, with the color red indicating the higher risks recorded and the color green denoting lower risk (map 7.4a). Map 7.2b shows the 80 percent posterior probability map of pro-FGM attitude, which indicates the statistical significance associated with the total excess risk. The color white indicates a negative spatial effect (associated with a reduced risk of pro-FGM attitude), black a positive effect (an increased risk), and gray a nonsignificant effect. However, the total spatial residuals in maps 7.2 and 7.4 in both data sets show that much of the variation in pro-FGM attitude remains unexplained.

The spatial effects of South Kurdufan in 2012/13 were greatly attenuated after multiple adjustments of other risk factors. This attenuation indicates that perhaps the higher number of pro-FGM participants living in the state was inflated by other factors such as self-identity, income, and education.

Discussion

To our knowledge, our research is the first and largest epidemiological study in a high-FGM-prevalence country in Sub-Saharan Africa that has examined geographic variation, at the state level, of an attitude shift toward FGM practice in an adult population. We used data from the 2012/13 and 2014 DFID Sudan Household Health Surveys on a large, nationwide sample. Overall, the proportion of pro-FGM was 18.3 percent in 2014 compared with 27.6 percent in 2012/13, including a striking variation across self-perceived Sudanese cultural identity groups and states of residence, ranging in 2014 from 1.3 percent in Northern state to 55.3 percent in South Darfur. Our findings also point to the crucial role of demographic, socioeconomic, political, cultural, and spatial factors surrounding the practice of FGM in these higher-FGM-prevalence settings. In fact, we found that people with a lack of education, low income, large family size, residence in rural areas, some trust in local government, and strong tribal identity were more likely to be associated with a positive attitude toward the continuation of FGM. Individuals from South Darfur were more likely to have a positive attitude toward the continuation of FGM when compared to Northern state in 2014. This result was somewhat surprising given the historical association between the north of Sudan and FGM, but possibly it was a product of the fact that those peripheral states suffer from the lowest levels of socioeconomic development in Sudan (associated with individual characteristics more likely to increase support for FGM).

Between 2012/13 and 2014, although the national percentage of pro-FGM decreased dramatically, South Darfur data showed it to be a lower prevalence area in 2012/13 but a higher prevalence area in 2014 (55.3 percent).

Sennar changed from the highest prevalence area in 2012/13 to a lower prevalence area in 2014. The proportion of pro-FGM remained stable at a low level during the same period in states such as Kassala and Khartoum.

Looking at these sudden shifts of attitude at the state level provides more evidence that monitoring attitude shifts of pro-FGM using national proportions can mask within-country variability, which may not be useful for design and implementation of policies and interventions locally. These findings provide novel evidence to support the notion of rapidly shifting attitude toward the abandonment of FGM. The notable decrease in the practice of cutting observed between the 2006 and 2010 Sudan Household Health Surveys and the shift in attitude demonstrated in data from the 2012/13 and 2014 DFID Sudan Household Health Surveys together make a compelling case for the creation of specific FGM-abandonment policies by public health policy makers in order to avert a growing burden of health dangers (*Sudan Tribune* 2014).

Several factors likely contribute to the changing attitude in the practice of FGM in these higher-FGM-prevalence states for both pro-FGM and anti-FGM groups. Pro-FGM groups primarily cite the importance of FGM as a requisite for a good marriage, a perpetuation of tradition, or a part of Sudan's culture and Islamic religious instruction. Anti-FGM groups point to the extensive educational campaign by the government and NGOs raising awareness of health dangers associated with FGM practice (DFID 2013; *Sudan Tribune* 2014). The rapidly changing role of women in the Sudanese societies, with increasing access to education and involvement in the democratic process and labor force, particularly in urban areas, also might contribute to the dramatic changes in anti-FGM attitude and the move toward its eradication (Ahmed, Al Hebshi, and Nylund 2009; Hernlund and Shell-Duncan 2007; Mackie and LeJeune 2009; Shell-Duncan 2008; Yoder, Abderrahim, and Zhuzhuni 2004).

In high-FGM-prevalence countries such as Sudan, the attitudes of pro-FGM and anti-FGM populations can be leveraged to promote the reduction of FGM. To do so, exploring what people think about the practice is essential. Does support vary across groups with different social and economic backgrounds? Do women and men share the same opinions? What are the perceived benefits of FGM and the reasons that women and men believe it should continue? In our study, we extensively examined confounding factors that might intermingle with each other in complex modeling to explore the pro-FGM determinants as compared with the exploratory analysis undertaken by UNICEF (2013).

Previous studies have shown that changing attitudes in Sudan toward FGM are helping reduce the prevalence of the practice (DFID 2013; *Sudan Tribune* 2014). According to UNICEF (2013), more than 50 percent of Sudanese women believe the practice should be discontinued amid growing awareness of its health dangers. Comparing data from the 2006 and 2010 Sudan Household Health Surveys shows a notable decrease in the practice of cutting over four years, with a further decrease expected according to UNICEF. The 2010 Sudan Household Health Survey indicated that the state of Kassala had the highest prevalence of

FGM in the country, whereas the 2012/13 and 2014 DFID Sudan Household Health Survey data show that the same state is associated with a lower proportion of pro-FGM attitude (*Sudan Tribune* 2014; UNICEF 2013). A possible explanation of this finding is that respondents in higher-FGM-prevalence states want the practice to be discontinued. These findings have significant policy implications. The support for this practice is decreasing and provides a valuable opportunity for its eventual abandonment.

The Sudanese government has introduced some regulations to stop the practice of FGM, but it remains widespread, particularly in rural communities (UNICEF 2013). The eradication of FGM is complicated further by cultural and societal pressures and by religious sensitivities surrounding the issue. In fact, our study's findings show that lack of education, larger family size, some trust in the local government, self-identity, willingness to vote in a general election, and residence in certain states were factors associated with a higher risk of pro-FGM attitude in the four years of the study. The finding that lack of education is a risk factor for pro-FGM attitude might be related to decision-making power, which supports the view that women maintain a traditional and restricted role. According to Kandala, Nwakeze, and Kandala (2009), women's sexuality is influenced by their limited decision-making power and the decision-making power is a function of their economic independence. As in Nigeria (Kandala, Nwakeze, and Kandala 2009), these findings support previous findings that consider FGM to be a social convention that may not be influenced by modernization (education or religion), therefore reconfirming that modernization (education or religion) also has limited influence on the likelihood of FGM in Sudan.

In comparison to other countries in the region, the practice of circumcision in Sudan is widespread. In 2010, the prevalence of female circumcision in Sudan was 88 percent (DFID 2013; *Sudan Tribune* 2014; UNICEF 2013), or 12.1 million girls and women who have undergone FGM. Globally, this prevalence ranges as low as 1 percent in Cameroon and as high as 98 percent in Somalia (UNICEF 2013). Our findings on FGM attitudes are corroborated by previous studies. Findings from UNICEF (2013) show that girls and women with no education are nearly four times more likely to support the continuation of FGM than girls and women with secondary or higher education. Our findings in Sudan echo this trend: lack of education is a risk factor for pro-FGM attitude even after multiple adjustments of other risk factors.

People's attitudes toward FGM vary widely across and within countries. Among higher-FGM-prevalence countries, UNICEF (2013) reports that in Guinea (with a prevalence rate of 96 percent), 19 percent of girls and women think FGM should stop compared with 42 percent of boys and men; in Eritrea, 60 percent of girls and women regard FGM as a religious requirement; in Côte d'Ivoire, 41 percent of girls and women of Voltaique–Gur background support the continuation of FGM compared with 3 percent of Akan girls and women; in Liberia, girls and women from the poorest households are twice as likely to have experienced FGM as those from the richest households; in Ethiopia, 41 percent of girls and women with no education support the continuation of FGM compared with 5 percent of girls and women with secondary or higher education; in Burkina Faso, 76 percent of girls and women have been cut compared with 9 percent who favor the continuation of FGM; and in The Gambia, 82 percent of girls and women who have undergone FGM think the practice should continue compared with 5 percent of girls and women who have not been cut.

Our study of Sudan found strikingly large differences between states and socioeconomic and cultural factors. However, when we controlled for many other factors that might have confounded the relationship between the attitudes about FGM and these factors in a Bayesian multivariate model, many of the previously observed associations such as urban–rural residence were no longer statistically significant. This finding suggests that most of these associations were not real (chance) because they did not account for one important risk factor: the environment in which the individual lived (spatial factors).

Our study of the 2012/13 and 2014 DFID Sudan Household Health Survey data sets has shown that factors of significant importance in FGM attitudes are lack of education, low income, large family size, trust in tribal leaders and local government, tribal identity, and state of residence. The highest levels of support for FGM in both data sets were found in the states of White Nile and South Darfur, where more than half of the population think the practice should continue. However, in states where FGM prevalence is higher (for example, Kassala), the majority of people think the practice should end.

Ethnicity and religion are among the most widely cited reasons for the continuation of FGM. In our study, we also made similar findings, with respondents citing ethnicity (importance of tradition) and good marriage as main reasons for pro-FGM attitude. Although FGM varies by ethnicity, Mackie and LeJeune (2009) argue that ethnic differentiation is not a significant motivating factor in more than a few isolated contexts. They argue that FGM is more likely to be practiced in order to gain acceptance and recognition within one's own community—as a means of belonging, rather than of differentiation. Ethnic differentiation seems to be more a consequence than a cause of the practice, and this is confirmed by our study given the higher percentage of pro-FGM respondents who cited the requirement of a good marriage as one of the reasons for the continuation of FGM.

Another commonly cited justification for FGM is religion, but this was not the case in our study. Among Bambara in Mali, for example, religious obligation often plays a role in a family's decision to practice FGM (Mackie and LeJeune 2009). Despite the fact that no religious scriptures actually require FGM, communities sometimes consider the practice a requirement to make a girl spiritually pure. Data on the role of religion are difficult to interpret because in many cases, religion, tradition, and chastity are correlated. A study in Somalia illustrates that, for some, the concepts of "religion," "to remain a virgin in order to be married," and "tradition" are "not fundamentally different," because "infibulation creates a barrier that preserves virginity, which Muslims consider the will of God and therefore religious" (Gruenbaum 2001, 50). Household surveys routinely show respondents citing a multitude of reasons directly or indirectly related to religion, health, cleanliness, tradition, and control of female sexuality, among others, as reasons for the practice of FGM (Mackie and LeJeune 2009).

An ethnic or religious explanation of FGM is not sufficient. First, it is practiced in a wide variety of ethnic and religious groups. Second, the practice is not necessarily universal within the broad descriptive group, but is often practiced only within a number of subgroups (Mackie and LeJeune 2009). With regard to religion, previous studies in Burkina Faso and Nigeria (Karmaker et al. 2011) showed that both Christian and Muslim communities who practice FGM often believe that their holy books require FGM. Yet nearby communities of the same religion may not engage in FGM, and worldwide, most Christians and most Muslims do not follow the practice.

The role of religion in the perpetuation of FGM has been widely debated. In a WHO (1999, v) report, religious obligation is described as an important factor in the decision to practice FGM, but it is typically just one of several elements within a "mental map." That map incorporates the stories, beliefs, values, and codes of conduct of society, which are in fact "interconnected and mutually reinforcing and, taken together, form overwhelming unconscious and conscious motivations" for its continued practice (Ahmadu 2000, 295). Arguments have been made that challenging the religious sanctity of FGM in isolation from other motivating elements may help change attitudes but will have little effect on behavior, because religion is only one of several factors that maintain the practice. In contrast, because these factors are "interconnected and mutually reinforcing," disconnecting FGM from one factor may help disconnect it from the others (Mackie and LeJeune 2009). Alternatively, all effects—religion, tradition, piety, and purity—may be disconnected from FGM by a single authoritative source, such as a charismatic local leader who confidently declares the practice to be unacceptable, given that one of the factors associated with pro-FGM attitude in our study was trust in local government (Mackie and LeJeune 2009).

As occurs in many countries that practice FGM, our study found that pro-FGM respondents justified its practice in order to secure a proper marriage, which was the most common reason offered across practicing communities and was offered despite wide variation in factors such as ethnicity, culture, religion, severity of cutting, symbolic reasons for the practice, ritual, or lack of ritual, as documented in Hernlund and Shell-Duncan (2007) and Mackie and LeJeune (2009). Previous studies in the field of anthropology found that those who practice FGM illustrate that marriageability plays an important role in the rational and prudent decision making of mothers to cut their daughters. "[M]otivated by love and concern for their daughters' future, well-meaning women [in the Arab Republic of Egypt] have perpetuated the custom and have insisted on inflicting pain on their daughters out of a firm belief in the physical and moral benefits of this operation as a guarantee of marriage and consequent social and economic security" (Hernlund and Shell-Duncan 2007, 29–35; Mackie and LeJeune 2009). In Sudan, "[n]o matter how clever the public education message on the hazards of female circumcision or how authoritative the religious source that says it is unnecessary, parents know it is necessary, if it is the prerequisite for their daughter's marriageability and long-term security" (Gruenbaum 2001, 192; Mackie and LeJeune 2009). Tradition and marriageability are correlated, according to social convention theory, which is discussed later in this section.

Marriageability as a reason to maintain the practice of FGM is given more often in countries of low FGM prevalence (Greenbaum 1997; Gruenbaum 2001; Shell-Duncan 2008; Shell-Duncan, Walter, and Leunita 2000; WHO 1999). Marriage itself is especially important because of the socioeconomic conditions that may characterize many practicing communities. In many areas where FGM is practiced, patriarchal economic customs and institutions make marriageability necessary to secure the long-term financial security of daughters and their families (Greenbaum 1997; Gruenbaum 2001; Mackie and LeJeune 2009; Shell-Duncan, Walter, and Leunita 2000; WHO 1999). In some places, the family may depend on a substantial bride price for their economic well-being (Greenbaum 1997; Mackie and LeJeune 2009). Because state-funded social security protections cover only a tiny fraction of the population in Sudan, marriage is a woman's primary source of material subsistence beyond early adulthood. Yet even if women had full economic independence, many likely would still pursue marriage and child-bearing and be exposed to FGM (Mackie and LeJeune 2009; Shell-Duncan, Walter, and Leunita 2000).

All of the reasons discussed about the continuation of FGM are society-level variables and are better captured by the geographic location of the survey respondents, incorporated into our analysis as a spatial factor. However, these society-level variables can be explained in part by social convention theory as it is applied to FGM (Mackie and LeJeune 2009). The social convention theory also might explain the roles of self-enforcing beliefs, social norms, moral norms, and over-determining factors that can further be considered to address unexplained observations and develop a more refined understanding of the practice of FGM (Mackie and LeJeune 2009). Policies should capitalize on these findings, and local, tribal, religious, and government leaders should be involved in continuing programs of action.

Limitations to the Study
Some limitations to our study deserve discussion. First, the cross-sectional nature of the 2012/13 and 2014 DFID surveys does not allow for establishing temporality and causality of the observed associations. However, given the nature of our independent variables of interest (state of residence and cultural, demographic, and socioeconomic factors) associated with attitudes toward FGM, the potential for reverse causation should be minimized.

Second, the analysis was based on nationally representative samples of Sudanese, so the generalizability and applicability of these findings to other populations or other Sub-Saharan African countries warrants further investigation.

Finally, the phrasing in the household surveys of the question of attitudes toward FGM might have some implications (that is, saying what the interviewer would like to know) for participant responses to these sensitive questions. However, these types of questions have been used in surveys since 1989, when UNICEF (Multiple Indicator Cluster Surveys [MICS] data) and ICF International (Demographic Health Surveys [DHS]) modules on FGM included similar questions on whether or not the practice should continue. The 2012/13 and 2014 DFID Sudan Household Health Surveys posed questions such as "Do you think this practice should continue?" or "Should it be discontinued?," followed by precoded responses, including "continued" and "discontinued" and ambivalent choices such as "not sure," "refuse to answer," and "don't know."

As in other survey topics, the phrasing of the questions has evolved over time. Earlier surveys of MICS and DHS included a larger set of attitudinal questions, not only inquiring whether FGM practice should continue but also requiring reasons behind the opinion given, whether that opinion had changed, and views on perceived benefits or inconveniences of the practice. Answers to questions capture a respondent's opinion at one point in time and in the context of responding to a formal survey. Among those who say they favor the discontinuation of FGM, the intense exposure to campaign messages against the practice may prompt them to report what they perceive to be the correct answer, rather than their true opinion (UNICEF 2013). Moreover, even a truthful response at one point in time fails to take into account that someone's opinion may change on exposure to new information about the practice or to the opinions of others (UNICEF 2013). This issue has been documented in Senegal and The Gambia, where "there is a broad range of realities inhabited by those who participate in FGM/C in this region—ranging from strong support to strong opposition, but with the potential movement over time by an individual or even community from one category to another, and potentially back again" (Hernlund and Shell-Duncan 2007, 44; UNICEF 2013). Hernlund and Shell-Duncan (2007, 44) add that "the construction of a person's 'opinion' about the practice is more correctly an ongoing positioning vis-à-vis fluctuating needs and realities, representing contingencies that affect decision-making."

Therefore, we cannot rule out the possibility that our findings might have been somewhat biased by the shift in attitude over time and the lack of many other important confounders that were not measured by these two surveys. Nevertheless, this is the largest study that has examined both bivariate and multivariate association of attitudes toward FGM aside from the UNICEF (2013) study that was limited to the exploration of bivariate associations.

Concluding Remarks

This is the first and largest study to examine the geographic variation of pro-FGM in an adult population from Sub-Saharan Africa. We found several consistent associations between sociodemographic and cultural variables and pro-FGM attitude in the data sets of the 2012/13 and 2014 DFID Sudan Household Health Surveys. The overall percentage of people with a positive attitude toward the perpetuation of FGM practice fell from 27.5 percent in 2012/13 to 18.3 percent in 2014. The spatial analysis showed distinct patterns in pro-FGM attitude across Sudan's states, pointing to the potential influence of demographic, cultural, socioeconomic, and spatial factors and to an increasing effect of time and age of the individual, which are all driving the ongoing decline in FGM prevalence. Importantly, the government of Sudan, its development partners, policy makers, and public health practitioners can use this geographic information on pro-FGM mapping not only for planning and educational purposes, but also in the decision-making process for the allocation of public resources to the most affected areas in Sudan. Our findings give a window of opportunity for a public health policy on FGM abandonment in Sudan.

Factors associated with pro-FGM are varied and complex: lack of education, low income, large family size, trust in tribal leaders and local government, tribal identity, and residence in While Nile or South Darfur states. The eradication of FGM must involve the identification of issues that sustain the practice in different localities, and subsequent action should be supported either by logical persuasion following aggressive health education or by legislation.

Notes

1. For more information, visit http://www.kmgehtiopia.org.
2. For more information, visit http://www.tostan.org.

References

Ahmadu, F. 2000. "Rites and Wrongs: An Insider/Outsider Reflects on Power and Excision." In *Female "Circumcision" in Africa: Culture, Controversy, and Change*, edited by B. Shell-Duncan and Y. Hernlund, 283–312. Boulder, CO: Lynne Reiner Publishers.

Ahmed, S., S. Al Hebshi, and B. V. Nylund. 2009. "Sudan: An In-Depth Analysis of the Social Dynamics of Abandonment of FGC." Special Series on Social Norms and Harmful Practices. Innocenti Working Paper 2009–08, United Nations Children's Fund Innocenti Research Centre, Florence.

Belitz, C., A. Brezger, T. Kneib, and S. Lang. 2012. *BayesX Software for Bayesian Inference in Structured Additive Regression Models Version 3.0.2* (accessed March 17, 2017). https://www.uni-goettingen.de/en/bayesx/550513.html.

DFID (U.K. Department for International Development). 2013. *Business Case–DFID Sudan Free of Female Genital Cutting*. London. https://devtracker.dfid.gov.uk/projects/GB-1-203407.

Fahrmeir, L., and S. Lang. 2001. "Bayesian Inference for Generalized Additive Mixed Models based on Markov Random Field Priors." *Applied Statistics* (JRSS C) 50: 201–20.

Greenbaum, D. 1997. "Intellect without Morality? (Letter to the Editor)." *Anthropology Newsletter*, February 2.

Gruenbaum, E. 2001. *The Female Circumcision Controversy: An Anthropological Perspective.* Philadelphia, PA: University of Pennsylvania Press.

Hamilton, A., and N.-B. Kandala. 2016. "Geography and Correlates of Attitude toward Female Genital Mutilation (FGM) in Sudan: What Can We Learn from Successive Sudan Opinion Poll Data?" *Spatial and Spatio-temporal Epidemiology* 16: 59–76.

Hernlund, Y., and B. Shell-Duncan. 2007. "Contingency, Context, and Change: Negotiating Female Genital Cutting in the Gambia and Senegal." *Africa Today* 53 (4): 43–57.

Kandala, N.-B. 2014. "Genital Mutilation (Practices Common in Sudan, Senegal, Egypt, Somalia, Ethiopia and Some Other African Countries)." In *Genital and Perianal Diseases: A Color Handbook,* edited by T. F. Mroczkowski, L. E. Millikan, and L. C. Parish, 382–91. Boca Raton, FL: CRC Press.

Kandala, N.-B., and Komba, P. 2014. "Geographic Variation of Female Genital Mutilation and Legal Enforcement in Sub-Saharan Africa: A Case Study of Senegal." *American Journal of Tropical Medicine and Hygiene* 92 (4): 838–47.

Kandala N.-B., N. Nwakeze, and S. N. I. I. Kandala. 2009. "The Spatial Distribution of Female Genital Mutilation (FGM) in Nigeria." *American Journal of Tropical Medicine and Hygiene* 81 (5): 784–92.

Karmaker, B., N.-B. Kandala, D. Chung, and A. Clarke. 2011. "Factors Associated with Female Genital Mutilation in Burkina Faso–Policy Implications?" *International Journal for Equity in Health* 10 (1): 20.

Mackie, G., and J. LeJeune. 2009. "Social Dynamics of Abandonment of Harmful Practices: A New Look at the Theory." Special Series on Social Norms and Harmful Practices, Innocenti Working Paper 2009–06, United Nations Children's Fund Innocenti Research Centre, Florence.

Macro International. 1997. *Female Genital Cutting: Findings from the Demographic and Health Surveys Program.* Calverton, MD: Macro International.

Shell-Duncan, B. 2008. "From Health to Human Rights: Female Genital Cutting and the Politics of Intervention." *American Anthropologist* 110 (2): 225–36.

Shell-Duncan, B., O. O. Walter, and A. M. Leunita. 2000. "Women without Choices: The Debate over Medicalization of Female Genital Cutting and Its Impact on a Northern Kenyan Community." In *Female "Circumcision" in Africa: Culture, Controversy, and Change,* edited by B. Shell-Duncan and Y. Hernlund, 108–28. Boulder, CO: Lynne Rienner.

Sudan Tribune. 2014. "FGM on Decline in Sudan as Attitudes Shift: UNICEF." February 13, (accessed September 2, 2014). http://www.sudantribune.com/spip.php?iframe&page = imprimable&id_article = 49935.

UNICEF (United Nations Children's Fund). 2013. *Female Genital Mutilation/Cutting: A Statistical Overview and Exploration of the Dynamic of Change.* New York: UNICEF.

WHO (World Health Organization). 1999. *Female Genital Mutilation–Programmes to Date: What Works and What Doesn't—A Review.* Geneva: WHO.

Yoder, P. S., N. Abderrahim, and A. Zhuzhuni. 2004. *Female Genital Cutting in the Demographic and Health Surveys: A Critical and Comparative Analysis.* Calverton, MD: ORC Macro.

CHAPTER 8

The Effect of Decentralization Policies on Inequalities of Public Service Delivery in Sudan

Zintis Hermansons and Bashir Ahmad

Considerable horizontal (geography-based) inequalities exist with regard to how people perceive service provision in Sudan. A recent study using the 2013 U.K. Department for International Development (DFID) Sudan household survey data shows that the majority of respondents, including those in Khartoum, think that services outside Khartoum are less accessible and of inferior quality to those provided in the city (Crowther et al. 2014a, 2014b).

Service delivery in Sudan is organized in a decentralized manner; most of the services are delivered at the state level or jointly with the government. The aim of this chapter is to inquire whether the way in which Sudan has organized decentralization and subnational governance could explain or give insight into regional inequalities regarding public service delivery. Presently, Sudan is a (nominally) federal country consisting of 18 states, and this analysis concentrates on the state level.

This chapter aims to look specifically at fiscal decentralization and to use it as a filter to address two underlying factors: political economy and institutional design. In other words, inequalities in public service delivery might have a systemic component involving institutions, structures, and actors that has determined how these inequalities came about and continue to persist.

In the sections that follow, we give a brief overview of the existing state of governance in Sudan, as well as insights into research conducted on governance and service delivery. The following section outlines the theoretical, legal, and administrative framework of fiscal decentralization, exploring its political economy with regard to the center versus the periphery. This framework can be used to understand the main finding of this chapter—that the marginalization of Sudan's peripheries affects how fiscal decentralization is being implemented and that it necessarily has a negative effect on the ability of the states to secure service delivery.

Existing Research on Governance and Service Delivery in Sudan and Proposed Methodology

Authors of a recent study using 2013 DFID Sudan household survey data (see chapters 2, 3, and 4 of this volume and Crowther et al. 2014a, 2014b) conclude that considerable vertical (income-based) and horizontal (geography-based) inequalities exist regarding the way people perceive service provision in Sudan. Applying econometric analysis involving three sets of indicators (actual service provision, perceptions, and sociodemographic characteristics of respondents) to explain perceptions about public service quality, they test whether the trust factor has an important effect. The authors conclude that trust in government and actual service providers can play a role independent of actual service provision in forming perceptions.

In a different approach, covered in chapter 6 of this volume, Hamilton and Svensson use econometric approaches and 2013 DFID Sudan household survey data and conclude that a failure in service delivery leads to people falling into poverty, which in effect explains why people perceive service provision as being bad. Moreover, the authors argue that perceiving service delivery as bad leads to people not trusting government and not participating in policy making, which opens the door for the government to neglect the issue of service provision.

Concentrating on the issue of education in another recent study, Nour (2013) looks particularly at the demand side for education. His analysis of enrollment and completion rates finds that economic reasons (per capita income and poverty rate), demographics, and degree of urbanization all are significant predictors of service quality and access (Nour 2013). The above-mentioned studies, however, have not touched on a crucial aspect of public service delivery: political economy. In other words, inequalities of public service delivery might be systematically linked—both caused and determined (perpetuated) by the way in which decentralization has been implemented.

The role of political economy can be analyzed by applying widely used "problem driven analysis" to "enhance understanding and resolve a particular problem at the project level, or in relation to [a] specific policy issue" (DFID 2009, 13). It encompasses the framework shown in table 8.1.

Econometric analysis helps discover causalities beyond public perceptions. But at the same time, a broader framework is needed to put into context the fact that whatever the mechanisms accounting for poor perceptions of public service delivery, the actual statistics about service delivery indicate that it is a de facto problem. One of the main reasons for this outcome is the lack of adequate resource flows, which has very serious implications for any international aid efforts. The tool, adopted for the purpose of analyzing service delivery in Sudan, consists of the framework shown in table 8.2.

The framework in table 8.3 can be used to analyze more specifically how the marginalization of Sudan's peripheries is related to fiscal decentralization.

Table 8.1 Three Layers of Problem-Driven Governance and Political Economy Analysis

What vulnerabilities/challenges?		Evidence of poor outcomes to which GPE weaknesses appear to contribute	For example, repeated failure to adopt sector reforms; poor sector outcomes; infrastructure identified as constraint to growth but not effectively addressed; continuous food insecurity. Corruption continues to undermine the business climate even after anticorruption law.
Governance and political economy analysis	Institutional and governance arrangements and capacities	What are the associated institutional setups and governance arrangements?	Mapping of relevant branches of government, ministries, agencies, and SOEs and their interaction; existing laws and regulations; policy processes (formal and de facto rules). What mechanisms are intended to ensure integrity and accountability and to limit corruption?
	Political economy drivers	Why are things this way? Why are policies or institutional arrangements not being improved?	Analysis of stakeholders, incentives, rents/rent distribution, historical legacies, and prior experiences with reforms, social trends, and forces (for example, ethnic tensions), and how they shape current stakeholder positions and actions.

Sources: Adapted from Fritz, Levy, and Kaiser 2009 and DFID 2009.
Note: A more sophisticated version of this framework is presented in Fritz, Levy, and Ort (2014). GPE = governance and political economy; SOEs = state-owned enterprises.

Table 8.2 Three Layers for Analyzing Service Delivery in Sudan by Applying Problem-Driven Governance and Political Economy Analysis

What vulnerabilities/challenges?		Evidence of poor outcomes to which GPE weaknesses appear to contribute	Inequalities in public service delivery with regard to quality and accessibility across Sudan's regions.
Governance and political economy analysis	Institutional and governance arrangements and capacities	What are the associated institutional setups and governance arrangements?	Mapping of decentralization system as primary means of providing services; references to legal system and procedural practice.
	Political economy drivers	Why are things this way? Why are policies or institutional arrangements not being improved?	Analysis of center–periphery hypothesis (marginalization of peripheries) as the main obstacle responsible for systematic service delivery failure.

Source: Adapted from Fritz, Levy, and Kaiser 2009.
Note: GPE = governance and political economy.

Table 8.3 Strategies of Subversion Regarding Decentralization

Domain	Actions at the central level
Political	Resist relinquishing control to subnational from opposition through increase in appointments.
Administrative	Divest certain administrative responsibilities, unless they offer high levels of visibility to key voters.
Fiscal	Limit ability of subnational officials to finance their administrative responsibilities by reductions and restrictions in intergovernmental transfers or by limitations on taxation or delays to improving donor funding.

Source: Adapted from Resnick 2014.

Governance in Sudan: A Macro Perspective on Service Delivery

Sudan's persistent inability to address crises and conflicts are issues that have dominated scholarly attention. "If governance can be defined as the art of conflict management, and good governance as 'the proper functioning of a system of conflict management,' the crisis of governance in the post-colonial Sudan is the art of conflict-generation" (Kok 1996, 555). Sudan scores particularly poorly on a multitude of governance indicators—especially regarding the level of violence and political instability (see figure 8.1). Indeed, it fits neatly with what de Waal (2007a, 4) characterizes as Sudan's "turbulent state," meaning "the second most persistent fact in Sudanese political history is the inability of any one elite faction to establish unchallenged political dominance over the state."

If one examines percentile ranks for all components of the World Bank's (2015b) worldwide governance indicators for Sudan, Sudan clearly is one of the worst-performing countries of Sub-Saharan Africa. The "government effectiveness" component is the most applicable for looking at public service delivery, although it captures other issues as well. As figure 8.1 shows, the government has become less effective every year for the past five years: in 2008, the percentile rank for this indicator was 8.25, whereas in 2013, it had dropped to 3.35. That drop means that in 2013, only 3 percent of 215 countries surveyed were doing the same or worse, but 97 percent had better conditions. Generally, this result indicates that governance in Sudan is in very poor condition, and indeed ongoing conflicts among other things provide evidence for this statistical finding.

In addition, data on financial resources available to service provision indicate that after the secession of South Sudan in 2011, Sudan was in a very disadvantageous position. This situation relates mostly to the considerable loss of revenue from the oil industry, which can affect financing service delivery. Moreover, the unstable security conditions and conflicts at the periphery, and "the oversized

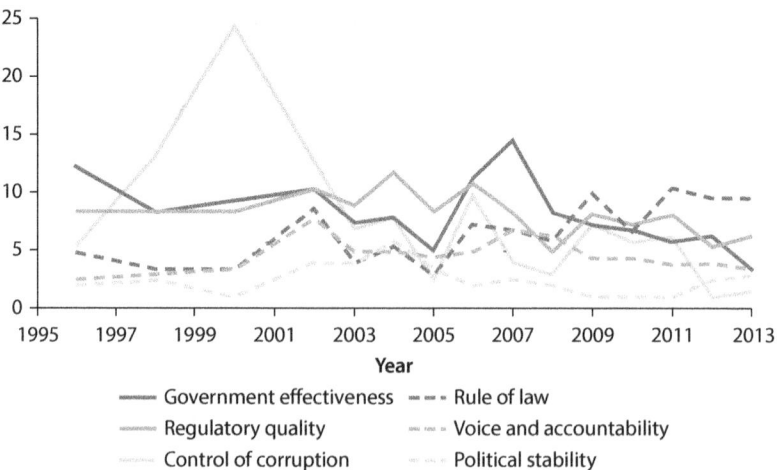

Figure 8.1 Worldwide Governance Indicators for Sudan, Percentile Ranks

Source: Based on World Bank 2015b.

federal and state government and the patronage system created by the regime," create extra pressure on the budget (Sharfi 2014, 320).

Table 8.4 shows that a loss of oil revenues has had a long-term negative effect on government revenue generation, thus potentially affecting the ability of the government to finance service delivery at the pre-2011 level. A separate econometric study regarding the influence of oil on Sudan's economy concluded that—given Sudan's dependence on oil—oil price fluctuations had a major effect on overall macroeconomic indicators and macroeconomic stability in the period from 1999 to 2009 (Ebaidalla 2014). Moreover, despite South Sudan's secession, oil is still a major source of revenue, and potential future discoveries indicate that oil could be an important factor in how the country performs economically (Ebaidalla 2014).

Internationally comparable statistics for Sudan's government finances cannot be accessed easily—Sudan is not included in the International Monetary Fund's *Government Finance Statistics Yearbook*, for instance—and the available data are mostly out-of-date. However, in figure 8.2, we present statistics on

Table 8.4 Sudan's Central Government Revenues
percentage of GDP

Revenue source	2010	2011	2012	2013	2014	2015	2016	2017	2018
Total revenues and grants	19.3	18.0	9.8	10.1	11.8	12.1	12.1	12.2	12.4
Revenue	18.7	17.7	9.4	9.4	11.3	11.4	11.4	11.5	11.7
Oil revenue as share of revenue	11.5	10.4	1.5	1.7	1.3	1.1	1.0	1.0	1.1
Grants	0.6	0.3	0.4	0.7	0.5	0.7	0.7	0.7	0.7

Source: Based on IMF 2014.

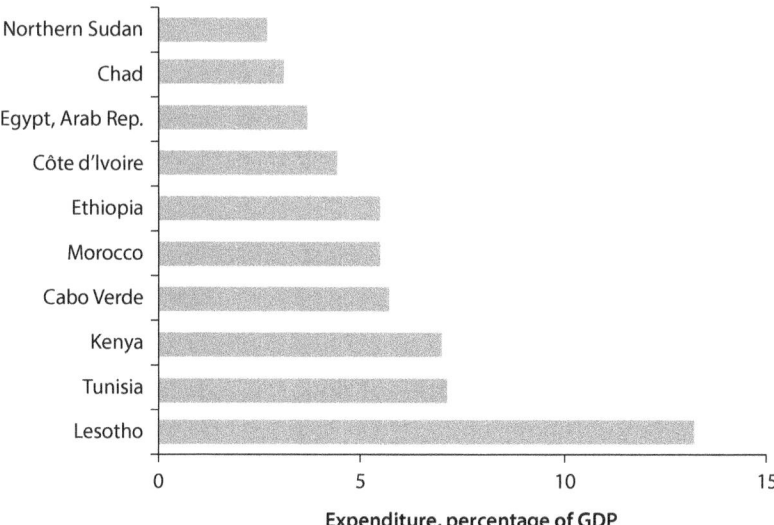

Figure 8.2 Public Education Spending, 2005–08

Source: Based on World Bank 2012.

educational spending, which give an approximate idea of the extent to which Sudan finances service delivery compared with other countries in the region.

Theoretical Framework: Decentralization and Service Delivery

Service delivery in Sudan is organized in a decentralized manner, so understanding how the institutional system works in practice is vital. The aim, nevertheless, is not to be prescriptive in pointing out whether decentralization is the best way for institutionalized governance to achieve better service delivery, because that has already been done in a recent analysis of the governance system in Sudan (Hilal, McHugh, and Trithart 2014). Our aim, rather, is to inquire whether the way in which Sudan has organized decentralization and subnational governance can explain or give insight into regional inequalities in public service delivery. An additional factor is how decentralization might be related to the fact that when asked to evaluate the quality of services, almost all respondents in the region indicated that quality was not "adequate" or that it could be characterized as "poor" (see chapters 2, 3, and 4 of this volume and Crowther et al. 2014a, 2014b). The issue of decentralization is also appealing, because research has been conducted that describes how decentralization is realized in Sudan and how it affects the way donors address the issue of enhancing access to public services (see Moreno-Torres 2005).

Consequently, we offer the following hypothesis, which contains both factual and explanatory components. The factual part of our hypothesis is that decentralization efforts have not been effective in bringing better service delivery. In other words, the fact that the public perception of service delivery is poor has much to do with the failures of decentralization. The explanatory component is that the center–periphery hypothesis, rephrased, would mean that the elites in Khartoum have used decentralization as an instrumental means to retain power and wealth in Khartoum and regions closely associated with this dominant center. Our contribution to the established center–periphery debate, which focuses mostly on violent conflict as an outcome, is a different kind of framework.

What does decentralization entail? It comprises three different avenues: (a) political decentralization, when political authority is passed to subnational elements; (b) fiscal decentralization, when subnational governments have their own revenues and, with the help of central government transfers, must secure delivery of a large part of their public services; and (c) regulatory decentralization, when local institutions act according to a national government mandate, but transfer of financial resources or political authority is not involved (Ahmad and Brosio 2009).

Any possible effects of decentralization depend heavily on how decentralization is realized, how authority is passed to local levels, and, in turn, to what extent local municipalities are financially independent. Faguet (2014) notes that the academic literature on decentralization as a governance practice and its effects is vast, with hundreds of published academic works over the past 40 years. The basic themes include the effects of decentralization on investment levels, public service provision, the education and health sectors, macroeconomic stability, and the quality of governance.

With regard to the relationship between decentralization and service delivery—in the case of decentralized political authority to local communities, for instance—getting local leadership to become accountable is easier because devolved power eventually forces leaders to deliver public services properly (Ahmad et al. 2005, Mehrotra 2006). In other words, "decentralization may result in better service delivery. The decentralization of the provision of social services, such as education, health, water, and sanitation, may improve service delivery" (Ekpo 2007, 2). According to this approach, once power to provide public service delivery is transferred to the local level, it forces local leadership to perform well because of accountability pressures. However, many factors affect how decentralization functions and is implemented, which in turn have direct effects on its outcomes.

In essence, the idea of how fiscal decentralization is connected to service delivery relies on the notion that decentralization can trigger pressure for greater accountability and that "accountability and transparency in government actions can also be enhanced by bringing expenditure assignments closer to revenue sources" (de Mello Jr. 2000, 365). Additionally, a potential technical advantage exists as well: decentralization reduces information and transaction costs, because identifying how to spend resources for service delivery is easier at the local level (de Mello Jr. 2000).

Unfortunately, academic analysis on the relationship between decentralization and service delivery in Sudan is scarce. Political decentralization has been explored as a tool for democratization and formation of political oppositions (Green 2011) and the way it may take into account cultural and ethnic diversities (Duany 1994). With regard to decentralization and service delivery, there is plenty of literature on other Sub-Saharan countries (Conyers 2007; Dafflon and Madies 2012; Garcia and Rajkumar 2008). One of the reasons might be the difficulty in obtaining reliable and timely data on service delivery because of Sudan's multiple, severe, and protracted conflicts. For instance, the World Bank launched a service delivery indicators project for Africa in 2010, but did not include Sudan (World Bank 2015a). Notably, a complete vacuum exists regarding literature on decentralization and service delivery in Sudan.

Fiscal Decentralization and Service Delivery in Sudan: Exploring Institutional Design and Available Data

We concentrate on state-level analysis of the 18 states and nearly 200 localities that make up modern-day Sudan.

With regard to decentralization, 2005 marked a significant turning point. However, Sudan's 1998 national constitution (National Assembly 1998) and the 2005 interim national constitution (National Assembly 2005)[1] have more or less the same content and emphasis on decentralization. For instance, article 177(1) of the interim constitution states, "The Republic of the Sudan shall be decentralized and composed of states"; and, consequently, article 178(2) states,

"The state shall promote and empower local government." The interim constitution (schedule C) stipulates exclusive executive and legislative powers for states to deliver various services, among them the most basic—housing, health, and education. (See annex 8A for how service delivery responsibilities are divided between national and state levels.) The interim constitution also stipulates competence of states to raise revenues by local taxes. For a thorough account of how decentralization has been included in the constitutions of Sudan since 1953, see Mo (2014).

Since 2005, the Comprehensive Peace Agreement brought new detail and emphasis to what decentralization in Sudan should look like (Government of Sudan 2005). The agreement's protocol on wealth sharing laid out principles on how wealth was to be shared between the north and the south of the country, including transfers to states, and stipulated an oil and nonoil revenue-sharing mechanism among Sudan's states. Fiscal decentralization thus gained prominence regarding service delivery and was explicitly stated in the interim constitution as well (article 1.8).[2]

With regard to decentralization and service delivery, Sudan's states thus have a degree of autonomy in collecting certain local taxes, and the central government is responsible for sharing nationally collected revenues in the form of transfers to states. Consequently, states are responsible for basic service delivery. However, in practice, despite the legal system's focus on decentralization, the evidence and analysis show that decentralization is limited in practice.

Various reports, such as that of the International Monetary Fund (Flamini 2012), question whether fiscal decentralization has become a reality at all. The International Monetary Fund found that indicators used to assess fiscal decentralization (total revenues, tax revenue, total expenditures, and compensation) show that in 2010, the central government retained 71–97 percent of the execution powers on each of the four fiscal indicators, and this trend persisted throughout the period from 2000 to 10 (Flamini 2012).

Moreover, Sudan suffers from a vertical fiscal imbalance: states are incapable of financing their own expenditures using their own revenues from local taxes and fees. Between 2000 and 2010, the vertical fiscal imbalance increased from 25 percent to 70 percent, such that in 2010, 70 percent of state expenditures on average were financed by national government transfers, ultimately the consequence of vertical fiscal imbalance (Flamini 2012).

Because states are heavily dependent on central government transfers, the allocation of these transfers is of utmost importance. According to Flamini (2012), evidence shows that horizontal fiscal imbalance also exists: transfers per capita allocated to the top recipient state were on average six times higher than the lowest recipient during the period 2000 to 2010. Blue Nile, River Nile, and Northern were the top recipients, whereas North Kurdufan, Red Sea, and South Darfur received the least (Flamini 2012). The latest *Human Development Report* for Sudan reveals that those allocations are inconsistent with the level of development (UNDP Sudan 2012). Similarly, the latest poverty estimates show that North Kurdufan, Red Sea, and South Darfur received the least amount of government transfers, yet have the highest poverty estimates among Sudan's states (IMF 2013).

The formula regarding how government transfers should be allocated includes specific development and performance indicators to assess the need of each state (Shibly 2013). However, in relation to Sudan, the World Bank (2011, 23) concluded, "It cannot be established how actual transfer levels are arrived at; neither can the use of the formula being confirmed." Thus, allocation appears to be politically determined by the government's favoring certain states.

The above-mentioned empirical evidence shows that fiscal decentralization may be formally enshrined, but it is not a practical reality in Sudan. The main, negative result of that situation is the shortage and unequal distribution of resources across the states of Sudan. In 2010, the World Bank's large-scale public expenditure tracking survey focusing on health (as agreed with the government of Sudan) sought to determine to what extent and how health services were financed and delivered (World Bank 2011, 3). The sample represented both well-developed states, such as Khartoum, and least-developed states, such as South Kurdufan.

Obviously, the bulk of the survey's findings related to specific mechanisms for how money reaches health facilities, but it also found that service delivery depends on the total amount of money available. Health expenditure per capita, for example, was four times higher in Blue Nile, one of the most developed regions, than in North Kurdufan, one of the least-developed regions. The World Bank concluded: "Fiscal decentralization, while key to the vision of the CPA [Comprehensive Peace Agreement] and INC [interim national constitution], poses a number of challenges to revenue management. To fulfill service delivery responsibilities, subnational levels need adequate revenue to conduct expenditure assignments and address regional/local needs" (World Bank 2011, 3).

With regard to service delivery, results from the 2013 DFID Sudan household survey shows that people in Sudan are not satisfied with service quality and accessibility (see chapters 2, 3, and 4 of this volume and Crowther et al. 2014a, 2014b). The survey covered 11 services: (a) public schools, (b) public hospitals, (c) piped water, (d) sanitation, (e) electricity, (f) courts, (g) police, (h) local committees, (i) religious courts, (j) state-level public administration, and (k) federal-level public administration. Most of the services are delivered at the state level or jointly with the government (see annex 8A). Two basic trends can be discerned. First, when asked to evaluate the quality of services, respondents in almost all states indicated that quality was not "adequate" or that it was "poor." Second, the respondents were asked to answer a specific question about whether they perceived service accessibility to be less accessible than in Khartoum. The answers indicate that the majority of respondents, including those in Khartoum, thought that services outside Khartoum were less accessible (see chapters 2, 3, and 4 of this volume and Crowther et al. 2014a, 2014b).

Indeed, the pattern of how decentralization has been realized might well explain the results of the survey, because the states lack the necessary resources and those resources are unequally distributed. Such allocation leads (a) to poor performance in quality of services and (b) because of unequal distribution, to poor accessibility of services outside the state of Khartoum.

Figures 8.3 and 8.4 depict the correlation between money transfers to states and perceptions in service quality. The pattern of how resources are distributed is reflected in how respondents to the 2013 DFID Sudan household survey

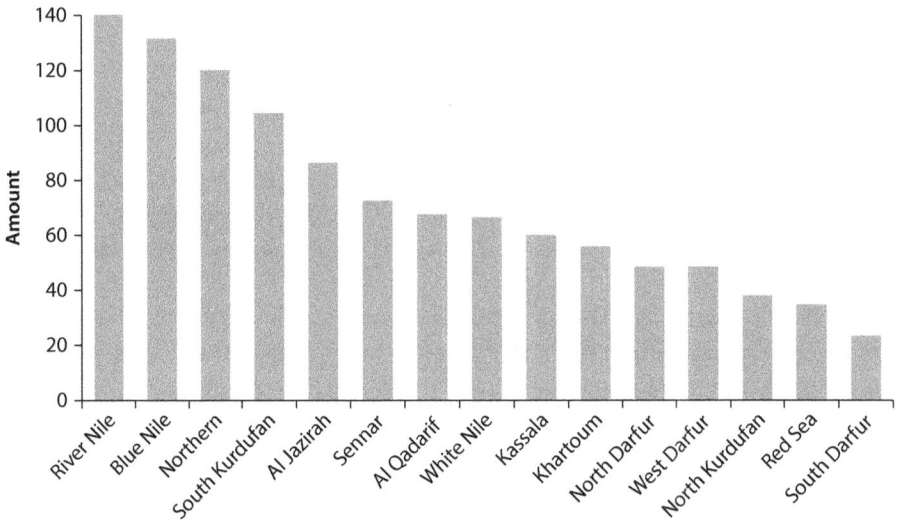

Figure 8.3 Per Capita Central Government Transfers, by State, 2000–10 Average
SDG, millions

Source: Adapted from Flamini 2012.
Note: SDG = Sudanese pound.

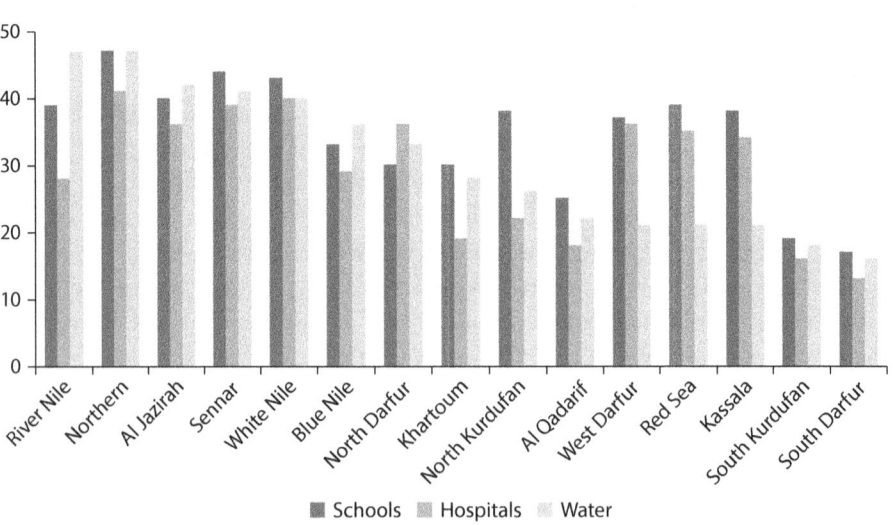

Figure 8.4 Perceived Quality of Services

Sources: Crowther et al. 2014a, 2014b.
a. Data from the 2013 U.K. Department for International Development Sudan household survey are sorted by how respondents evaluated the quality of water services.

evaluated quality of services. In general, a clear divide exists between northern states and marginalized states of the south.

Literature on fiscal decentralization in Sudan is vast (see, for example, Bell and Ahmed 2005; Bongo 2013; El-Badawi and Suliman 2010; Flamini 2012; Shibly 2013), but it is united by the common finding that Sudan has experienced vertical and horizontal fiscal imbalances for decades, imbalances that negatively affect service delivery. However, this literature is mainly preoccupied with discussing technical difficulties that impede decentralization.[3] We would like to go beyond technical findings and ask a more politically oriented question: What explains this long-lasting pattern of the central government in trying to maintain power and marginalizing particular regions?

Decentralization and the Center–Periphery Hypothesis

Alex de Waal (2007a, 2007b) proposes five hypotheses to explain Sudan's intractable conflicts. Among them is the center–periphery hypothesis, which has two versions in academic and investigative literature: either (a) a deliberate conspiracy exists among administrative, military, and commercial elites to exploit the provinces; or (b) those who accumulated power in the center during colonial times continue to do so at the expense of the peripheries (de Waal 2007a, 2007b). Actually, an argument has been made that Sudan is a case of a "marginalizing state" (Ylönen 2009, 43). Ylönen (2009) offers a thorough discussion of how marginalization of peripheries has occurred in various ways.

The practice of revenue sharing and fiscal decentralization also fits into this kind of pattern in a modified way. If the center–periphery hypothesis holds—that regions become marginalized as capital and wealth are accumulated at the expense of the regions—then wealth sharing, in a way that it is not properly distributed or that is distributed in a biased way, is just another version of the center–periphery hypothesis. If one thinks about consequences, marginalization policy inevitably leads to conflicts and insurgencies (for instance, see recent addition in Badmus 2011). In other words, the argument is that the way fiscal decentralization has been carried out leads to poor service delivery, which can be explained by recourse to a center–periphery framework.

Our aim is not to detail the specific ways in which the center–periphery mechanism works in decentralization (it would indeed require detailed qualitative analysis), but rather to look at supporting literature and argue that considering the center–periphery hypothesis in the particular context of decentralization and service delivery is worthwhile. Briefly looking at the history of how decentralization was carried out in Sudan is valuable to understand the center–periphery pattern. But for reasons of space, we will restrict ourselves to the regime of Colonel Jaafar Nimeiri (1969–85) in which decentralization can be seen as having taken a large-scale approach that affected current establishments.

During the Nimeiri period, in 1971, the Local Government Act was passed, which established provincial administration. The system did not work, however, because delegated responsibilities to local governments did not match budgetary allocations, and one of the explanations for the failure was that central government did not want to give up its power (Rondinelli 1981). In 1980, Nimeiri introduced a new system of subnational governance. Interestingly, an article written by a member of the People's Assembly described it, explaining that the "creation of these governments is designed to curtail centripetal forces by encouraging rural development and by building up services to the benefit of the regions" (Alassam 1983, 120). However, an argument has been made that the system was simple manipulation: the idea was to set up ineffective regional governments just to get support from people and to show that the government was willing to share power (Al-Teraifi 1991). The government never really cared about the regions and, furthermore, "perhaps no other country in Africa has embarked on such varied experiments with decentralization as has the Sudan, in a bid to garner popular support for authoritarian regimes" (Mohammed 2006, 54).

A rigorous quantitative study of how Sudan's central government allocated resources to the states between 1971 and 2002 concluded that revenues were directed toward national goals, thus neglecting the peripheries, and overall that policy can be described as one of marginalization (Mohammed 2006). With regard to revenue sharing, there is a particular tendency to neglect the Darfur region, whereas the northern region has obviously been favored by the government (Flamini 2012; Mohammed 2006).

After Nimeiri, and the 1989 coup, the government of Sudan continued with decentralization schemes in 1991 and 1994, finally consolidating them in the 1998 constitution. However, scholars argue that Sudan has enacted substantial legislation regarding local government, but "the phenomenon has much to do with the desire of central government to manipulate the system to serve the political ends of incumbent governments than with genuine endeavors to serve the interests of local communities" (Abdul-Jalil, Mohammed, and Yousuf 2007).

In this context, *The Black Book*, released anonymously but later attributed to Seekers of Truth and Justice (2002), importantly documents detailed statistics about the hegemony of the northern region over the whole country. The book consists of two parts, one released in 2000 and the other in 2002, and became politically significant in the context of the war that escalated in Darfur from 2003. Among such factors as the central government's favoring the northern region in practically every area of power sharing, the book also mentions fiscal decentralization and notes that the mechanism is set up such that 76 percent of the representatives of the National Council for Distribution of Resources come from the northern region (Seekers of Truth and Justice 2002). A good account of how the three northern tribes acquired hegemony in taking government posts despite the enormous ethnic diversity of the country can be found in Musa (2010).

Nevertheless, much speculation has arisen about whether the analysis and data provided in *The Black Book* (Seekers of Truth and Justice 2002) are accurate.

There also have been academic attempts to verify its claims. One study (Cobham 2005) tried to determine not only whether budget allocation was biased toward the northern and Darfur regions, but also whether development outcomes signaled reasons for concern about the pattern mentioned in *The Black Book*. Exploring the patterns of budget allocation and various indicators of health and education, the author concluded that "data offer strong support for the view that the government of Sudan has—through discriminatory allocation of finance—promoted deepening inequality among regions, undermining human development outcomes in the East and West of the country especially" (Cobham 2005, 476).

The debate about marginalization has changed since South Sudan's secession in 2011, but it has not changed substantially. If one applies broad macroeconomic perspective to the question of how Sudan is governed, then some scholars contend that Sudan resembles an "extractive state," meaning that President Omar al-Bashir has concentrated political and economic power in Khartoum; persistently favors a development path that excludes most of the regions; and favors an economic path of supporting huge dam projects, labor-intensive gold mining, and oil and gas exploration, an approach that does not result in countrywide development (Wohlmuth et al. 2014).

Interestingly, de Waal (2013), in the context of marginalization, has examined whether anything close to a popular uprising that could induce regime change could happen in Sudan. He argues that in drawing a map of power relations, one has to apply the thinking of a political marketplace where the battle to secure patronage is constant. The consequence of this type of competitive clientelism promotes ethnicization, separatism, and grievances and obviously does not lead to the possibility of a unified civic uprising in the peripheries; he thinks that this is one of the main reasons that the Arab Spring left Sudan untouched (de Waal 2013).

In addition, a separate study argues that Sudan stands out as an outlier with regard to insurgencies, arguing that none of them have led to power seizure or change of power structure (D'Agoôt 2013). Instead, a new imperative of the identity-based goals—such as the attainment of autonomy or power-sharing arrangements—has taken prominence (D'Agoôt 2013).

However, despite insurgencies, Musso (2012) argues that, in the political landscape, the current regime has acquired almost undisputed hegemony that has penetrated the social, political, and economic spheres. The regime has managed to demobilize the opposition effectively and create a situation where opposition neither supports government nor opposes it (Ali 2014).

Using the DFID Sudan household survey data on political affiliation, we attempt to test for the current regime's dominance and to look at whether the way in which financial resources have been distributed regionally in the framework of decentralization is correlated with the patronage system. Do higher amounts of central government transfers lead to greater support for the ruling party in the states?

Table 8.5 indicates that in almost all states, the ruling National Congress Party enjoys undisputed support, which is in line with the argument presented previously. However, we also can detect that a center–periphery divide exists for party affiliation. That means that patronage is weaker in Sudan's peripheries, leading to smaller amounts of money transfers and less favorable outcomes in service delivery.

With regard to Sudan's future, the secession of South Sudan has redirected the world's attention to that country, but the center–periphery question is still an issue and could pose further threats to development in Sudan if unresolved (Temin and Murphy 2011). To deal with it, the government (as well as international institutions) needs to emphasize governance where discussion has been framed more in the context of conflict and its implications rather than in applying center–periphery thinking (Temin and Murphy 2011). Along the same lines, Kock (2011) argues that after the secession of South Sudan, the center–periphery issue is Sudan's "national question." "These relations will have to be negotiated with renewed vigour by power brokers and leaders inside Sudan, as a new chapter in Sudanese history begins" (Kock 2011, 7). Thus, in future analysis of fiscal decentralization and service delivery, center–periphery thinking should occupy a prominent role.

Table 8.5 Contingency Table on Party Affiliation in Sudan
percentage

State	Umma	NCP	PCP	DUP	Communist	No party	Other	Total
White Nile	8	67	3	6	0	16	1	100
Sennar	13	63	2	5	0	17	1	100
Kassala	9	60	2	8	1	16	4	100
Northern	12	59	3	14	1	9	3	100
North Kurdufan	7	52	4	6	0	30	1	100
Red Sea	15	51	5	6	4	12	7	100
Blue Nile	14	51	13	6	0	14	1	100
Al Jazirah	8	46	3	8	1	27	7	100
River Nile	9	46	2	10	3	28	2	100
Al Qadarif	23	45	9	9	0	9	5	100
South Kurdufan	38	38	9	9	1	6	0	100
West Darfur	17	36	14	6	3	20	3	100
South Darfur	23	32	7	8	3	24	2	100
North Darfur	19	32	9	13	5	20	2	100
Khartoum	7	15	4	16	5	45	9	100
Total	14	44	5	9	2	22	4	100

Source: Based on data from the 2013 U.K. Department for International Development Sudan household surveys.
Note: Respondents were asked, "Which political party do you think you would be most likely to support, if elections were held tomorrow?" DUP = Democratic Unionist Party; NCP = National Congress Party; PCP = Popular Congress Party.

Conclusions

This analysis seeks to explore governance and service delivery in Sudan using a decentralization framework in general, with particular attention to fiscal decentralization, and to explain what the state of service delivery is in Sudan and why. The analysis shows that fiscal decentralization can be seen only on paper.

The analysis indicates that Sudan's states have experienced a growing vertical fiscal imbalance, meaning that their own revenues are not sufficient to cover their responsibilities to deliver services; consequently, they are heavily dependent on central government transfers. The transfers also have created a horizontal fiscal imbalance, in which western and southern states have been marginalized and continuously receive less than northern states. Thus, vertical fiscal imbalance creates a shortage of money, but horizontal imbalance only exacerbates the ability of states to deliver public services. The 2013 DFID Sudan household survey results, which also covered service delivery, might be explained by this pattern. Additionally, if one looks at development indicators of neglected states, then the unfair system undoubtedly creates negative effects for development per se.

To explain why fiscal decentralization has not worked and favors particular regions, we have applied the center–periphery hypothesis. We modified the hypothesis by stating that accumulating wealth in the center and marginalizing peripheries is practically the same as giving no wealth to others; yet decentralization is about wealth sharing. By looking at the academic literature that discusses decentralization and wealth sharing, the center–periphery hypothesis is one of the main explanatory arguments. We conclude that since the secession of South Sudan, the center–periphery issue will continue to be important for Sudan and needs to be taken into account when analyzing decentralization and service delivery.

Annex 8A Distribution of Responsibilities among Different Levels of Government in Sudan

National competencies	*State competencies*	*Concurrent competencies*
National defense	Professional associations	State constitution
Foreign affairs	Tertiary education, education policy, and scientific research	State police and prisons
Nationality and naturalization		Local government
Passports and visas	Health policy	State information, state publications, and state media
Immigration	Urban development, planning, and housing	
Currency, coinage, and exchange control	Trade, commerce, and industry	Social welfare
	Delivery of public services	State civil service
Constitutional court and other national courts	Banking and insurance	State judiciary
	Bankruptcy and insolvency	State land and natural resources
National police and prisons	Disaster management	Cultural matters within the state
Postal services	Electricity generation and water and waste management	Regulation of religious matters
Aviation and navigation		Internal and external borrowing

table continues next page

National competencies	State competencies	Concurrent competencies
National lands and national natural resources	Information, publications, media, broadcasting, and telecommunications	Management of state lands
		Provision of health care
Central bank	Environmental management	Regulation of businesses
National debt	Relief, repatriation, resettlement, rehabilitation, and reconstruction	Management of state natural resources and forestry resources
National states of emergency		
International and interstate transport	International and regional agreements on culture, sports, trade, investment, credit, loans, grants, and technical assistance	Primary and secondary schools
		Agriculture within the state
National economic policy and planning	Financial and economic policies and planning	Intrastate public transport and roads
		Population policy and family planning
Management of the Nile waters and transboundary waters	Gender policy	State referenda
	Water resources other than interstate waters	
National information, publications, and telecommunications regulations	State courts responsible for enforcing national laws	Town and rural planning
		Traditional and customary law
	Land regulation	
National elections		

Source: Adapted from Hilal, McHugh, and Trithart 2014.

Notes

1. The new constitution is under discussion.
2. The protocol on wealth sharing, Article 1.8, states: "Revenue sharing should reflect a commitment to devolution of power and decentralization of decision making in regard to development, service delivery, and governance."
3. For example, the composition of a formula to establish the correct financial need of the states for governmental transfers, low capacity of the states to collect revenues, underdeveloped public administration in the states, poor management of funds, and more are discussed also.

References

Abdul-Jalil, M., A. A. Mohammed, and A. Yousuf. 2007. "Native Administration and Local Governance in Darfur: Past and Future." In *War in Darfur and the Search for Peace*, edited by A. de Waal, 25–74. Cambridge, MA: Harvard University Press.

Ahmad, E., and G. Brosio. 2009. "What Do We Know? Evidence on Decentralization and Local Service Provision." In *Does Decentralization Enhance Service Delivery and Poverty Reduction?* edited by E. Ahmad and G. Brosio, 1–22. Cheltenham, U.K.: Elgar.

Ahmad, J., S. Devarajan, S. Khemani, and S. Shah. 2005. "Decentralization and Service Delivery." Policy Research Working Paper 3603, World Bank, Washington, DC.

Alassam, M. 1983. "Regional Government in the Sudan." *Public Administration and Development* 3 (2): 111–20. doi:10.1002/pad.4230030203.

Ali, H. I. 2014. "Whither Sudan?" *Contemporary Arab Affairs* 7 (3): 380–97. doi:10.1080/17550912.2014.932110.

Al-Teraifi, A. 1991. "Regionalisation in the Sudan: Characteristics, Problems and Prospects." In *Sudan after Nimeiri*, edited by P. Woodward, 92–128. London: Routledge.

Badmus, I. A. 2011. "Contesting Exclusion: Uneven Development and the Genesis of the Sudan's Darfur War." *Journal of Alternative Perspectives in the Social Sciences* 3 (3): 880–912.

Bell, M., and M. Ahmed. 2005. "The Government of Sudan: Intergovernmental Policies and Issues." Working Paper 11, George Washington Institute of Public Policy, Washington, DC. http://www.gwu.edu/~gwipp/papers/wp011.pdf.

Bongo, S. 2013. "Fiscal Decentralization in Gadarif State: Did It Realize the Promise?" University of Gadarif, Sudan. http://www.ecineq.org/ecineq_bari13/FILESxBari13/CR2/p150.pdf.

Cobham, A. 2005. "Causes of Conflict in Sudan: Testing the Black Book." *European Journal of Development Research* 17 (3): 462–80. doi:10.1080/09578810500209254.

Conyers, D. 2007. "Decentralisation and Service Delivery: Lessons from Sub-Saharan Africa." *IDS Bulletin* 38 (1): 18–32. doi:10.1111/j.1759-5436.2007.tb00334.x.

Crowther, N., K. Okamura, C. Raja, D. Rinnert, and E. Spencer. 2014a. "'Quo Vadis, Sudan?' A Preliminary Analysis of the 2013 DFID Household Survey." Interim report, London School of Economics and Political Science, London.

———. 2014b. "Inequalities in Public Services in the Sudan: Using a Perceptions-Informed View to Drive Policy in Education, Health and Water Provision." LSE Master of Public Administration (MPA) Capstone Report, London School of Economics and Political Science, London. http://r4d.dfid.gov.uk/Output/195649/Default.aspx.

Dafflon, B., and T. Madies. 2012. *The Political Economy of Decentralization in Sub-Saharan Africa: A New Implementation Model in Burkina Faso, Ghana, Kenya, and Senegal*. Washington, DC: World Bank.

D'Agoôt, M. 2013. "Understanding the Lethargy of Sudan's Periphery-Originated Insurgencies." *Small Wars & Insurgencies* 24 (1): 57–83. doi:10.1080/09592318.2013.740229.

de Mello, L. R., Jr. 2000. "Fiscal Decentralization and Intergovernmental Fiscal Relations: A Cross-Country Analysis." *World Development* 28 (2): 365–80. doi:10.1016/S0305-750X(99)00123-0.

de Waal, A. 2007a. "Sudan: The Turbulent State." In *War in Darfur and the Search for Peace*, edited by A. de Waal, 1–35. Cambridge, MA: Harvard University Press.

———. 2007b. "Sudan: What Kind of State? What Kind of Crisis?" Occasional Paper 2, Crisis States Research Centre, London School of Economics and Political Science, London. http://www.justiceafrica.org/wp-content/uploads/2007/04/DeWaal_Crisis_States_2.pdf.

———. 2013. "Sudan's Elusive Democratisation: Civic Mobilisation, Provincial Rebellion and Chameleon Dictatorships." *Journal of Contemporary African Studies* 31 (2): 213–34. doi:10.1080/02589001.2013.786901.

DFID (U.K. Department for International Development). 2009. "Political Economy Analysis: How to Note." Practice paper, DFID, London. http://www.gsdrc.org/docs/open/PO58.pdf.

Duany, W. 1994. "The Problem of Centralization in the Sudan." *Northeast African Studies* 1 (2): 75–102. doi:10.1353/nas.1994.0008.

Ebaidalla, E. M. 2014. "The Effects of Oil Price Volatility on the Sudanese Economy." *Eastern Africa Social Science Research Review* 30 (1): 1–26. doi:10.1353/eas.2014.0000.

Ekpo, A. 2007. "Decentralization and Service Delivery: A Framework." Report for the African Economic Research Consortium. Department of Economics, University of Uyo, Nigeria. http://www.africaportal.org/dspace/articles/decentralization-and-service-delivery-framework.

El-Badawi, I., and K. Suliman. 2010. "Toward an Equitable Inter-Governmental Transfer System for the Sudan." *Sudan Journal of Economic and Social Studies* 8 (1): 107–53.

Faguet, J.-P. 2014. "Decentralization and Governance." *World Development, Decentralization and Governance* 53 (January): 2–13. doi:10.1016/j.worlddev.2013.01.002.

Flamini, V. 2012. "Fiscal Decentralization: Trends, Challenges and Perspectives." IMF Country Report 12/299, International Monetary Fund, Washington, DC. https://www.imf.org/external/pubs/ft/scr/2012/cr12299.pdf.

Fritz, V., B. Levy, and K. Kaiser, eds. 2009. *Problem-Driven Governance and Political Economy Analysis: Good Practice Framework.* Washington, DC: World Bank. http://siteresources.worldbank.org/EXTPUBLICSECTORANDGOVERNANCE/Resources/PGPEbook121509.pdf.

Fritz, V., B. Levy, and R. Ort, eds. 2014. *Problem-Driven Political Economy Analysis: The World Bank Experience.* Washington, DC: World Bank.

Garcia, M., and A. S. Rajkumar. 2008. *Achieving Better Service Delivery through Decentralization in Ethiopia.* Washington, DC: World Bank.

Government of Sudan. 2005. *2005 Comprehensive Peace Agreement.* United Nations Mission in Sudan, Khartoum. http://unmis.unmissions.org/Default.aspx?tabid=515.

Green, E. 2011. "Decentralization and Political Opposition in Contemporary Africa: Evidence from Sudan and Ethiopia." *Democratization* 18 (5): 1087–105. doi:10.1080/13510347.2011.603476.

Hilal, T., G. Mchugh, and A. Trithart. 2014. "Governance in the Sudan: Options for Political Accommodation in the Republic of Sudan." Briefing Paper 7, Governance and Peacebuilding Series, Conflict Dynamics International, Cambridge, MA. http://www.cdint.org/documents/CDI-Governance_in_the_Sudan_full_report_English.pdf.

IMF (International Monetary Fund). 2013. "Sudan: Interim Poverty Reduction Strategy Paper." IMF Country Report 13/318, Washington, DC. http://www.imf.org/external/pubs/ft/scr/2013/cr13318.pdf.

———. 2014. "Sudan: First Review under the Staff-Monitored Program." IMF Country Report 14/249, Washington, DC. http://www.imf.org/external/pubs/ft/scr/2014/cr14249.pdf.

Kock, P. 2011. "The Politics of Resources, Resistance and Peripheries in Sudan." Occasional Paper 86, South African Institute of International Affairs, Johannesburg. http://www.saiia.org.za/occasional-papers/the-politics-of-resources-resistance-and-peripheries-in-sudan.

Kok, P. 1996. "Sudan: Between Radical Restructuring and Deconstruction of State Systems." *Review of African Political Economy* 23 (70): 555–62. doi:10.1080/03056249608704223.

Mehrotra, S. 2006. "Governance and Basic Social Services: Ensuring Accountability in Delivery through Deep Democratic Decentralization." *Journal of International Development* 18 (2): 263–83. doi:10.1002/jid.1219.

Mo, K. 2014. "Contested Constitutions: Constitutional Development in Sudan 1953–2005." Working paper, Chr. Michelsen Institute, Bergen, Norway. http://www.cmi.no/publications/file/5265-contested-constitutions-constitutional-development.pdf.

Mohammed, A. A. 2006. "The Problem of Uneven Regional Development in the Northern Sudan." *Fletcher Forum of World Affairs* 30 (1): 41–60.

Moreno-Torres, M. 2005. "Service Delivery in a Difficult Environment: The Child-Friendly Community Initiative in Sudan." U.K. Department for International Development, London. http://www.eldis.org/fulltext/CFCI-Sudan-casestudy.pdf.

Musa, A. M. 2010. "Marginalization and Ethnicization in the Sudan: How the Elite Failed to Stabilize a Diverse Country." *Contemporary Arab Affairs* 3 (4): 551–62. doi:10.1080/17550912.2010.522113.

Musso, G. 2012. "Electoral Politics and Religious Parties in Sudan: An Analysis of the April 2010 Election." *African Conflict and Peacebuilding Review* 2 (1): 58–86. doi:10.2979/africonfpeacrevi.2.1.58.

National Assembly. 1998. Constitution of the Republic of Sudan. http://www.icrc.org/ihl-nat.nsf/0/d728f18be88d9482c1256dc600507f33/$FILE/Constitution%20Sudan%20-%20EN.pdf.

———. 2005. Interim Constitution of the Republic of Sudan. https://unmis.unmissions.org/Portals/UNMIS/CPA%20Monitor/Annexes/Annex%201-%20Interim%20National%20Constitution%20of%20Sudan%20-%20FIXED.pdf.

Nour, S. S. O. M. 2013. "Development and Social Justice: Education, Training and Health in Sudan." Working Paper 2013-013, United Nations University–Maastricht Economic and Social Research Institute on Innovation and Technology, Maastricht, Netherlands. http://merit.unu.edu/publications/wppdf/2013/wp2013-013.pdf.

Resnick, D. 2014. "Urban Governance and Service Delivery in African Cities: The Role of Politics and Policies." *Development Policy Review* 32 (S1): S3–S17. doi:10.1111/dpr.12066.

Rondinelli, D. A. 1981. "Administrative Decentralisation and Economic Development: The Sudan's Experiment with Devolution." *Journal of Modern African Studies* 19 (4): 595–624. doi:10.1017/S0022278X00020188.

Seekers of Truth and Justice. 2002. *The Black Book: Imbalance of Power and Wealth in Sudan*. Translated by Abdullahi Osman el-Tom. 2004. http://orientemiedo.files.wordpress.com/2009/10/justice-and-equality-movement-the-black-book.pdf.

Sharfi, M. H. 2014. "The Dynamics of the Loss of Oil Revenues in the Economy of North Sudan." *Review of African Political Economy* 41 (140): 316–22. doi:10.1080/03056244.2013.876982.

Shibly, M. M. 2013. "Fiscal Transfers: Towards a Pro-Poor System—Assessment of the Existing Inter-Governmental Fiscal Transfers System in Sudan." Policy paper, United Nations Development Programme Sudan, Khartoum. http://www.sd.undp.org/content/dam/sudan/docs/policy_roundtable/doc/Final%20%20Research%20Paper%20Assessment%20of%20Existing%20Inter-Governmental%20Fiscal%20Transfer%20System.pdf.

Temin, J., and T. Murphy. 2011. "Toward a New Republic of Sudan." Special Report 278, United States Institute of Peace, Washington, DC. http://www.usip.org/sites/default/files/SR278.pdf.

UNDP (United Nations Development Programme) Sudan. 2012. *Sudan National Human Development Report 2012*. Khartoum: UNDP Sudan. http://www.sd.undp.org/content/dam/sudan/docs/Sudan_NHDR_2012.pdf.

Wohlmuth, K., A. Gutowski, M. Kandil, T. Knedlik, and O. O. Uzor, eds. 2014. *Macroeconomic Policy Formation in Africa: Country Cases*. Münster, Germany: Lit Verlag.

World Bank. 2011. *Sudan: Public Expenditure Tracking Survey (PETS)—Case Study of the Health Sector*. Report 67712-SD. Washington, DC: World Bank. http://www-wds.worldbank.org/external/default/WDSContentServer/WDSP/IB/2012/11/29/000386194_20121129010150/Rendered/PDF/NonAsciiFileName0.pdf.

———. 2012. *The Status of the Education Sector in Sudan*. Washington, DC: World Bank.

———. 2015a. *Service Delivery Indicators*. Washington, DC: World Bank. http://www.sdindicators.org/where-are-we-now/.

———. 2015b. *Worldwide Governance Indicators*. Washington, DC: World Bank. http://data.worldbank.org/data-catalog/worldwide-governance-indicators.

Ylönen, A. 2009. "On Sources of Political Violence in Africa: The Case of 'Marginalizing State' in Sudan." *Política y Cultura* 32 (July): 37–59.

CHAPTER 9

Still Far from Development: Humanitarian Assistance Policy and Practice in Darfur between 2004 and 2014

Dragana Marinkovic

Introduction

Darfur has been considered a humanitarian emergency for almost 12 years. Although the conflict there continues, changes, and evolves, the attention on Darfur, in particular by Western media, has moved elsewhere to new conflicts, such as the one in Syria. Humanitarian assistance to Darfur is also diminishing, despite the fact that the conflict continues and that no feasible peace agreement is in sight. The government of Sudan has successfully managed to resist international humanitarian intervention in the forms of both aid and protection and, in this way, to hide Darfur from the eyes of the international public. The government has accomplished this by restricting access to Darfur, expelling agencies from Darfur, and strictly controlling the programming and aid that goes to its five states. In addition, the government has pushed for a policy shift from humanitarian to development aid under the pretext that the war in Darfur is over. This approach has resulted in a shift in aid policy toward reconstruction and development in an environment not conducive for such a policy. It also has resulted in the withdrawal of peacekeepers and a consequent lack of protection for the affected population. These developments have left many in Darfur vulnerable and on their own, faced with a predatory government, conflict, and a lack of basic means to make a living.

This chapter explores the trajectory of humanitarian assistance to Darfur from 2004—when, after the signing of the ceasefire agreement, there was a significant scaling up of the emergency response to the crisis in Darfur—until 2014. The chapter aims to illustrate the ways in which the political influence of the Sudanese government hampered the ability of humanitarian agencies and peacekeepers to provide adequate assistance and protection to the affected populations and to demonstrate the effect of that obstruction on the people on the ground. The government has attempted to obstruct the work of the international agencies in two main ways: first, by acting forcefully through restrictions, expulsions, and various bureaucratic obstacles, and second, by pushing for a policy shift from humanitarian aid to development assistance under the pretext that the situation in Darfur is stable enough and suitable for a development-oriented strategy. This shift happened despite the lack of a feasible peace agreement that could have been accepted by the majority of the warring parties. The government efforts rendered international agencies unable to protect and provide adequate humanitarian assistance to affected populations. The consequences were detrimental to the conflict-affected populations, who found themselves in a situation in which the majority were unable to secure livelihoods for themselves because of the ongoing conflict, while humanitarian assistance and protection were constantly diminishing. At present, similar circumstances remain. Notably, the government was not the only actor that contributed to the obstruction and failure of humanitarian work in Darfur; many rebel groups played roles as well. This chapter, however, focuses primarily on the Sudanese government and explores its role in this complex environment.

To illustrate the overarching conclusion, this chapter combines quantitative insights from the U.K. Department for International Development (DFID) Sudan household survey along with qualitative data. First, the chapter looks at why the African Union–United Nations Hybrid Operation in Darfur (UNAMID) was and still is unable to provide adequate protection to conflict-affected populations despite its mandate to do so. The chapter describes the history of UNAMID's gradual politicization on the ground, its failures, and the reasons behind them, showing how the government used both of the previously described techniques to prevent UNAMID's work. The chapter then examines the challenges that humanitarian agencies face in Darfur, showing how the restrictions and expulsions as well as the policy shift from humanitarian to development assistance had negative consequences for the conflict-affected populations. The chapter draws a broader conclusion that the Sudanese government's overall resistance to international intervention has been successfully operationalized through the promotion of the idea that the war in Darfur is over. International agencies, and in particular Western donors, fell into the trap of supporting an illegitimate and unfeasible peace agreement that the government subsequently used to implement strategies to obstruct the work of humanitarian agencies.

This chapter focuses on Darfur alone for several reasons. Darfur has been called one of the worst humanitarian emergencies in the world by a number of United Nations (UN) officials (UN News Centre 2004). It has been considered a humanitarian emergency for almost 12 years. Spending on humanitarian aid in Sudan overall is substantial, and in 2013 alone more than US$635 million went to Sudan (UN OCHA 2013), a great percentage of which was allocated to Darfur. Therefore, Darfur represents an important case for the study of humanitarian policy. Understanding how conflict and politics interact with humanitarian assistance policy there may shed light on important aspects of humanitarian policy overall.

The chapter points to an important issue related to using data for decision making in (humanitarian) policy in fragile contexts. First, it emphasizes the importance of data collection in places like Darfur, where data are not only scarce but also difficult to make available or public. The chapter illustrates how political factors contribute to information obscurity, which may affect important policy decisions. Efforts such as the DFID household survey allow for a peek into new pieces of information that may be crucial to create a more complete picture of the situation on the ground. Triangulating that information with other narratives, including the official government narrative, allows for an improved understanding of conflict dynamics and, in particular, people's perceptions of the conflict.

Methodology

The methodology used for this chapter consists of qualitative research that includes reviews of various documents from a variety of international donors and agencies, newspaper articles and other press releases, academic literature, and expert interviews with academics and practitioners. The quantitative component involved descriptive statistical analysis of the data from a public perception survey conducted in 2013 in Sudan and provided to the author by DFID Sudan; descriptive statistical analysis of funding data gathered by the United Nations Office for the Coordination of Humanitarian Affairs (UN OCHA); and displacement data from the United Nations High Commissioner for Refugees.

Darfur presents a particular research challenge because of the general lack of credible data. International organizations have had substantial difficulty gathering complete data because of the constantly changing dynamics of the ongoing conflict in the past 12 years. When data exist, they usually remain under the control of the Sudanese government, which prohibits access to or publication of any information that would jeopardize its reputation. Thus, international organizations often do not publish potentially informative data. The lack of available information keeps the conflict in Darfur further isolated and off the agenda of the international community. Examples of data withheld by the international community under the pressure of the Sudanese government are plenty, ranging from UNAMID's unwillingness to publish data on human rights violations (Reeves 2014c) to the hesitation of the United Nations International Children's Emergency Fund to publish shocking data on child malnutrition (Reeves 2014a). The public perceptions survey conducted by DFID in 2013 presents a fairly complete data set. However, some information from it may not be credible; many respondents might not have answered the survey questions truthfully because they may have felt that doing so would pose a threat to their safety (Crowther et al. 2014).

Darfur in Context

The most recent conflict in Darfur escalated in 2003, although communal conflicts had been present before then (Brosché 2008). The drivers of conflict in Darfur are many and complex, and determining a single root cause is difficult

(Pantuliano and O'Callaghan 2006). As de Waal (2007, 36) explains, "disorder in the peripheries does not pose a threat, either economically or politically, to the class that prospers at the center of Sudan." Tubiana (2011, 227) points out that Darfur's inhabitants have long felt that they are contributing to the country's wealth while not receiving anything in return. The inequality has manifested itself both in the lack of provision of government services and in the strong sense of discrimination felt by Darfurians (Tubiana 2011, 227).

The Black Book, published by the members of the Islamist movement Seekers of Truth and Justice (2000), who later founded the Justice and Equality Movement (JEM), a rebel group in Darfur, states that "since Independence, Darfur has not secured a single developmental scheme which could finance a single Local Administrative Area for three months" (Seekers of Truth and Justice 2000). This points both to the grievances and to the neglect of the center toward the periphery. Education also exemplifies the inequality. As *The Black Book* (Seekers of Truth and Justice 2000) notes, in Western Darfur, primary schools remained closed for two years because of a lack of books and of money to pay staff, and only 4,211 children were able to take the primary school examination. That number is less than the total "number of primary school leavers in a single Local Administrative Area in the Northern Region" (Seekers of Truth and Justice 2000).

Apart from the neglect of the center toward Darfur, ethnic tensions over land and resources have contributed significantly to the conflict. The Sudanese government has manipulated these tensions and attempted to recruit proxies for fighting from various ethnic groups (Tubiana 2011). The conflict has produced mass killings, mass displacement, and rape and has left people in the region unable to sustainably provide for their own livelihood. Various experts estimated the death toll to be around 300,000 in 2014, but it is likely much higher (Banco 2014). In the same year, more than 2 million people were displaced. Mass rape has been used as a weapon of war with an estimated 200 women raped in a single attack on Tabit in 2014 (Reeves 2014c).

Effects of the Conflict on Livelihoods in Darfur

Conflict in Darfur has had a detrimental effect on people's ability to secure their own livelihoods, sometimes irreversibly changing the ways in which people obtain income by destroying stable sources of essential commodities and creating vulnerability among the population. For example, in a study of villages in North, West, and South Darfur, Young et al. (2005) describe how between 2001 and 2004, systematic attacks on villages caused the destruction of livestock, homes and farms, human capital (through deaths, the separation of families, and violence against women), social capital (by undermining of support groups in the community), and natural resources (through contamination of water or destruction of land). All of those actions significantly hampered the ability of communities to develop survival strategies. Not only have the communities experienced failed production, closed market routes, the inability to gain access to natural resources, and the inability of migrant workers to send remittances, but also the communities have had to constantly change and evolve their strategies to adapt to the context of conflict. These factors made it difficult for the humanitarian agencies working in Darfur and other conflict-affected areas to assist these populations (Young et al. 2005). There was and still is a general lack of information about who are the vulnerable people and why, and those impediments to information exist both because of the government's unwillingness to provide adequate data and because of the constantly changing conflict patterns (Feinstein International Center 2011). Therefore, Darfur has experienced a significant increase in chronic vulnerability, especially among the displaced, "who are failing to achieve sustainable livelihoods despite ongoing processes of urbanization and livelihood adaptations" (Feinstein International Center 2011, 15). In some areas, the preconflict sources of livelihood have disappeared altogether (Buchanan-Smith and Jaspars 2007). The study of North and West Darfur found that large numbers of people became dependent on brick-making as a common source of daily labor, as well as petty trade, collection of natural resources, looting, and theft (Buchanan-Smith and Jaspars 2007).

Local institutions and communities have changed significantly, and that change affects not only people but also the work of humanitarian agencies. For example, local institutions ceased to exist, local leaders often have been killed or have fled, and many preconflict community-based groups are no longer in place. Over the course of 2004, many new international organizations and nongovernmental organizations (NGOs) went to Darfur as part of an accelerated mobilization of emergency responses. Some new support groups in different communities emerged as well (Jaspars 2010). The new local governance systems have interacted in various ways with the system of international humanitarian aid, with a mixed record of success. For example, one of the problems mentioned in the Feinstein International Center study is that international NGOs have "ignored or even shunned local capacity" (Feinstein International Center 2011, 11). Moreover, local institutions working with the United Nations did not have the capacity and flexibility needed to address the challenges of the crisis (Feinstein International Center 2011). Politicization was a problem; many camps for internally displaced persons (IDPs) were highly politicized, and aid distribution was based on adherence to different groups.

In addition to looking at how conflict affects livelihoods in Darfur, one must consider how changes and adaptations in livelihoods affect conflict. The role that humanitarian actors and NGOs play is crucial to consider given that humanitarian aid and other forms of assistance are not isolated from local dynamics and instead constitute the political economy of conflict (Middleton and O'Keefe 2006). A study conducted by Young et al. (2007) describes some of the ways in which changing livelihood strategies affect conflict. In South Darfur, for example, livestock production and maintenance often has become impossible because the disruption of many migratory routes and the collapse of many previously existing markets make earning a living difficult for pastoralists. Furthermore, the prevailing lack of security has prompted many pastoralists to sell their livestock and take up arms.

The mass selling of livestock led to a decrease in prices. The resulting inability to maintain a livelihood from livestock production prompted many to engage in agriculture, a choice that led to land ownership disputes. Competing land claims generated further conflict related both to land issues and to the exploitation of natural resources (Young et al. 2007).

Shrinking Humanitarian Space and Security and the Effect on Assistance

Physical security is one of the major constraints for obtaining a sustainable livelihood in Darfur, and international agencies have largely been inadequate in protecting people because of politically driven access constraints, capacity gaps, and, to an extent, a lack of understanding of local dynamics. This section provides further insights on Darfur related to security. It shows that UNAMID has failed spectacularly to protect civilians and has fallen under the influence of the Sudanese government. As many humanitarian agencies have experienced in Darfur, UNAMID has been gradually pushed out of Darfur and prevented from protecting civilians with the excuse that the situation has stabilized.

In 2013, the U.K. Department for International Development conducted a survey on public perceptions in Sudan that covered a variety of issues, including governance, corruption, public services, female genital mutilation, conflict, and humanitarian aid.[1] The survey results give interesting insights into the situation in 2013. Of 422 respondents in Darfur alone, more than 80 percent personally have seen war and 41 percent have received some form of humanitarian aid (Crowther et al. 2014). War has been the major cause of displacement (Crowther et al. 2014). Results from a question asking interviewees about the reasons they had to leave their homes show that war was the most predominant reason, pointing to high levels of insecurity in the region (figure 9.1) (Crowther et al. 2014).

Significant restrictions on movement because of a lack of security reduced people's ability to secure their own livelihood. In Darfur, individuals are mainly unable to gain access to markets, to collect natural resources such as wood and water, to start farming, to migrate to obtain work, or to obtain humanitarian assistance (Buchanan-Smith and Jaspars 2007). Insecurity is produced by a combination of factors ranging from ceasefire violations (Young et al. 2005), banditry and looting as a form of obtaining a living (Buchanan-Smith and Jaspars 2007), sexual harassment and violence in IDP camps (Amnesty International 2013), government targeting of local activists and civilians (Small Arms Survey 2014), and random attacks by the Sudanese Armed Forces on IDP camps (Amnesty International 2013).

Apart from the Sudanese Armed Forces and government forces, security in Darfur is provided mainly by UNAMID, which is the African Union and United Nations hybrid operation in Darfur. UNAMID's main mandate is the protection of civilians, but it also includes protection and cooperation related to humanitarian assistance, the implementation of peace agreements, and the promotion of human rights and the rule of law (UNAMID n.d.). UNAMID cooperates with

Figure 9.1 Reasons for Leaving Home, Darfur
percent

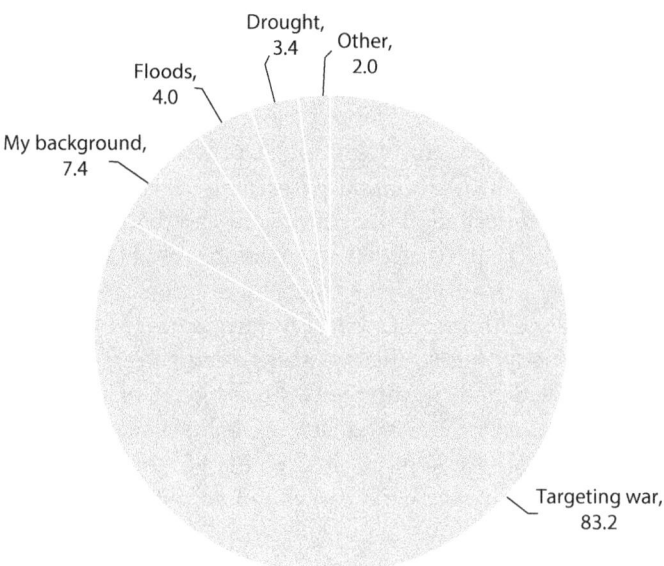

Source: Based on data from the 2013 U.K. Department for International Development Sudan household survey.
Note: "Targeting war" refers to the reason for leaving home as either war or targeting of people because of their background.

the Sudanese government police, who are also present in government-controlled areas. Although UNAMID has some effect on civilian protection, promotion of community policing, and response to gender-based violence and other security concerns, the mission has faced significant constraints and has largely been unable to adequately protect civilians (UN 2014).

From the very outset in 2007, UNAMID faced difficulties in its work. First, even before the mission officially started, many (including military analysts) argued that UNAMID's mandate was overstretched (Jibril 2010) and not well thought out (de Waal 2007). There was "little attention paid to the concept of operations and a strategic goal" (de Waal 2007, 11) by UNAMID, whereas there was a broad assumption by many political leaders and activists that UNAMID would be able to provide security and protection to the people in Darfur. Thorough analysis of the situation on the ground was never conducted or requested by the Sudanese government. There was only a quick review mission that lasted 11 days in 2007 (de Waal 2007). Thus, expectations for UNAMID at the outset were unreasonably high and led to disappointment later in the outcomes of the mission.

The Sudanese government opposed the deployment of UNAMID from the beginning and has continued to obstruct its work. Some of the early obstructions included delaying approval of the list of UN contributors to the force, refusing troops from certain countries and accepting only African contributors, refusing to grant various movement permissions, and attempting to disable communication networks (Human Rights Watch 2007). This resistance is not new. Sudanization of aid workers (replacing international staff with Sudanese nationals) from the 1980s and 1990s, later interpreted by aid agencies "as in line with the developmental aims of capacity building" (Duffield 2002, 85), entailed similar restrictions and resistance. The government controlled recruitment of staff; allowed only limited posts to be filled by international staff members; and set significant restrictions on access, citing security grounds (Duffield 2002).

Throughout its time in Darfur, and particularly as of 2012, UNAMID has been compliant with almost all of the restrictions and demands of the Sudanese government (Loeb 2013). In particular, the mission would ask for Sudanese government approval for almost all of its troops' movements despite the fact that UNAMID is officially authorized to travel to most areas (Loeb 2013). The mission has been extremely passive in requesting more access, in releasing crucial information about Sudanese government attacks on UNAMID and civilians, and in providing accurate reports on human rights violations (Lynch 2014). When UNAMID patrols are kept at checkpoints for too long while a crisis is happening, they often "turn back too easily" and do not persist in trying to gain access (United Nations 2014).

This not only leaves the populations vulnerable but also erodes public trust in the mission and its neutrality. People's trust in the peacekeepers and the police is very low, and a majority among the conflict-affected population perceived the mission to be ineffective. For example, one of the inhabitants of Dali, a town in North Darfur, explained: "These peacekeepers have been here for three or four years. Since they entered our country, they have not helped us in any way. They can't stop the government or those who attack us. They are just there. Today, they come take information. Tomorrow, more information. It's too much talk" (IRIN News 2008).

The fact that UNAMID's mandate includes support for the Darfur Peace Agreement and that it also supports the Doha Document for Peace in Darfur (DDPD) also puts the mission in a compromising position. Because neither peace agreement has been signed by all the warring parties, the mandate essentially puts a supposedly neutral mission in the position of taking sides (Loeb 2013). That situation has created significant mistrust among various rebel groups who have actively prevented UNAMID's access to different areas and who have attacked peacekeepers multiple times (Loeb 2013).

All of those problems result in numerous failures to provide protection. Some of the most recent examples include the rape of more than 200 women and girls in Tabit, North Darfur, by Sudanese government soldiers in October 2014. The government denied the incident and prevented UNAMID from conducting an investigation (Loeb 2015). UNAMID later reported publicly that it found no evidence of mass rape. An internal report leaked afterward showed that investigations were severely hampered by government intimidation (Reeves 2014a). Another example is the abduction in March 2013 of three buses of displaced residents from Darfur accompanied by UNAMID (Lynch 2014).

Although sometimes there is no protection at all for civilians, what protection exists is often not sufficient. For example, women are sometimes offered protection by UNAMID police, but they do not trust the police and are not familiar with how the UN police operate. They often are offered protection that is incomplete; police officers will accompany women to natural resource collection sites but will not accompany them into forested areas where they are often attacked (Thompson, Okumu, and Eclai 2014).

Those examples not only illustrate the mission's inability to provide security, but they also point to the fact that there is no security in Darfur, despite government claims that the situation has improved in many areas. For example, IDPs in Sirba, West Darfur, have called for UNAMID to establish a base there because of extreme insecurity, attacks by the Sudanese government, and local disputes, but UNAMID states that it has been absent because the government reported that the security situation in the area is stable (Reeves 2014b). Such examples point to the significant ability of the Sudanese government to manipulate information and portray a false situation of security by blocking access and preventing investigations.

The situation in a majority of the areas in Darfur cannot be described as stable. As recently as January 2015, there were 21,000 newly displaced people registered across camps in Darfur (UN 2015a). The government has proved unwilling to actually provide security to the people, and attacks on IDP camps, aerial bombardments, and rape all have been techniques deployed by the government in many of the areas under its control. The areas controlled by various rebel movements have access restrictions that prevent aid workers from obtaining information, and little is known about the security and needs of the population in those areas.

Despite all the evidence that the ongoing conflict is not coming to an end, talks of UNAMID's withdrawal from Sudan have already started. At the request of the Sudanese government, UNAMID will begin downsizing its troops in the areas that are "relatively safe and stable" (UN 2015b, 18). Downsizing will be based on benchmarks relating to the government's ability to provide security in other areas of Darfur (UN 2015b). This is clearly problematic but also representative of the broader pattern of humanitarian assistance in Darfur. The government has attempted to present the situation as less grave than it is and is pushing humanitarian actors out of the country despite the ongoing fighting and the lack of any feasible peace agreement in sight. The major outcome is an increase in vulnerable populations who will be left unprotected in terms of both physical security and livelihood. Although UNAMID has provided inadequate security since its deployment, a withdrawal would mean complete isolation for the conflict-affected populations.

Politicization of Humanitarian Aid, Push for Long-Term Solutions, and Effect on Assistance

> [N]ot to fully understand, or take into account, the political objectives of assistance, the politics of the causes of any given emergency and the political objectives of those who are afflicted by it, is to simultaneously reduce the effectiveness of humanitarian intervention. (Middleton and O'Keefe 2006, 543)

The Sudanese government historically has been able to exert significant control over international humanitarian and development agencies operating in Sudan. From the experience of the Operation Lifeline Sudan–North in the 1990s—having to face the trade-off between complying with the government's requirements or jeopardizing its work in the south—until today, when the government heavily controls not only access but also programming of international humanitarian agencies, the history of humanitarian operations seems to follow a familiar trend.

Complementary to this is the Western change in aid policy during the early 1990s from purely relief to the idea of linking relief to development and promoting self-sufficiency, a shift that caused damage to those in need both in the 1990s and more recently (Duffield 2002). Earlier, in the 1990s, international agencies attempted to take on a developmental relief approach and support employment and self-sufficiency among displaced southerners in northern Sudan, but the agencies ended up supporting further subordination of southerners and the government's need for cheap labor, particularly in agriculture (Duffield 2002). Today, developmental efforts in Darfur come from this deeply rooted idea of self-sufficiency but can also be ascribed to the frustration with a never-ending humanitarian emergency and constant reduction in funds for humanitarian assistance. Coupled with the claims of the Sudanese government that development, rather than humanitarian, assistance is necessary in Darfur, the international community gains a great excuse to reduce assistance, and the Darfur population suffers from a deadly combination of factors.

The implications of the Sudanese government's political influence on humanitarian aid agencies are significant for the populations on the ground. Since the expulsion of 13 NGOs in 2009, most of the population living outside of the government-controlled areas has not been reached by international humanitarian actors, and the precise effect of the loss of access has been difficult to measure because the expulsions reduced the ability of international humanitarian agencies to monitor the humanitarian situation (Loeb 2013). The UN Secretary General's report suggested that in 2011, an estimated 300,000 people in need were "beyond the reach" of humanitarian agencies (Loeb 2013, 25; UN 2011a).

The Sudanese government's logic for expulsions was that the presence of international agencies contributed to the indictment of President Omar al-Bashir, the secession of South Sudan, and the proliferation of IDP camps in Darfur (Loeb 2013). The response of the international community to the expulsions was weak. The international community focused on addressing the lost capacity rather than addressing the expulsions themselves. UN officials at the time stated that a stronger political response with regard to the expulsions would have led only to the expulsion of more NGOs and to less access overall (Loeb 2013). The government also profited from an "apologetic stance post-expulsion" (Loeb 2013, 26). There was a shift of rhetoric from humanitarian aid to development, and the government realized "'how passive the [international agencies were] and how aggressive the [government of Sudan] could be'" (Loeb 2013, 27).

The shift from relief to development rhetoric was particularly detrimental for the populations in need in Darfur. As figure 9.2 shows, humanitarian aid to Sudan overall decreased significantly, and since 2009, the total amount has been more than halved.

The decline in total funding is hardly a result of an improved humanitarian situation. Between 2013 and 2014, according to the UN reports (UN 2013, UN OCHA 2014a), the number of people in need has increased, from 4.4 million in 2013 to 6.9 million in 2014.

Additionally, with the expulsions of NGOs and the introduction of development rhetoric, the Early Recovery and Reintegration sector appeared for the first time in 2010 in the consolidated appeal for funding from UN OCHA. As figure 9.3 indicates, the funding for that sector was highest in 2010 and, despite a decline in the following year, continued to be funded relatively steadily from 2012 onward. This sector deals with finding durable solutions for IDPs and refugees, a policy that is in line with the government's politics.

The food and livelihoods sector has always been funded more heavily than others, but it has experienced a steady decline, as shown in figure 9.4.

The changes in funding previously noted, although potentially driven by the changing situation in Darfur, are less likely to be the outcome of an improved situation than of the fact that the Sudanese government dictates the type of intervention according to its political objectives. The government's opposition to the work of humanitarian agencies is reflected in the Darfur Recovery and Reconstruction Strategy (Darfur Regional Authority 2012) that came about as a result of the Darfur Joint Assessment Mission in 2012 and the DDPD.

Figure 9.2 Total Humanitarian Aid to Sudan, by Year, 2002–14

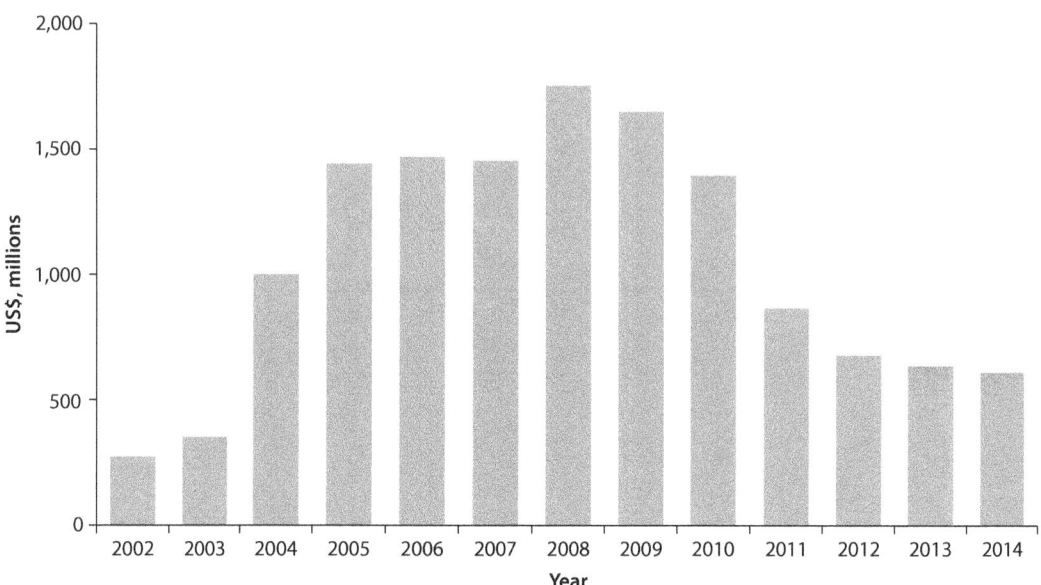

Source: Based on data from the United Nations Office for the Coordination of Humanitarian Affairs Financial Tracking Services website.

Figure 9.3 Funding for Reintegration and Recovery, 2010–15

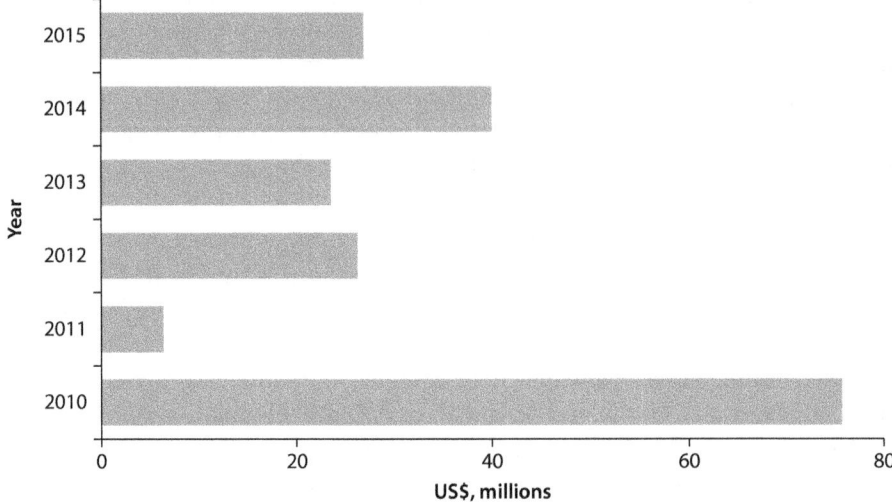

Source: Based on data from the United Nations Office for the Coordination of Humanitarian Affairs Financial Tracking Services website.

Figure 9.4 Funding for Food and Livelihoods Sector, 2002–14

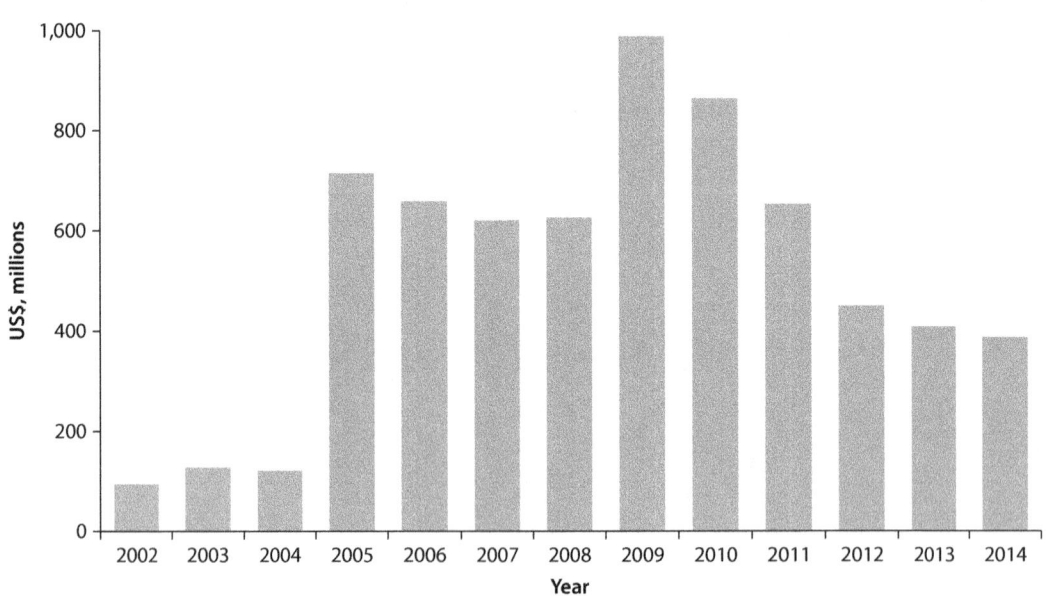

Source: Based on data from the United Nations Office for the Coordination of Humanitarian Affairs Financial Tracking Services website.

The Darfur Recovery and Reconstruction Strategy (Darfur Regional Authority 2012) strongly condemns the long-term provision of food and other humanitarian assistance not designed to contribute to development. The document states that "protracted relief aid has done little to address the root causes of the crisis, nor has it enabled the people of Darfur and their government to more meaningfully dictate their own recovery and rehabilitation" (Darfur Regional Authority 2012, xviii). Although such a shift to more long-term solutions is desirable, the government has not shown a real intention to commit to creating conditions conducive for recovery and development. A number of reasons have led to this conclusion.

First, the document, which also was supported by many international actors, including the United Nations Development Programme and the World Bank, states that the report was produced following various consultations with civil society, the population, and local governments. Nonetheless, during the three conferences in Doha, members of civil society were present, but there was no willingness to truly include them in the process and they were not given a chance to modify or change the document, which had already been prepared by the international mediators (ICG 2014). "The DDPD largely failed to incorporate its views, and civil society participants felt increasingly manipulated" (ICG 2014, 4). This speaks to the fact that the DDPD and the documents that followed from it were not a reflection of the real needs or the perspective of civil society. Second, the DDPD was never the government's serious commitment to a political solution in Darfur as shown both by the number of signatories (only one umbrella rebel group) and by the government's lack of willingness to compromise on any part of the document (ICG 2014). The lack of prospects for the DDPD's success also has been reflected in the very limited funds committed for its implementation by the international community (ICG 2014).

Effect of Political Pressure on Returns and Reintegration

Voluntary return and resettlement were presented as a primary priority in the Darfur Recovery and Reconstruction Strategy. The document states that the Voluntary Return and Resettlement Commission is charged with encouraging individuals to return and with compensating them for lost or unrestored property (Darfur Regional Authority 2012). It also states that the IDPs should expect "increased service provision in areas of return'" (Darfur Regional Authority 2012, 21) and appropriate infrastructure. The compensation for returns would be in the form of plots of land on which individuals must reside if they also want to be assisted in rebuilding houses. The report strongly states that these types of compensation have been very successful in towns such as Nyala and are already being expanded into other settlements, such as Geneina (Darfur Regional Authority 2012). Although the report broadly mentions issues of land title and ownership and lack of security, it does not refer to them specifically when discussing return and resettlement. However, those issues are some of the major concerns among IDPs, shown particularly by the subsequent refusal of refugees from Chad to participate in the March 2013 conference in Darfur that was intended to address the concerns of IDPs and refugees and their voluntary return (*Sudan Tribune* 2013). Refugees from three camps in Chad (Treguine, Bredjing, and Kounongou) explained that the security situation is not conducive to return and that the Darfur Regional Authority needs to address the problems in the region before any such conference can take place. The timing of the conference was questioned by IDPs in Darfur as well. Many of those refugees stated that the conditions in the region were not conducive to return and suggested that the conference was a government-led effort to dismantle IDP camps (*Sudan Tribune* 2013).

UN strategies have incorporated government priorities in their programs to a significant degree. In 2014, UN OCHA identified durable solutions for IDPs and refugees in Sudan as one of its strategic priorities and dedicated 8 percent (US$81 million) of its total funding for this strategic objective with a total of 2,346,080 people targeted (UN OCHA 2014a). In 2012, the Governance, Infrastructure and Economic Recovery Sector was established, from which, in 2013, a total of more than US$42 million in resources was deemed necessary, including US$37.7 million for Darfur (UN 2013). In the years 2012, 2013, and 2014, the UN set as a priority finding durable solutions for IDPs and refugees, and UN OCHA's 2012 strategy reflects this idea particularly, recognizing that "improving security conditions indicate that elements of early recovery and durable solutions programming needs to be incorporated into the humanitarian programme ... that the aid operation in Sudan needs to be rationalized and that current humanitarian funding levels—which are among the highest in the world—are unlikely to be maintained in years to come also compel such an approach" (UN 2011b, 41).

Despite the increasing financial dedication of the international community, the statistics from the United Nations High Commissioner for Refugees show that the number of returned IDPs went into decline, particularly from 2011 until 2013 (table 9.1).[2] To understand this fully, one must question what a "returned IDP" means in practice. As many examples show, identifying a person as a returned IDP does not necessarily mean that the person has permanently moved back to his or her place of origin. A substantial number of people engage in temporary return, in which they move back to their land to cultivate it and provide for themselves and their families in order to supplement food aid that is in decline,

Table 9.1 Returned and Existing IDPs by Year, 2006–13

Year	2006	2007	2008	2009	2010	2011	2012	2013
Total number of returned IDPs	11,955	84,834	21,081	166,900	143,000	279,325	91,554	19,471
Total number of IDPs	1,325,235	1,250,000	1,201,040	1,034,140	1,624,100	2,422,520	1,873,300	1,873,300

Source: Based on data from the United Nations High Commissioner for Refugees Statistical Online Population Database.
Note: IDP = internally displaced person.

because they no longer are able to survive on humanitarian assistance alone (Hovil 2014). Reports also indicate that the Sudanese government moves people back to their villages for short periods of time to show to the international community that returns are taking place (Hovil 2014). These obviously do not constitute return in the real sense of the word and give the wrong perception not only to outsiders but also to the international aid workers within Darfur whose access to information and certain locations is severely limited.

These temporary returns in Darfur present a substantial security threat for those who engage in it. Because land rights issues remain largely unresolved, returning IDPs are often attacked by the new land occupiers and by armed militias. The returning IDPs tend to make deals with armed militias and various rebel groups whereby, in exchange for the right to cultivate the land seasonally, IDPs need to give a percentage of their harvest to the rebel groups (Hovil 2014).

Supporting return, reintegration, and the finding of durable solutions for the IDPs presents a dangerous dilemma for the international humanitarian actors. On the one hand, both the Sudanese government and the major (Western) donors apply pressure to move away from IDP camps and the dependency-breeding provision of humanitarian aid. On the other hand, pushing for return at a stage when conditions are not conducive clearly risks an even more dangerous alternative for the people in question. Major criticisms around this topic focus on the lack of international attention on the issues of rapid urbanization in Darfur. As de Waal (2009) explains, "the crisis in Darfur is the latest in a long series of such episodes in Sudanese history and can also be seen as an instance of the accelerated traumatic urbanization of society." Regardless of the political solution, many IDPs in Darfur most likely will remain in urban areas. According to de Waal (2009), about a third of the population in IDP camps is integrated into the urban areas economically. The pressure on the cities, and on Nyala in particular, is growing as the infrastructure and services prove unable to support the growing population, and IDPs in urban areas are becoming more vulnerable. Another complication to the issue is pointed out by Assal (2008) through the example of Khartoum but also applies to other growing urban areas such as Nyala. Assal notes a lack of integration that creates isolated communities (mostly IDPs) and contributes to a polarization between the different groups based on ethnic or tribal identities and political affiliations, which is linked to economic grievance issues. So far, the international community has focused mainly on providing aid in camps and rural areas and has not dedicated much attention to this growing urban problem. The Sudanese government has been developing a Nyala master plan, but major criticisms note the lack of involvement and consultation of the affected population in this plan (Buchanan-Smith and McElhinney 2011). The international humanitarian agencies have had very limited engagement on this front with either the population or the government, despite the fact that in this area, long-term strategy might be a more viable and useful option.

Conclusion

This chapter argues that despite the existing need for humanitarian assistance in Darfur, humanitarian agencies are slowly withdrawing and aid is being shifted toward reconstruction and development in a conflict environment that is not conducive to such a policy. The Sudanese government's continuous resistance to the presence of humanitarian actors in the country has resulted in only 6,850 international aid workers being present in Darfur as of November 2013 compared with 17,700 before the expulsion in 2009 (UN OCHA 2014b). Most of the Western donors in the country have, yet again, fallen into the trap of supporting an unfeasible peace agreement in Darfur from which many of the policies detrimental to conflict-affected populations emerged. These include reduction in necessary food aid, pressure on IDPs to return to dangerous environments, refusal by UNAMID to provide protection, and more. Although, clearly, humanitarian assistance in Darfur has been provided for a very long time and no end to the war is in sight, switching to a development-oriented policy and reducing vital humanitarian assistance in the midst of conflict is highly problematic. Some lessons can be drawn from the 1980s and 1990s in Sudan because the government's resistance to humanitarian assistance has long historical roots. However, humanitarian agencies on the ground have limited capacity to act on their own, and strong international pressure is needed to prevent the Sudanese government from pushing its dangerous agenda forward.

Finally, by illustrating the complexity of the situation in Darfur, the chapter points to both the need for and the importance of data to shed more light on the region that has to an extent been kept isolated for a long time. Although an assumption that new data will lead to better humanitarian policy decisions may be far fetched, given the extent and complexity of the decisions, the improved understanding may serve as an incentive to at least question the current trajectory of humanitarian policy in Darfur.

Notes

1. The survey data set was provided to the authors by the DFID statistical adviser.
2. Data are from the United Nations High Commissioner for Refugees Statistical Online Population Database, http://www.unhcr.org/en-us/statistics/country/45c06c662/unhcr-statistical-online-population-database-sources-methods-data-considerations.html?query=Statistical%20Online%20Population%20Database.

References

Amnesty International. 2013. "10 Years On: Violations Remain Widespread in Darfur." Briefing Paper AFR 54/007/2013, Amnesty International, New York.

Assal, M. 2008. "Urbanization and the Future of Sudan." *African Arguments*, January 29 (accessed March 22, 2015), http://africanarguments.org/2008/01/29/urbanization-and-the-future/.

Banco, E. 2014. "After 7 Years, United Nations Prepares to Drastically Cut Peacekeeping Force in Darfur." *International Business Times*, December 26 (accessed August 31, 2015), http://www.ibtimes.com/after-7-years-united-nations-prepares-drastically-cut-peacekeeping-force-darfur-1767626.

Brosché, J. 2008. *Darfur–Dimensions and Dilemmas of a Complex Situation*. Uppsala, Sweden: Uppsala University, Department of Peace and Conflict Research.

Buchanan-Smith, M., and S. Jaspars. 2007. "Conflict, Camps and Coercion: The Ongoing Livelihoods Crisis in Darfur." *Disasters* 31(Suppl 1): S57–76. doi:10.1111/j.1467-7717.2007.00349.x.

Buchanan-Smith, M., and H. McElhinney. 2011. "City Limits: Urbanisation and Vulnerability in Sudan—Nyala Case Study." Humanitarian Policy Group, Overseas Development Institute, London.

Crowther, N., K. Okamura, C. Raja, D. Rinnert, and E. Spencer. 2014. "'Quo Vadis, Sudan?' A Preliminary Analysis of the 2013 DFID Household Survey." LSE Master of Public Administration (MPA) Capstone Report, London School of Economics and Political Science, London. http://r4d.dfid.gov.uk/Output/195649/Default.aspx.

Darfur Regional Authority. 2012. *Developing Darfur: A Recovery and Reconstruction Strategy*. Report produced by the government of Sudan, State of Qatar, United Nations Development Programme, World Bank, and African Union–United Nations Hybrid Operation in Darfur (UNAMID).

de Waal, A. 2007. "Darfur and the Failure of the Responsibility to Protect." *International Affairs* 83 (6): 1039–54.

———. 2009. "Do Darfur's IDPs Have an Urban Future?" *African Arguments*, March 31 (accessed May 15, 2015), http://africanarguments.org/category/making-sense-of-sudan/humanitarian/page/2/.

Duffield, M. 2002. "Aid and Complicity: The Case of War-Displaced Southerners in the Northern Sudan." *Journal of Modern African Studies* 40 (1): 83–104. doi:10.1017/S0022278X01003822.

Feinstein International Center. 2011. "Navigating without a Compass: The Erosion of Humanitarianism in Darfur." Briefing Paper, Tufts University, Medford, MA. http://dl.tufts.edu/catalog/tufts:UA197.005.005.00009.

Hovil, L. 2014. "'It Is a Joke.' Ongoing Conflict in Sudan's Darfur Region and Controversies over 'Return.'" Research paper, International Refugee Rights Initiative, New York. http://www.refugee-rights.org/Publications/Papers/2014/ItsAJoke.pdf.

Human Rights Watch. 2007. "UNAMID Deployment on the Brink: The Road to Security in Darfur Blocked by Government Obstructions." Joint NGO Report, Human Rights Watch, New York.

ICG (International Crisis Group). 2014. "Sudan's Spreading Conflict (III): The Limits of Darfur's Peace Process." Africa Report 211, International Crisis Group, Brussels.

IRIN News. 2008. "Darfur Peacekeepers Offer No Protection—IDPs." October 20. http://www.irinnews.org/report/80999/sudan-darfur-peacekeepers-offer-no-protection-idps.

Jaspars, S. 2010. "Coping and Change in Protracted Conflict: The Role of Community Groups and Local Institutions in Addressing Food Insecurity and Threats to Livelihoods. A Case Study Based on the Experience of Practical Action in North Darfur." HPG working paper, Humanitarian Policy Group, Overseas Development Institute, London.

Jibril, A. 2010. "Past and Future of UNAMID: Tragic Failure or Glorious Success?" HAND Briefing Paper, Human Rights and Advocacy Network for Democracy, Darfur Relief and Documentation Centre, Geneva.

Loeb, J. 2013. "Talking to the Other Side: Humanitarian Engagement with Armed Non-state Actors in Darfur, Sudan, 2003–2012." HPG Working Paper, Humanitarian Policy Group, Overseas Development Institute, London.

———. 2015. "Mass Rape by Army in Darfur: Sudanese Army Attacks against Civilians in Tabit." Report, Human Rights Watch, New York. https://www.hrw.org/report/2015/02/11/mass-rape-north-darfur/sudanese-army-attacks-against-civilians-tabit.

Lynch, C. 2014. "They Just Stood Watching." *Foreign Policy*, April (accessed May 8, 2015), https://foreignpolicy.com/2014/04/07/they-just-stood-watching-2/.

Middleton, N., and P. O'Keefe. 2006. "Politics, History and Problems of Humanitarian Assistance in Sudan." *Review of African Political Economy* 33 (109): 543–59.

Pantuliano, S., and S. O'Callaghan. 2006. "The 'Protection Crisis': A Review of Field-Based Strategies for Humanitarian Protection in Darfur." HPG Discussion Paper, Humanitarian Policy Group, Overseas Development Institute, London.

Reeves, E. 2014a. "Malnutrition Data for Darfur Still Being Withheld." *Sudan Tribune*, February 10 (accessed June 11, 2015), http://www.sudantribune.com/spip.php?article49907.

———. 2014b. "UNAMID's Failure and the Issue of Security in Darfur." *Sudan Tribune*, July 31. http://www.sudantribune.com/spip.php?article51869.

———. 2014c. "The UNAMID Internal Report on Mass Rape in Tabit." *Sudan Tribune*, November 21 (accessed June 11, 2015), http://www.sudantribune.com/spip.php?article53100.

Seekers of Truth and Justice. 2000. *The Black Book: Imbalance of Power and Wealth in Sudan*. Part I. Translated by Abdullahi Osman el-Tom. 2004.

Small Arms Survey. 2014. "Darfur Peace Process Chronology." Human Security Baseline Assessment for Sudan and South Sudan, Geneva. http://www.smallarmssurveysudan.org/fileadmin/docs/facts-figures/HSBA-Darfur-Peace-Process-Chronology-2014.pdf.

Sudan Tribune. 2013. "Darfur Refugees Refuse to Attend Conference amid Security Fears." March 22 (accessed July 24, 2015), http://www.sudantribune.com/spip.php?article45934.

Thompson, M., M. Okumu, and A. Eclai. 2014. "Building a Web of Protection in Darfur." *Humanitarian Exchange* 60: 24–27. http://odihpn.org/wp-content/uploads/2014/02/HE_60_web_1.pdf.

Tubiana, J. 2011. "The War in the West." In *The Sudan Handbook*, edited by J. Ryle, J. Willis, S. Baldo, and J. M. Jok, 223–41. Suffolk, U.K., and Rochester, NY: James Currey Ltd. UN (United Nations).

UN (United Nations). 2011a. "Report of the Secretary-General on the African Union–United Nations Hybrid Operation in Darfur." Policy Paper S/2011/814, UN, New York. http://www.un.org/en/peacekeeping/missions/unamid/reports.shtml.

———. 2011b. *Sudan: United Nations and Partners Work Plan 2012*. Khartoum: UN Office for the Coordination of Humanitarian Affairs, Sudan.

———. 2013. *Sudan: United Nations and Partners Work Plan 2013*. Khartoum: UN Office for the Coordination of Humanitarian Affairs, Sudan.

———. 2014. "Special Report of the Secretary-General on the Review of the African Union–United Nations Hybrid Operation in Darfur." Policy Paper S/2014/138, UN, New York. http://www.un.org/en/peacekeeping/missions/unamid/reports.shtml.

———. 2015a. "Humanitarian Bulletin Sudan." Issue 4, January 19–25, 2015. http://reliefweb.int/report/sudan/sudan-humanitarian-bulletin-issue-04-19-25-january-2015-enar.

———. 2015b. "Special Report of the Secretary-General on the African Union–United Nations Hybrid Operation in Darfur." Policy Paper S/2015/163, UN, New York. http://www.un.org/en/peacekeeping/missions/unamid/reports.shtml.

UNAMID (African Union–United Nations Hybrid Operation in Darfur). n.d. "Protecting Civilians, Facilitating Humanitarian Aid and Helping Political Process in Darfur." UNAMID website (accessed October 10, 2015), http://www.un.org/en/peacekeeping/missions/unamid/.

UN News Centre. 2004. "Sudan: Humanitarian Situation in Darfur One of Worst in the World–UN Officials." May 4 (accessed August 30, 2015), http://www.un.org/apps/news/story.asp?NewsID=10615&Cr=sudan&Cr1=#.VeMXb_mqqko.

UN OCHA (UN Office for the Coordination of Humanitarian Affairs). 2013. "Sudan 2013." *Financial Tracking Service* (accessed July 24, 2015), https://fts.unocha.org/appeals/413/summary.

———. 2014a. *Revised Strategic Response Plan.* June. https://www.humanitarianresponse.info/system/files/documents/files/revision_2014_sudan_srp.pdf.

———. 2014b. "Sudan: Darfur Profile." March. http://reliefweb.int/sites/reliefweb.int/files/resources/Darfur_Profile_10Mar14_A3_portrait.pdf.

Young, H., K. Abdalmonium, M. Buchanan Smith, B. Bromwich, K. Moore, and S. Ballou. 2007. "Sharpening the Strategic Focus of Livelihoods Programming in the Darfur Region: A Report of Four Livelihoods Workshops in the Darfur Region." Report, Feinstein International Center, Medford, MA.

Young, H., A. M. Osman, Y. Aklilu, R. Dale, B. Badri, and A. J. A. Fuddle. 2005. *Darfur: Livelihoods under Siege.* Medford, MA: Feinstein International Famine Center, Tufts University.

Conclusion: Can We Use Survey Data?

Can perceptions-based surveys provide a basis for sound decision making and improve understanding of the context in which policy making is conducted? Even in ideal settings, those of stable and politically liberal contexts, there are concerns that well-designed surveys may suffer from intentional or unintentional biases. In fragile and conflict-affected contexts, these biases may be compounded and exacerbated. Therefore, how useful are surveys? Using evidence from Sudan, this volume has demonstrated that, under certain conditions, survey data can be a useful source in shaping programs and understanding the policy context.

Theory suggests that the development of data sets that provide insights into the opinions, perceptions, and experiences of the general public or marginalized groups can generate incentives for better decision making. Such development is likely to empower large latent groups—such as the broad coalition of taxpayers and civil society—to make more effective political demands in relation to smaller and more organized groups—such as business associations, trade unions, and lobbies—that are usually more effective at collecting evidence privately and using this to influence policy.

The insights of theory will only work in practice if such data can be collected in a reliable and valid way. As the experience in Sudan shows, it is possible to devise strategies to minimize the risks of generating unreliable or invalid survey data. Once a reasonably robust dataset has been developed, a range of econometric techniques (especially regression analysis) can then be used to yield important insights into the perceptions and experiences of different subsets of the population.

As the chapters covering specific policy issues demonstrate, regression analysis can provide important insights into who (a) trusts traditional institutions, (b) perceives having good access to different services, (c) supports female genital mutilation, and (d) is more likely to experience bribery and corruption; and, indeed, why these could be. Larger themes, such as the impact of governance arrangements (for example, decentralization) and conflict, can also be analyzed using these techniques alone and in combination with a wide variety of other sources. Furthermore, this triangulation of the survey data findings with other qualitative and quantitative sources, inherent in the exploration of large cross-cutting themes, provides additional assurance of the validity of the survey data.

Clearly, the fact that surveys can be used effectively in a challenging context like Sudan does not prove that they will be effective in other contexts. Each survey is unique and faces a set of technical and non-technical challenges that vary across contexts and time. However, the fact that good quality survey data can be generated in a difficult context like Sudan provides evidence that data collection is not the preserve of more stable environments. In fact, the returns of such a survey are much greater in these contexts since they are carried out so infrequently.

As the data revolution and the advent of the Sustainable Development Goals of 2015 herald an increasing need to solicit the perceptions and experiences of program beneficiaries, the need to develop and deploy good quality survey instruments will increase. We believe that this volume has provided an important proof of context that this type of endeavor is both feasible and useful in fragile contexts. In combination with other important data collection tools, this approach can be used to enrich the evidence base of decision making in these settings.

Environmental Benefits Statement

The World Bank Group is committed to reducing its environmental footprint. In support of this commitment, we leverage electronic publishing options and print-on-demand technology, which is located in regional hubs worldwide. Together, these initiatives enable print runs to be lowered and shipping distances decreased, resulting in reduced paper consumption, chemical use, greenhouse gas emissions, and waste.

We follow the recommended standards for paper use set by the Green Press Initiative. The majority of our books are printed on Forest Stewardship Council (FSC)–certified paper, with nearly all containing 50–100 percent recycled content. The recycled fiber in our book paper is either unbleached or bleached using totally chlorine-free (TCF), processed chlorine-free (PCF), or enhanced elemental chlorine-free (EECF) processes.

More information about the Bank's environmental philosophy can be found at http://www.worldbank.org/corporateresponsibility.